Early
Literacy
for
Under-Fives

Early Literacy for Under-Fives

Karen Boardman

1 Oliver's Yard
55 City Road
London EC1Y 1SP

2455 Teller Road
Thousand Oaks, California 91320

Unit No 323-333, Third Floor, F-Block
International Trade Tower Nehru Place
New Delhi – 110 019

8 Marina View Suite 43-053
Asia Square Tower 1
Singapore 018960

Editor: Delayna Spencer
Production Editor: Gourav Kumar
Copyeditor: Joy Tucker
Proofreader: Sarah Cooke
Indexer: KnowledgeWorks Global Ltd
Marketing Manager: Lorna Patkai
Cover Design: Wendy Scott
Typeset by KnowledgeWorks Global Ltd
Printed in the UK

Library of Congress Control Number: 2023932561

British Library Cataloguing in Publication data

A catalogue record for this book is available from the British Library

ISBN 978-1-5297-7035-3
ISBN 978-1-5297-7034-6 (pbk)

At Sage we take sustainability seriously. Most of our products are printed in the UK using responsibly sourced papers and boards. When we print overseas, we ensure sustainable papers are used as measured by the Paper Chain Project grading system. We undertake an annual audit to monitor our sustainability.

This book is dedicated to all the ECEC practitioners who play, sing, dance and read.
Thank you!

CONTENTS

CONTENTS

ABOUT THE AUTHOR

Karen Boardman is Head of Department of Early Years Education at Edge Hill University, Ormskirk, Lancashire. She has worked in the field of early childhood education and care (ECEC) for over 35 years in leadership and management roles and as a nursery nurse (NNEB), nursery/reception and primary teacher in a wide range of settings.

Karen is an advocate for literacy provision, early reading and all teaching that is meaningful for young children and their families to inspire and enthuse their learning and development. She is also passionate about the wonderful work that ECEC practitioners do every day in settings all over the world.

ACKNOWLEDGEMENTS

With sincere thanks to all the ECEC practitioners, teachers and leaders for their time, commitment and contributions to the Early Reading Research project. Thank you for talking to me and sharing your thoughts, pedagogy and provision in supporting under-fives with their early literacy development.

I would also like to thank my colleagues at TACTYC for suggesting that I write this book. I hope this is what you thought it would be!

Lastly, this book is dedicated to all ECEC practitioners who play, sing, dance and read with our youngest children. Thank you for doing the wonderful work you do every day for every child.

1

INTRODUCTION

Literacy – A Diverse Perspective

Welcome to *Early literacy for under-fives*. This book intends to encourage some reflective thinking about the breadth and depth of literacy learning for under-fives and will support you with some 'refocusing' on all aspects of literacy provision, beyond the teaching of reading and writing. There is an emphasis placed on early reading for under-fives throughout the early chapters in this book, given there is currently no established definition to support students, practitioners, aspiring early years professionals or early years teachers with their understanding of what early reading is, and the **pedagogy** that sits alongside this for very young children under the age of five. I refer to pedagogy here as both the act of 'teaching' and the underpinning theories, beliefs, ethics, policies and, indeed, the debates that shape our approaches to provision – why we do what we do and how. This will be discussed in further detail in Chapter 2.

I believe that it is important to discuss and refocus perceptions of early reading for under-fives because there is already a wealth of literature and research surrounding the teaching of early reading, phonics and **holistic** literacy, which is usually linked to the concerns relating to reading attainment in the UK (and also in Australia and European countries). The policy approach to the teaching of reading, advocating **systematic synthetic phonics (SSP)** in schools is now widely acknowledged, yet still fiercely debated. This also includes reception children (aged four and five years) and children in Year 1 classrooms in England who are expected to complete the DfE Phonics Screening Check at Key Stage 1 (beginning from 2012 onwards). Much of the literature surrounding early reading is largely focused on struggling readers or the mechanics of reading – how children learn to read (the teaching of SSP), supporting confident readers and engaging readers in 'reading for pleasure'. These are all important aspects of reading, yet they do not present the whole picture of being a reader, particularly for under-fives. Often, these aspects separate the importance of communication and language from the core concepts of early reading. This book conveys all the important elements of early reading and ensures that it sits within the context of early literacy.

Levy (2011, p. 1) suggests that reading is one of the 'crucial components of early years education'. By this Levy means that the importance of teaching reading in early years education often has a stronger emphasis, due to the wider impact on young children becoming readers, how children learn to read and the provision for early years, given this is also linked with much wider social and **cultural literacy** implications essential for all children's learning and development. This is an important point to raise because literacy – communication, language, comprehension, reading and writing – has such a diverse perspective. Diverse in that the breadth of literature and perceptions about literacy is immense, with many multidisciplinary perspectives (for example, psychological, linguistic, educational, cultural, social, economic and political), a wide range of opinions and some established practice from grounded child development theories. Therefore, for very young children, literacy is not just about those who are able to read and write or focused on those who struggle with reading and writing. Many researchers (Larson & Marsh, 2013; Levy, 2016; Marsh, 2014; Nutbrown et al., 2005) advocate that the processes involved in learning to read also influence our interactions within wider communities and, as such, impact on the moral, cultural and social structure of these communities. The National Literacy Trust in the UK promotes a **socio-cultural** approach to literacy, suggesting that young children's reading and writing skills cannot be developed in isolation, but are often underpinned with an understanding of language developed through conversations and interactions with others. The National Literacy Trust evidence review *Literacy and life expectancy* (Gilbert et al., 2018) highlights that children born into communities with the most serious literacy challenges (most likely from deprived areas) often perform worse at school, are then later on in life less financially well off, which subsequently leads to poorer health and the lowest life expectancy rates in England. This research builds on their earlier *Literacy changes lives* (Dugdale & Clark, 2008) report, which established a link between literacy and life chances, physical and mental health, economic well-being, family life, civic engagement and crime. Therefore, it is hugely important to emphasise how literacy and literacy attainment, in particular, may have wider implications for future life chances of young children, adopting a social justice viewpoint, which may explain the increased focus on early reading from policy-makers globally. The United Nations (2006) proposes that social justice is a view that everyone deserves fairness – equal economic, political and social rights, and opportunities across the world. When focused on literacy, we therefore have a responsibility to provide access to and engagement with the whole range of literacy experiences for all our young children from birth.

Intrinsically, literacy is considered by many researchers to be a necessity that is vital for young children's lifelong learning (Flewitt, 2013; UNESCO, 2016; Morrisroe, 2014). The United Nations Educational, Scientific and Cultural Organization (UNESCO) defines literacy as:

> a fundamental human right and the foundation for lifelong learning. It is fully essential to social and human development in its ability to transform lives. For individuals, families, and societies alike, it is an instrument of empowerment to improve one's health, one's income, and one's relationship with the world.
>
> (UNESCO, Education Homepage, 2016)

This definition explains how literacy is an entitlement, a 'human right' and the 'foundation for lifelong learning' – placing the emphasis on literacy as transformative, social, cultural, leading to improved future life chances. The UNESCO Education Position Paper in 2004 earlier explained that:

> Literacy is the ability to identify, understand, interpret, create, communicate and compute, using printed and written (and visual) materials associated with varying contexts. Literacy involves a continuum of learning to enable an individual to achieve his or her goals, to develop his or her knowledge and potential and to participate fully in the wider society.
>
> (UNESCO, 2004, p. 13)

This international definition outlines how complex literacy is for all professionals and highlights further how literacy (speaking, listening, reading and writing) is linked to meaningful participation within the wider community, rather than just a set of skills to be 'learned by', or 'taught to' young children in schools. It is also important to reflect on how these skills of learning to read are being measured, why they need to be measured at all and by whom. This debate will be outlined in further detail later in Chapter 5.

Rose suggests in the *Independent review of the teaching of early reading* (2006, p. 39) that literacy is defined as 'four strands of language – reading, writing, speaking and listening', which is aligned with UNESCO and other international definitions of literacy. The Rose review (Rose, 2006) highlighted that these four strands are all interwoven and mutually beneficial, which means that young children's early communication skills are very much dependent upon social interactions within families and communities: arguably more so for under-fives. Thus, literacy skills are critical in helping young children to make sense of their world and their own place in it. From the time young children wake up to the time they go to sleep, very young children are constantly interpreting and making meaning within their cultural and social worlds. As the world is continuously changing and evolving, it is crucial that the very nature of all literacy practices – including 'emergent' literacy, 'digital' literacies and early reading definitions – are reviewed, as these also advance and will often require amendments over time. As such, this is a good point to begin an introduction to literacy for under-fives text, which considers all aspects of the literate journey in today's society; from early interactions, play, listening and understanding, communication, speech and language, sound discrimination, reading and writing.

The 'Legacy' of Literacy in Context for Under-Fives

The legacy of literacy, which includes decades of research-informed practice and contemporary international perspectives, provides the context for this book and its particular stance on early reading for under-fives. Literacy has an important legacy, in that it has been well researched over many decades from many perspectives – socio-cultural (Street, 2006); **emergent literacy** (Blythe, 2011; Clay, 1991); environmental print (Goodman, 1996; Nutbrown & Hannon, 2003); family literacies and new literacies, including

digital literacy worlds (Bearne, 2003; Marsh, 2016). These perspectives will be explored in depth later in Chapters 8 and 9. Subsequently, given this legacy, we now have a broad knowledge about how children learn to be literate – but this is also still developing, with new research emerging. We already know that the fundamental principles of how children learn in the early years is based on play and playful pedagogies – through inter-actions, conversations and **multisensory**, experimental and meaningful experiences – both in settings and at home within families and communities (Hamer, 2011, 2012; Moyles, 2010; Nutbrown et al., 2005). This is why early years environments globally have principles focused on 'enabling environments', with a variety of safe play spaces for children to play, explore, create and learn independently and socially, both indoors and outdoors. Wood (2013) highlights that literacy interactions embedded within these rich, playful and enabling environments are already well established within research.

The Early Years Foundation Stage (EYFS) (DfE, 2017, 2020), *Development Matters* (Early Education, 2012), *Development Matters: non-statutory curriculum guidance for the Early Years Foundation Stage* (DfE, 2020) and *Birth to 5 Matters* (Early Education, 2021) documen-tation in England outlines the overarching principles and characteristics of effective learning (CoEL) to support child-centred holistic approaches for all areas of learning. These characteristics are rooted in how children develop and learn. Many researchers (Flewitt et al., 2015; Gopnik & Schlulz, 2004; Stewart, 2011; Stewart, 2012; Wohlwend, 2015) emphasise that these playful experiences sit alongside meaningful contexts in order to support under-fives with acquiring literacies through their play. The impor-tance of meaningful contexts as a concept for literacy is explored in more detail in Chapters 3, 10 and 11. Equally, Wohlwend (2015) suggests that literacy is not an output to be measured, but is grounded in socio-cultural experiences, which are connective for young children – linked to their social worlds and local family contexts. Yet, the debate on how to teach children to read and write, based on the principles of language acquisi-tion, language comprehension and word recognition, has rumbled on for centuries and is worryingly measured and politicised (Cushing, 2022; Wyse & Bradbury, 2022). It is easy to get caught up in these debates, even though they usually offer a narrow defini-tion of literacy.

There have already been several decades of controversy and emotive disputes sur-rounding how early reading should be taught to young children (Brooks, 2003; Chall, 1967; Ehri, 2002; Hall, 1987; Rose, 2006; Torgeson et al., 2006). Consequently, these (often heated) debates have led to a particular standpoint that SSP ought to be the pre-ferred approach to support young children as 'readers' and as 'writers' (Johnson & Wat-son, 2005; Rose, 2006). This particular stance increased the political and economic focus of SSP, which led to schools in England (and more recently, Australia, Egypt, Lebanon and Jordan) being directed to teach SSP and only SSP to teach reading. The wealth of lit-erature is heavily focused on SSP as **decoding** to support reading, alongside **encoding** skills for spelling.

However, this narrow focus on teaching SSP seems to overlook the fact that under-fives are very much immersed in early reading environments, as readers and writers dur-ing their play and within their family environments, and are already able to recognise meaningful patterns, letters, sounds and images as part of their early reading journey from birth. Similarly, international perspectives on play do not advocate the formality of teaching phonics (or any other curriculum subject) to children under the ages of five and, in fact, suggest that this is not necessary until formal schooling begins, which is much later for many international children – often starting school at six or seven years old. These interesting debates will be presented in further detail in Chapter 5.

Current Policy and Practice in Literacy with Under-Fives

Current policy and practice in England is based on the *Early Years Foundation Stage* (EYFS) (DfE, 2007, 2021), which essentially is a statutory curriculum framework, beginning from birth to five years. Similarly, *Belonging, being and becoming: the early years learning framework for Australia* (DfET, 2019) also begins from birth. Most countries have documentation in place to support children's experiences that largely begin after the age of three, which encompass holistic values and the principles of care, learning and play – Wales, Scotland, France and Portugal. Equally, many central European and Scandinavian countries review their curriculum as guidance rather than a set of discrete learning outcomes or early learning goals (ELGs) to be achieved. *The Swedish School Law* (2010) and the pre-school curriculum put into place by the National Agency for Education (Skolverket 2018) is focused on the culture, physical, social and emotional strengths of pre-school children, with no formal targets or goals for literacy in place. This approach of holistic child-centred learning is forged in collaboration with parents and communities. The *Te Whariki Early childhood curriculum* of New Zealand (MoE, 2017) also prioritises social, physical and emotional interactions embedded in the community. In addition, the Reggio Emilia philosophy in Northern Italy places a heavy emphasis on the child-centred holistic, creative approach to learning and development. As such, the concept of literacy for under-fives is very much dependent upon the approach each country takes to **early childhood education and care (ECEC)**: an important stage in its own right or preparation for school education. Chapters 4 and 5 will explore these international perspectives in further detail to provide deeper understanding of current policy initiatives.

Nevertheless, given that the approach to literacy is based on the various curriculum frameworks already in place, literacy always seems to have the most persistent of policy drivers to influence practitioners in their pedagogy. Current policies place SSP as the prime approach to teaching reading, which – when aligned with Ofsted policies *Reading by six: how the best schools do it* (Ofsted, 2010), *Getting them reading early* (Ofsted, 2014) and the Ofsted inspection framework (2022) – inevitably influences practice and this leads to a detrimental impact on provision in early years settings (Boardman, 2019). The EYFS (DfE, 2017, 2020) ELGs also feature the prominence of SSP for literacy, reading and writing, which is entirely different to other international pre-school curriculum approaches. In addition, all initial teacher education (ITE) providers in England have an increased focus on SSP within the *Teachers' Standards* (DfE, 2011), the *ITT core content framework* (DfE, 2019) and the many iterations of the Ofsted inspection framework documentation, with serious ramifications for providers and settings if not achieved – failing their regulatory inspections being one aspect. Consequently, this predictably impacts on early years state-maintained, as well as private, voluntary and independent (PVI) settings, given that early years teacher status (EYTS) has also been considered to be part of early years initial teacher training (EYITT) since 2014. This key driver from the DfE and Ofsted policy-makers in England then heightens the concerns about **accountability**, falling standards and measured outcomes for literacy attainment. As such, this approach is then frequently debated by policy-makers globally, often resulting in new initiatives, such as toolkits for language development, teaching strategies for struggling readers, a variety of interventions to 'catch up' or 'close the gap' and new SSP programmes of study. Many international initiatives from the World Health Organization (WHO), United Nations Children's Emergency Fund (UNICEF), Inspiring Readers, Book Aid International and Zero to Three usually involve gifting or promoting access to picture books for parents and families and engagement in World Book Days, which are usually focused on the 'joy of reading' and reading for pleasure. Recently, campaigns such as 'Save with Stories' and 'Operation Storytime' have involved celebrities, authors, illustrators and teachers reading and sharing stories with children using digital media. These initiatives are grounded in encouraging children to engage with picture books and stories, largely due to the consistent narrative about struggling readers and children falling behind. For many educationalists access to books addresses many perceived inequalities. However, this book seeks to highlight how reading storybooks is just one important aspect of literacy and 'early reading' for under-fives. Yet, this is very much dependent upon your definition of early reading and what it means to 'be a reader' to support our understanding.

Under-Fives are 'Readers'

The definition of early reading in this book is sustained within research and knowledge enterprise (practitioner/teacher case studies) carried out with experienced early years practitioners/teachers in their settings across England over five years, from 2017–2021, to explore how graduate early years practitioners support the early reading development of under-fives. It is important to note that there is still a lot to learn about this approach and this definition of early reading for under-fives, yet it is a good starting point for this book. For example, the many varied and wonderful things that experienced early years practitioners do every day to support literacy environments and under-fives as readers is often misunderstood – both by the practitioners/teachers themselves and the wider community. If your definition of 'reading' is print based, focused on letters, sounds and words, then this may require some rethinking for under-fives. The definition of early reading in this book embraces the development from birth of 'readerly curiosity behaviours' (Boardman, 2021, p. 3) which includes access to communication, language, music, rhythm and rhyme in addition to handling resources, print texts, images and picture books. This also includes reading pictures and following images on tablets and other multimedia devices to enjoy and make meaning from these interactions – independently or essentially shared with adults and/or other children. These interactions become meaningful alongside the social, cultural and emotional benefits of shared storytelling, reading stories and engaging in musical activities, poetry, rhymes and songs to explore language patterns and communications. Under-fives are 'readers', as they delight in the sounds, textures, repeated rhymes and familiar pictures within their cultural worlds and take turns in their conversations during play.

How to Make the Most of This Book

The glossary of key terms presented at the end of this book will be useful as a reference to support your knowledge and understanding of literacy terminology, which is sometimes quite complex. Each chapter has a particular focus to enable the reader to dip in and out of the book as a graduated text, with key questions and reflections for continuous learning. The intention is that this essential book will guide you through your learning, similar to Bruner's (1960) model of a spiral curriculum. For example, Chapters 2 and 3 are focused on early reading, a definition to support the readers' understanding of what I propose that early reading is and the essential links with language, drawing on data from the research project. Later Chapters 5 and 6 move on to the focus of early reading and phonics, ensuring that this is indeed separated from early reading as a wider holistic literacy definition, yet embedding understanding of phonics and why it is important for children to engage with phonics in learning to read. Chapters 10 and 11 invite the reader to refocus back to early reading and the wider principles of literacy as a social justice or 'injustice' issue, including writing for under-fives to enable deeper and more meaningful learning overall, which will impact on your work in settings with under-fives.

Each chapter includes some key ideas and approaches, case studies (voices of professionals) with reflections and some suggestions for further critical thinking within the activities. It would be useful for you to document your learning with the use of a reflective journal while completing some of the activities featured in each chapter. This book is designed as your 'programme' textbook, encouraging you to unpick and rethink your pedagogy and provision for under-fives, related specifically to literacy. The principle of this book builds on a contemporary research project with reference to grounded and relevant perspectives from practitioners/teachers in settings working with under-fives. This book also explores some of the seminal child development and pedagogical theories – playful pedagogies alongside language, communication and literacy. The 'rethinking your pedagogy' sections offer deeper critical questions and scenarios to use for ongoing **continuing professional development (CPD)** and can also be used as reflection pieces during staff development sessions. To support further impact, it would be useful to take some of the critical questions and/or scenarios back to your settings/schools for further critique and deeper engagement with your pedagogy.

There is an increased emphasis throughout this book on meaningful literacy 'in context', as all-encompassing for children under five. In addition, the focus is on early reading – not pre-reading, which is distinct to this textbook, as it is always presented as early reading. The intention is that this will support all readers with their own professional development and understanding of the breadth and depth of literacy for under-fives.

What this book does not do is instruct how to 'teach' early reading and literacy. This book does not provide curriculum outlines, lesson plans or 'best-practice', yet does offer some useful suggestions for you to consider. This book is designed to support you in reflecting on your own pedagogy and shares some potential ideas for your future pedagogy. The intention is that hopefully you will feel empowered to continue to learn and explore further underpinning research to be able to articulate and rationalise to all stakeholders why you do the things you do and what works well for the children in your settings. This book does not advocate for any particular curriculum framework or approach (Froebel, Montessori, Reggio Emilia, Steiner/Waldorf etc.). This is deliberate, given that literacy learning is individual and unique to all. However, some of these principles will be interwoven throughout various chapters, where appropriate. Undeniably, literacy learning has immense social, emotional and cultural implications and doesn't really need a curriculum framework when you view early reading and literacy as every 'experience', 'routine' or 'moment'. Hold this thought as further detail will be explored later in Chapter 7. I do not profess to know everything about early reading and do not consider myself an expert in this field – much valuable research has already taken place and will continue to do so. However, I do offer a perspective from the five-year research project, based on what practitioners/teachers working with under-fives do in settings in England to support early reading development, which is new knowledge for this field. The study includes 147 survey responses, six focus group workshops, eight interviews and nine reflective zines (a reflective zine is an empty booklet for practitioners/teachers to write in daily, weekly or pertinent reflections in response to the research question). The research question is 'how do you support under-fives with early reading?' This book also makes some suggestions from the practitioners/teachers who took part in two focus group workshops to begin to craft a working definition of early reading that will be helpful for all readers.

The chapters are organised in such a way to enhance learning, reflection, discussion and action, acknowledging that practitioners/teachers already bring a lot of experience to this field.

Chapter 2, 'Early reading – what it is', provides some definitions about what is meant by early reading and what early reading is for under-fives. This definition will also be explained in relation to key terminology of speech, language and communication and the value of music, rhythm, rhyme and movement. These are essential interwoven links to literacy and early reading, often overlooked in the wider early reading and phonics **discourse**. This chapter explores a literacy-rich environment and how the environment can support early reading pedagogy.

Chapter 3, 'Early reading – what it is not', focuses on how the terminology of early reading is different to the teaching of phonics (used by policy-makers and many international organisations). This chapter shares experiences from graduate practitioners/

teachers about early reading with under-fives – their approaches and understanding of early reading, discrete from the teaching of phonics to highlight what early reading is not. This chapter also explores some working definitions of early reading from experienced practitioners.

Chapter 4, 'Understanding early reading in a wider literacy context', supports your understanding of early reading within the broader definition of literacy. It is important at this point in this book to clarify why it is vital for young children to engage in reading and writing and what this is for under-fives – such as, not always formally writing or reading, but mark-making and identifying images and sharing stories, making music, rhythm, rhyme, rap and so on. This chapter includes the breadth of literacy learning outdoors and literacy learning opportunities that can be accessed in museums, art galleries and places of interest.

Chapter 5, 'Early reading and phonics', outlines what the local and international policy stance is for teaching phonics and supports students with their understanding of the idea that phonics teaching is a small essential part of a much wider debate to enable children to be readers. This is an important chapter to support you with why you need to understand how and where the teaching of SSP 'fits into' the early reading and phonics debate and if it does at all for your work with under-fives.

Chapter 6, 'The deficit model of early reading and literacy', explores some 'labels' often used to describe children's attainment or perceived lack of attainment and situates these within an intervention approach of 'catching up' as being the norm for children under five. This chapter explains how this perception is often not underpinned by early years pedagogy or the principles of the EYFS, CoEL or any other international curriculum frameworks and invites the reader to do some deeper reflective critical thinking. The initiative and pedagogy of reading for pleasure in schools is also discussed within this chapter.

Chapter 7, 'Being a "reading" professional and a literacy advocate for under-fives', recommends what individual students/practitioners/early years teachers might like to do to support and advocate reading, writing and playful pedagogies for under-fives – how everyday activities and routines are all literacy learning opportunities. This chapter focuses on how we can encourage all children to be literacy learners, readers, writers and composers. This chapter also includes some suggestions for supporting and collaborating with parents, carers, families and communities as an advocate for literacy.

Chapter 8, 'Language and literacy – the bigger picture', reviews some bigger-picture thinking about language and literacy for lifelong learning. The context for why literacy is important for young children is reviewed in further depth. Literacy equality, diversity and inclusion is explored for some impactful pedagogy rethinking.

Chapter 9, 'Digital literacies and **multimodality**', draws upon digital literacies within the digital worlds of young children, introduces multimodality as an approach, the digital child and the concept of digital footprints. This chapter also explains how early reading is supported within digital literacies as playful pedagogy.

Chapter 10, 'Storytelling, not "herding sheep"', refocuses you on the value of storytelling and sharing picture books/multimodal interactive stories regularly within the routine of early years settings – not just as a 'herding sheep' activity. This chapter is also a reminder of how rhyming, rhythm, steady beat and music are also powerful early reading activities to support children as lifelong readers.

Chapter 11, 'Taking the lead on "literacy" for under-fives', provides some further stories from early years professionals in a wide range of settings to support your understanding of enhancing and leading literacy provision for under-fives. There are many literacy leaders already doing some great work in settings and schools.

Chapter 12 outlines some final thoughts with a section dedicated to planning your next steps for provision, with some signposts to further activity to support and promote literacy as a continuum of learning.

In Summary

This introduction has provided a very brief overview of literacy, introducing the 'legacy' of literacy – what we already bring to these discussions – and some of the contemporary international terminology relating to literacy for under-fives (emergent literacy, environmental print, digital literacies). These essential aspects provide the context for this book and its particular stance on early reading, which ensures that this is not just another book on literacy, but hopefully will be your established 'go to' book for the topic.

This chapter has also introduced some of the debates about policy from governments, policy-makers, regulatory bodies and international literacy organisations, to set the scene for further discussions on how these underpin provision or expectations for practice. Literacy is a socially desirable concept – in that it has influence and impact on wider aspects of our lives. As such, this then persuades us to define reading in our own way, as it is not self-evident and is dependent upon a perspective lens. Therefore, early reading has some additional complexities to explore for practice and provision for under-fives.

References

Bearne, E. (2003). Rethinking Literacy: communication, representation and text. *Reading, Literacy and Language, 37*(3), 98–103.

Blythe, S.G. (2011). *The genius of natural childhood: secrets of thriving children.* Hawthorn Press.

Boardman, K. (2019). The incongruities of 'teaching phonics' with two-year-olds. *Education 3–13, 47*(7), 842–853. doi: 10.1080/03004279.2019.1622499

Boardman, K. (2021). Why do early years educators engage with phonics policy directives in their work with under-threes in England? *Policy Futures in Education, 20*(1), 1–18. https://doi.org/10.1177/14782103211003221

Boardman, K. (2022). Where are the children's voices and choices in educational settings' early reading policies? A reflection on early reading provision for under-threes.

European Early Childhood Education Research Journal, *30*(1), 131–146. doi: 10.1080/1350293X.2022.2026437

Brooks, G. (2003). *Sound sense: the phonics element of the National Literacy Strategy.* Report to the Department for Education and Skills. DfES.

Bruner, J. (1960). *The process of education.* Harvard University Press.

Chall, J.S. (1967). *Learning to read: the great debate.* McGraw Hill.

Clay, M.M. (1991). *Becoming literate: the construction of inner control.* Heinemann Educational.

Cushing, I. (2022). Word rich or word poor? Deficit discourses, raciolinguistic ideologies and the resurgence of the 'word gap' in England's education policy. *Critical Inquiry in Language Studies.* doi: 10.1080/15427587.2022.2102014

Department for Education and Skills (DfES) (2007). *Practice guidance for hte Ealry Years Foundation Stage.* Nottingham: DfES Publications.

Department for Education (2017). *Statutory Framework for the Early Years Foundation Stage.* London: Department for Education.

Department for Education (2021). *Statutory framework for the early years foundation stage.* Available at: https://www.gov.uk/government/publications/early-years-foundation-stage-framework--2.

Department for Education and Training (DfET) (2019). *Belonging, being and becoming: the Early Years Learning Framework for Australia.* DfET.

Department for Education (DfE) (2011). *Teachers' Standards: guidance for school leaders, school staff and governing bodies.* July (introduction updated June 2013). DfE.

Department for Education (DfE) (2019). *ITT core content framework.* DfE.

Department for Education (DfE) (2020). *Development Matters: non-statutory curriculum guidance for the Early Years Foundation Stage.* Revised July 2021. DfE.

Department for Education and Skills (DfES) (2007). *Early Years Foundation Stage: learning and development requirements.* DfES.

Dugdale, G., & Clark, C. (2008). *Literacy changes lives: an advocacy resource.* National Literacy Trust.

Early Education (2012). *Development Matters in the EYFS: non-statutory guidance for the Early Years Foundation Stage.* Early Education.

Early Education (2021). Birth to 5 Matters: non-statutory guidance for the Early Years Foundation Stage. Early Years Coalition. Early Education.

Ehri, L.C. (2002). Phases of acquisition in learning to read words, and implications for teaching. *British Journal of Educational Psychology: Monograph Series*, *2*(1), 7–28.

Flewitt, R. (2013). Early literacy: a broader vision. TACTYC Occasional Paper. TACTYC.

Flewitt, R., Messer, D., & Kucirkova, N. (2015). New directions for early literacy in a digital age: the iPad. *Journal of Early Childhood Literacy*, *15*(3), 289–310. doi.org/10.1177/1468798414533560

Gilbert, L., Teravainen, A., Clark, C., & Shaw, S. (2018). Literacy and life expectancy: an evidence review exploring the link between literacy and life expectancy in England through health and socioeconomic factors. National Literacy Trust Research Report. National Literacy Trust.

Goodman, K.S. (1996). *On reading.* Heinemann.

Gopnik, A., & Schulz, L. (2004). Mechanisms of theory formation in young children. *Trends in Cognitives Sciences, 8,* 371–377. doi:10.1016/j.tics.2004.06.005

Hall, N. (1987). *The emergence of literacy.* Hodder & Stoughton.

Hamer, C. (2011). Face to face: why talking to babies, and giving them the chance to respond, will give them the best possible start. *Early Education,* Spring, 10–11.

Hamer, C. (2012). Parent–child communication is important from birth: NCT research overview. *Perspective: NCT's Journal on Preparing Parents for Birth and Early Parenthood,* January, 15–20.

Johnson, R., & Watson, J. (2005). *The effects of synthetic phonics teaching on reading and spelling attainment.* Scottish Executive Department. www.scotland.gov.uk

Larson, J., & Marsh, J. (Eds) (2013). *The Sage handbook of early childhood literacy.* 2nd ed. Sage.

Levy, R. (2011). Young children reading: at home and at school. Sage.

Levy, R. (2016). A historical reflection on literacy, gender and opportunity: implications for the teaching of literacy in early childhood education. *International Journal of Early Years Education,* 24(3), 279–293.

Marsh J.A. (2016). *The digital literacy skills and competences of children of pre-school age.* Media Education - Studi, ricerche, buone pratiche, 7(2), 178-195.

Marsh, J. (2014). Online and offline play. In A. Burn & C. Richards (Eds.), *Children's games in the new media age* (pp. 109–312). Ashgate.

Morrisroe, J. (2014). Literacy Changes Lives 2014: a new perspective on health, employment and crime. National Literacy Trust.

Moyles, J. (Ed.) (2010). *The excellence of play.* 3rd ed. Open University Press.

Nutbrown, C., Hannon, P., & Morgan, A. (2005). *Early literacy work with families: policy, practice and research.* Sage.

Nutbrown, C., & Hannon, P. (2003). Children's perspectives on family literacy: methodological issues, findings and implications for practice. *Journal of Early Childhood Literacy,* 3(2), 115–145. doi.org/10.1177/14687984030032001

Nutbrown, C., Hannon, P., & Morgan, A. (2005). *Early literacy work with families: policy, practice and research.* Sage.

Ofsted (2010). Reading by six: how the best schools do it. Ofsted.

Ofsted (2014). Getting them reading early. Ofsted.

Ofsted (2022). *Education inspection framework.* Ofsted.

Rose, J. (2006). Independent review of the teaching of early reading: final report. March. DfES.

Skolverket (2018). Curriculum for the compulsory school, preschool class and school-age educare. Revised 2018. National Agency for Education.

Stewart, M. (2012). Understanding learning: theories and critique. In L. Hunt & D. Chalmers (Eds.), *University teaching in focus: a learning-centred approach.* Routledge.

Stewart, N. (2011). *How children learn: the characteristics of effective early learning.* British Association for Early Childhood Education.

Street, B.V. (2006). Autonomous and ideological models of literacy: approaches from new literacy studies. *Media Anthropology Network*, 124–125. Redefining Literacy as a Social Practice.

The Swedish National Agency for Education (Statens skolverk) (2010) - Government.se

Te Whariki (2017). Early childhood curriculum. MoE.

Torgeson, C., Brooks, G., & Hall, J. (2006). A systematic review of the research literature on the use of phonics in the teaching of reading and spelling. Research Report 711. DfES.

UNESCO (2004). The Plurality of Literacy and Its Implications for Policies and Programmes. UNESCO Education Sector Position Paper. Paris: UNESCO.

United Nations Educational, Scientific and Cultural Organization (UNESCO) (2004). Education position paper. UNESCO.

United Nations, (2006). Department of Economic and Social Affairs. *Social Justice in an Open World: The Role of the United Nations*, ST/ESA/305, United Nations Publication, New York.

United Nations Educational, Scientific and Cultural Organization (UNESCO) (2013). *Literacy policy*. UNESCO.

UNESCO, Education Homepage, 2016. www.UNESCO.com

Wohlwend, K. (2015). Playing their way into literacies: reading, writing, and belonging in the early childhood classroom. Teachers College Press.

Wood, E. (2013). *Play, learning and the early childhood curriculum*. 3rd Ed. Sage.

Wyse, D., & Bradbury, A. (2022). Reading wars or reading reconciliation? A critical examination of robust research evidence, curriculum policy and teachers' practices for teaching phonics and reading. *Review of Education, 10*, e3314. doi.org/10.1002/rev3.3314

2

EARLY READING – WHAT IT IS

Chapter Objectives

This chapter outlines the concept of early reading. By the end of this chapter, you will:

- understand what early reading is and what this means for your provision for young children under five;
- consider the early reading experiences of under-fives, beginning from birth;
- review language, communication, critical thinking and social interactions within your understanding of early reading;
- think carefully about the meaning of pedagogy and understand this terminology;
- review your understanding of a literacy-rich environment to support early reading development.

Early Reading – What It Is

This chapter will introduce you to the concept of early reading – what it is and what this means for under-fives. The intention is to encourage you to reflect on your approach to literacy provision overall, with some potential new learning to support future thinking and provision. This chapter also provides some useful definitions and some examples about what is meant by 'early reading' and what early reading is, as a lived experience for under-fives. This definition will also be explained in relation to the wider concepts of speech, language and communication, including the value of music, rhythm, rhyme and movement. These are essential interwoven links to literacy and early reading, often overlooked in the wider discourse of early reading for very young children.

A considerable amount has already been written about early reading, with a continued emphasis surrounding the enduring phonics debate. This chapter is not concerned with the teaching of reading (teaching phonics) and is focused only on early reading – the early reading experiences of under-fives. We will also review the voices of experienced professionals and explore what they say about early reading pedagogy and provision in their settings, which is part of an ongoing national research project. The overall findings of the research project are embedded within this book.

Activity 2.1: Considering Early Reading

A useful place to begin is to start with some reflection on what you think early reading is:

How would you explain your current understanding of what early reading is for under-fives to a colleague?
How would you explain early reading provision to parents, carers and families?
What is early reading?

I would like to suggest that you begin your reflective journey at this point and perhaps start your journal to document your learning with space to add further thoughts after each activity. This is an important aspect of being a reflective practitioner, which involves being active (documenting your learning), dynamic (rethinking, reviewing), digging deeper through dialogue and responding to questions (which will also involve sharing your learning with others to make learning visible) and, where appropriate, adapting in response to your developing knowledge and understanding about how children develop and learn.

You could also leave a space to add more thoughts to this activity to build up your reflections over time and perhaps pose some questions of your own.

What is Early Reading?

It is usual to think about early reading with the focus on developing skills of reading – sometimes from the perspectives of emergent literacy, or pre-reading. However, this implies that children from birth are not reading – not yet engaging in the many early reading experiences that babies have from birth. It may surprise you that we already know that before birth and in the early weeks of their lives, babies are processing important information about sounds, tones and patterns of language – as well as being able to distinguish familiar adults' voices (Karmiloff & Karmiloff-Smith, 2001; Mampe et al., 2009). Babies are already tuning into their familiar adults and environments and setting their phonological experiences, as their brains are already sensitive to all types of rhythms. This knowledge frames our early reading understanding – but that is very much dependent upon your overall definition of 'reading'.

The complex literacy skills of reading (decoding and encoding print) and writing begin with babies' earliest communications. Research developed by Schore (2005) and Lally (2009) demonstrated that the 'foundations of competence in literacy, communication, critical thinking and social interaction are all shaped through the experiences babies have with those who care for them in their early years' (Lally, 2012, p. 11). Therefore, language, communication, critical thinking and social interactions are also a vital part of our early reading discussions. In addition, early language acquisition, which includes eye contact, gesture, non-verbal and verbal communications, impacts on all aspects of young children's development. We know from research by the Early Intervention Foundation (Law et al., 2017) that engaging in communication and language with significant adults supports children with understanding their emotions and communicating their feelings in order to build, establish and maintain relationships: to think symbolically. Symbolic thinking is essential for young children's language development because this supports very young children to understand abstract concepts, such as words, gestures, numbers, feelings, family members and relationships, etc. These concepts then become a real experience for many children and, as such, represent their own reality within their expressive language. For example, a young child may use the word 'toast' to mean all food or to tell the adult they are hungry, until they have learned the names of other foods, or they may use 'daddy' as a name for all adults.

Thus, literacy, and early reading learning in particular, does not begin in nursery or school settings, given that families are already supporting their children in a wide variety of ways from birth. Goodman (1996) suggests that, as practitioners, we often make the mistake of believing that 'literacy' is a new experience for young children, which is frequently not the case. Under-fives are already immersed in language-rich experiences in their family environments and are engaged in early reading. Research from Levy and Hall (2021) highlights that families often read aloud in a wide variety of ways to their children, such as shared reading activities, as part of their daily routine. These shared reading activities are meaningful physically, sensorily and emotionally and, as such, connect both the families and the young children from birth. Therefore, many children are already being supported with essential cultural language and early reading activities from birth in their home environments.

Case Study 2.1: Ten in the Bed

A parent/carer is singing to a five-month-old baby, making eye contact and physical contact by holding both hands together, while singing 'There were ten in the bed'. The song is 'There were ten in the bed and the little one said roll over, roll over, so they all rolled over and one fell out' and so on. The adult moves both the baby's arms together to 'roll over' each time the song gets to the 'roll over' words. This is not the first time the parent and baby have engaged in this fun singing activity and have already shared many songs, rhymes and games together from birth. On this occasion the adult stops halfway through the song. The baby makes a vocalised sound and further eye contact and also moves her arms. The adult says, 'Oh, so sorry, have we not finished yet?' and continues the song until the end. Baby smiles at the end of the song (as the baby is familiar with the rhythm of the last verse and the end of the song).

Case Study 2.2: Twinkle, Twinkle Little Star

A parent/carer is singing to a six-month-old baby, making eye contact and physical contact by cuddling, while singing 'Twinkle, twinkle little star'. The baby makes several vocal sounds and physically moves her body, displaying some annoyance. The parent/carer says 'Oh, you don't like that song do you, I forgot,' and then begins to sing 'The wheels on the bus'. The baby smiles and settles.

Case Study 2.3: The Bear Went Over the Mountain

A fifteen-month-old is watching a programme on children's television at home, which embeds Makaton sign language as a key feature. This programme is a favourite of this little one and she often asks for this programme by name during the day. She watched the rhyme 'The bear went over the mountain' and joined in with all the signing activities. The sign for bear (which is a teddy bear) is arms folded across. Later in the day, the little one asked to sing 'Round and round the garden' rhyme by doing the actions and saying 'garden'. The parent obliged and when the child reached the section of 'like a teddy bear' she signed this action with arms folded, saying 'teddy bear'.

Later, the fifteen-month-old was looking at a picture book and signed horse when she saw a horse on the page. The parent presumed the same programme had featured this 'learning' previously. As she turned the page, there was a teddy bear and the little one signed this, then went off to get her teddy bear. She put her teddy bear next to the storybook and signed 'The bear went over the mountain' rhyme while doing all the actions for the teddy bear.

Reflection Points

- What do these case studies tell you about language and communication for babies?
- How do these experiences link to early reading?

Let's think about how early reading experiences are apparent from birth. Cooper (2010, p. 5) suggests that there are nine steps of communication in *The early years communication handbook*:

1   interaction
2   play
3   listening
4   understanding
5   expressive language
6   speech and sound discrimination
7   speech

8   reading

9   writing.

The *communication pyramid* or *language development pyramid* (Child Development Centre, 2019) is often used by speech and language therapists. As you can see from Figure 2.1 below, the foundation for all communication skills is early interaction, pre-verbal and attention and listening.

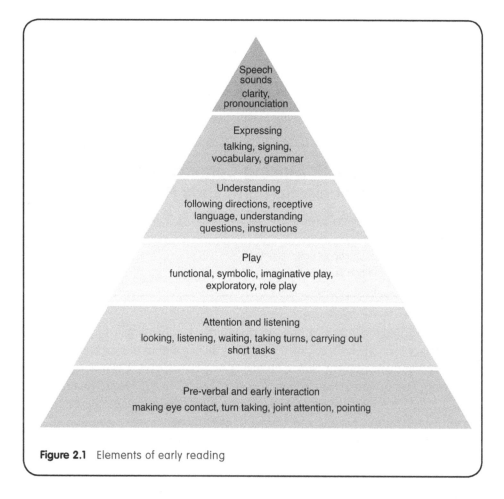

Speech
sounds
clarity,
pronounciation

Expressing
talking, signing,
vocabulary, grammar

Understanding
following directions, receptive
language, understanding
questions, instructions

Play
functional, symbolic, imaginative play,
exploratory, role play

Attention and listening
looking, listening, waiting, taking turns, carrying out
short tasks

Pre-verbal and early interaction
making eye contact, turn taking, joint attention, pointing

Figure 2.1 Elements of early reading

This matrix highlights the complexity of early reading, as there are many aspects that feature in the early reading domain, long before the focus gets to print-based reading and formal writing definitions – pre-verbal, early interaction, attention and listening, play, understanding, expressing, talking, pronunciation clarity. I suggest that this is all early reading as it is too intricate to separate language and communication from early reading, as is literacy as a whole concept – it is undistinguishable and blurry.

At this point, it is important to think about how early reading as a concept does not always need to link to books, despite the literature we read. Yet, it is understandable that there is a focus on how early reading links to the printed word for many. For example, Whitehead (1996) outlines this example of reading picture books:

> Babies and older toddlers respond to pictures and to print in books in a variety of ways; first with eye – gaze, smiles, gurgles and squeals, scratching at the paper, pointing and bouncing with enthusiasm. Eventually this develops into naming, joining in with the words, turning the pages and initiating real discussions about character, motives and plots as well as linguistic talk about letters, sounds and the conventions of print.
>
> (Whitehead, 1996, p. 66)

This can easily be an example of babies responding to songs, music or events in their home environment and demonstrates how gesture and language-reading behaviours can be observed.

Activity 2.2: Making Connections with Communication and Early Reading

How does the extract from Whitehead (1996) fit into the language/communication development ment pyramid?

What does this tell you about early reading?

How does this support your practice?

This socio-cultural focus, as a continuum from birth, highlights that very young children's literacy skills are both acquired and strengthened within mutual conversations, interactions and engagement with multimedia materials (Street, 1984). Literacy skills and, principally, early reading development is embedded in lived experiences, unique to each child. It is very important to note that this is, therefore, not dependent on the formal teaching of reading and writing skills promoted in many educational contexts for under-fives, but much more interactive and 'experienced' from birth. Remember that this particular form of literacy learning (reading and writing) is the result of decades of education policy documentation, prioritising one form of instruction over another, which often does not validate early reading in its own right. There is already a wealth of research focused on reading, which recognises that the early years of life are the most crucial, given this is often when young children's engagement with, and enthusiasm for reading activity is defined (Finnegan, 2016; Goswami, 2015; Knickmeyer et al., 2008).

So, what exactly does the term 'early reading' mean? It is highly problematic to establish an agreed definition, given that the overall concept of 'reading' is already open to a wide variety of definitions. Many research studies focus primarily on the mechanics of reading and therefore define reading as the ability to decode print (Hulme & Snowling, 2013;

Wyse & Goswami, 2008). However, further study suggests that reading includes, but is not just limited to, the decoding of print. For example, Levy (2016, p. 2) maintains that 'reading is not just the decoding of print and image but includes a capacity to extract information, engage with concepts, understand ideas and form opinions'. This suggests that young children need to 'do something' with the pictures, sounds, patterns and words to enable connections that are meaningful and part of their own experiences and environments. Marsh (2014) and Marsh et al. (2016) describe this as reading that goes beyond print. Therefore, early reading for under-threes is more than learning about print – it is 'familiar, connective, sensory, communicative and consequential' (Boardman, 2019, p. 6).

In addition, many researchers argue that reading is also multimodal (Bearne et al., 2007; Carrington, 2005; Ehri, 2002; Larson & Marsh, 2005; Marsh, 2008), offering a much more holistic definition of reading that embraces both visual and digital modes (Levy, 2009; Smith & Arizpe, 2016). Consequently, it is the interaction and engagement, context and comprehension that enables reading to be truly meaningful for very young children (Boardman, 2019; Levy, 2016; Sénéchal, 2006). This sets the tone firmly on what we do as practitioners in our early years environments to encourage all children, including those under the age of five, to engage with early reading.

The following extracts offer some definitions of early reading from experienced practitioners to consider at this point:

> Early reading is all those things you do to support children in their reading development – singing nursery rhymes to teach them about rhyming and that words have meaning, letters of their names and that there is print all around them.
>
> Early reading is all forms of positive communication. The patterns, rhythm and sounds that lead to early reading.
>
> The foundations you need to be able to read, achieved through listening and communication, modelling language, rhyming, environment and role play.
>
> Early reading is making sense of sounds and marks, translating their environment.
>
> Beginning to promote a love of reading through everyday practice.
>
> Early reading is complex and is often confused with phonics – where does early reading begin and end? For me early reading is the beginning bit before teaching phonics.
>
> Early reading is language based and where young children learn about language, print, letters, sounds and words. It is part of their play and learning in the environment.
>
> (Boardman, 2017)

Reflection Points

- Are these thoughts on early reading similar or different to yours?
- What do these definitions tell you about early reading?
- Why is every child's experience of early reading unique?

As you can see, there is already a focus and use of the language of 'foundations', communication – 'translating', 'leading to' and so on, within these definitions. If we consider reading *only* to be decoding text, then it is understandable that the focus prior to 'actual' reading and decoding printed words is often thought about in terms of pre-reading or foundations of literacy skills.

I define early reading as a much wider concept, which encompasses all aspects of how young children engage with communication, language and literacy. For example, through enjoying stories; reading within images and pictures (looking at and finding something useful and connective); exploring paper and screen texts; and 'understanding' how this works. Early reading is about having fun with language, sharing information to be able to make connections and use the information gathered – reciprocal interconnections (reciprocal here meaning shared and linked to real-life experiences that have meaning). For example, when reading picture books with under-threes and a familiar object is shared, the child then identifies this object and makes connections in their real life and uses language to expand on this connection from the picture book. Jordan (2010, p. 105) also suggests that reading as a concept involves 'complex interactions and reciprocity', highlighting that early reading needs to be considered 'within context above all else, to have value and meaning for very young children' (Boardman, 2019, p. 844). This is why I suggest that it is problematic to separate early reading from communication and language. Consequently, early reading is not a 'leading to' or 'later reading skill' but has value in its own right as *early reading*. It is important to begin to use this terminology with confidence and to understand what it means in relation to the whole reading debate.

For example, early reading activities may include (at the very least):

- engaging in communications, expressive, interactive and turn-taking in conversations from birth;
- an awareness of language, enrichment of children's language and vocabulary;
- enjoying songs and nursery rhymes (culturally appropriate);
- exploring and experimenting with language patterns in words, songs, poems;
- understanding that pictures/objects have meaning and relevance to young children;
- exploring rhyming patterns within rhymes and songs – continuing a rhyming string;
- listening to music, engaging in rhythm, dancing, singing;
- stamping, clapping to the steady beat, rhythm, rhyme or rap;
- enjoying puppets, role play, treasure baskets;
- matching images, objects, sounds;
- interest in and interacting with books, pictures, imagery, digital print – pointing to pictures, labelling objects;

- holding books, turning pages of a book, handling and manipulating interactive technology, tablets and ICT;
- shared book reading, story time, retelling stories – these activities are essential from birth;
- imaginative storytelling with small-world play, outdoors and natural resources;
- dance, music and movement, visual tracking physical play (balls, hoops, funnels, pipes, tyres);
- exploring and discriminating sounds, listening games;
- exploring pictures, print and words, paying attention to the text and the conventions of print, how pictures link to words;
- phonological awareness; **graphemes**; phoneme–grapheme correspondence – letter and sound correspondence and linking important letters of children's names, familiar objects.

Reflection Points

- Do you need to go back to your earlier definitions of early reading and add any further information?
- Are you clear about how early reading and reading definitions may be different?
- Think about why this might be confusing for practitioners/teachers or any educators and why this is the case.
- Can you think of any more examples of early reading activities to add to list above?

Early reading is 'reading' that is connective and meaningful for under-fives – not a discrete set of skills to be learned or taught. Early reading is everything that we do that offers meaning to children in their cultural lives – talking, singing, rhyming, rapping, listening, making music, enjoying stories and language patterns are a few examples.

How Might this Influence Your Pedagogy and Provision?

Now that we have explored some wide-ranging, yet relevant definitions, we need to be thinking about how this knowledge (new or existing) is going to influence your pedagogy and enhance provision for under-fives.

What is Pedagogy?

Pedagogy is often referred to as the act of teaching plus the theories, beliefs, policies and challenges underpinning this. Teaching with under-fives does not need to follow any formal way of working. Teaching for practitioners in early years is a much broader term that includes the variety of ways in which practitioners support young children in their daily development and learning. As such, this also includes all interactions with young children and play-based activities: 'communicating and modelling language, showing, explaining, demonstrating, exploring ideas, encouraging, questioning, recalling, providing a narrative for what they are doing, facilitating, and setting challenges' (Ofsted, 2015a, p. 35, n. 14; Ofsted, 2015b, p. 69, n. 61).

Pedagogy is actually what practitioners 'do and think' (Moyles et al., 2002, p. 5). 'It is the thinking behind teaching that is at the heart of pedagogy' (Papatheodorou & Potts, 2016, p. 112). Therefore, pedagogy is more than teaching – this also includes the resources chosen, the environment and layout of spaces, the structure and routine of the day, expectations and the curriculum. Moyles et al. (2002, p. 5) continue to highlight, in their *SPEEL: study of pedagogical effectiveness in early learning*, that pedagogy:

> connects the relatively self-contained act of teaching and being an early years educator, with personal, cultural and community values (including care), curriculum structures and external influences. Pedagogy in the early years operates from a shared frame of reference (a mutual learning encounter) between the practitioner, the young child and his/her family.

Furthermore, Formosinho and Formosinho (2016) suggest that pedagogy requires a synthesis between theory and practice and ethical provision – a knowledge and understanding of the interconnectivity of learning and teaching.

Activity 2.3: Thinking About Pedagogy

Think carefully about what pedagogy means in practice and focus on your own pedagogical approach.

- What is your pedagogical approach to early reading? Make some notes in your reflective journal.
- What will this look like and what will it feel like for the children?
- What will early reading look like in your environment?

Return to your reflective journal and outline your own pedagogical approach to early reading. Try to explain the influences on this approach and how these have impacted on your pedagogy. You might already be thinking about a literacy-rich environment as being integral to your pedagogical approach to early reading. It is important to be thinking about what a literacy-rich environment is to support early reading for under-fives.

A literacy-rich environment is an environment (classroom, nursery setting, infant room) that is immersed in and encourages, supports and enables communication (non-verbal and verbal, sign language) speaking, listening, reading and writing in a variety of authentic, meaningful ways – utilising print, images and don't forget the use of digital media. We also need to consider how we ensure that there is a strong purposeful home/setting link. You should be able to see it, feel it, as it ought to be visible in literacy-rich opportunities. For example, the environment might have on display some anchor charts (visual displays that capture ongoing learning for the children or children's drawings, mark-making etc.), word walls, communication pockets, labels for continuous provision and storage etc. A literacy-rich environment will also highly value children's own work, their everyday language and communications and ensure that this is always displayed at their level. We should also be asking the children's permission to display their work. Neaum (2017) suggests that a literacy-rich environment features high levels of talk and lots of conversations, alongside authentic literacy practices. For example, making lists, planning outings, reading texts, notes or emails, following directions, writing cards, filling in forms and many more. A literacy-rich environment will also have a strong focus on *access* for independent reading and writing, from birth – available at all times. Ideally this is also co-created with the children to connect their learning. For example, picture books, real books, images for all ages – not just baby board/cloth books in the baby or toddler room! Babies and toddlers should also be given access to real picture books and non-fiction books. To ensure context and relevance, the songs, rhymes, music, stories, picture books shared with young children ought to be familiar to their own worlds and culturally (and appropriately) relevant. For example, professionals need to consider why this song, book or story is being used at this point and how this will enhance the children's development and learning, rather than thinking about a random topic to cover this week or using the most popular storybook at the time to create a topic. A literacy-rich environment will support all aspects of communication, language and early reading in context.

Reflection Points

- Explore what this means for your environment:

'A literacy-rich environment will support communication, language and early reading in context.'

- What do you need to consider in order to plan for this?
- Do you need to refocus/focus on any particular areas?

Remember that reading is cultural and requires access to a wide range of early reading media to be significant. It is important to think about the images, representation and the materials within the resources for very young children. To illustrate, here is an example of a recent conversation with a parent about sharing books with her children:

I bought lots of books, cloth ones to put on the pushchair, plastic ones for the bath, bedtime books, floor time/tummy time books with lovely material and sensory experiences included. You can get such fabulous books now! I read all the time to my children. However, I noticed when I was reading with my twelve-month-old (he was pointing to the pictures in the book) that the objects in the books were, like, really random – a kite, a duck, a teapot, a whale, a rainbow. I was thinking and trying to explain what these are to him.

This is such an interesting conversation and one that I have all the time with parents/carers, families and practitioners, linked to my research of early reading. You might like to think about how often babies and young children see a kite, a whale or a rainbow in their lived experiences? Is it possible to have access to a kite or a teapot and understand what that is? We need to consider how we situate these images in children's understanding and how they have relevance or significance. Consequently, it is critical to carefully review your use of picture books and all early reading resources used with under-fives to ensure that there are no negative inferences. For example, relating to black or brown people, gender bias, religion or people with any disability – positive representation matters for all and must be something we continue to address in our pedagogy and provision.

Activity 2.4: Who Decides on the Images in Books for Babies?

Think carefully about who decides on the images in baby books?
What images should be included for babies to represent their meaningful worlds and value cultural diversity?
How does this discussion support your understanding of early reading?
Make some notes and find out more about the images in books for babies – you might like to visit a book shop (or online book shop) and read a few board books, cloth books and picture books designed for babies. It would be useful to think about how relevant they are to support babies with their early reading development and how representation is embedded.

Children need to see, access and engage with meaningful early reading activities at all times. Young children need to be supported by adults who take every opportunity to talk, listen, read and write – model the functions and forms of reading and writing for them and with them. This is vital for all young children, but especially important for under-fives who are learning rapidly about their place in the world from the images and experiences they access.

Reflection Points

- Why is access, relevance and meaning so important for under-fives?
- What does access involve?

Activity 2.5: Review of Your Own Early Reading Environment

Consider your own environment for early reading:

	All the time	Some of the time	Not yet
I provide authentic, meaningful, culturally relevant experiences			
I ensure there are lots of rhyming games, singing nursery rhymes, poems, songs, music			
I regularly check the relevance, context and meaningfulness of all the songs, rhymes, poems and rhymes we sing			
I provide examples of environmental print, labels, images – real and meaningful to children			
I actively engage in talking and listening with young children and often say more than is necessary by narrating, explaining, highlighting things of interest			
I use a lot of books with photographs to encourage talk, interaction			
I provide plenty of indoor and outdoor literacy-rich experiences			
I provide open-ended creative tasks			
I plan for lots of time to talk, interact and for turn-taking in conversations			
I encourage enrichment of children's language and vocabulary			
I provide opportunities to explore and experiment with language patterns in words, songs, poems. I provide lots of opportunities for children to have fun with language			

	All the time	Some of the time	Not yet
I provide games that explore rhyming patterns within rhymes and songs – continuing a rhyming string			
I provide regular links with home/families			
I provide relevant and interesting 'reading' materials to support home/families with their understanding of early reading			
I provide a variety of musical activities/resources, such as music bags, which are available at all times			
I provide and plan for lots of activities that include stamping, clapping to a steady beat, rhythm, rhyme			
I provide puppets, role play, treasure baskets			
I ensure that all adults show an interest in and interact with books, pictures, imagery, digital print, pointing to pictures, labelling objects with children			
I provide independent access to enable children to hold books, turn pages of a book, handle and manipulate interactive technology, tablets and ICT			
I plan for lots of shared book reading, story time activities, retelling stories			
I provide activities which explore and discriminate sounds, listening games, nature walks, music, etc.			
I ensure that adults encourage exploration of pictures, print and words, paying attention to the text and the conventions of print, how pictures link to words			
I engage in plenty of talk with children often – I support all children			

	All the time	Some of the time	Not yet
I provide many opportunities for writing and model writing as often as I can			
I label children's displays of their own work and ensure that the children decide what the label says about their work and do this with the children observing, scripting			
I review all my interactions with children, parents and families often to ensure that I am supporting accurate and positive representation			

The early reading environment is much more than just providing resources and opportunities, but that is a good starting point. It is essential to read picture books, share stories and tell stories often – this activity offers the most 'complex' of communication, language and literacy opportunities. Remember that this can also be done with digital texts and images, but is most effective with eye contact, gesture, facial expressions etc. It is vital to consider that when we read to children or sing with children, we do so for all the same reasons that we talk to very young children – to bond, support, reassure, explain, inform, inspire, clarify, comfort etc. When we read aloud and share stories, images and picture books with very young children, we are also building up their listening skills, their language and vocabulary and supporting early reading. Logan et al. (2019) propose that it is highly beneficial to read with young children from birth and they suggest that those children that are not read to at home may miss out on as many as 1.4 million words as compared to children who are read to. A very strong assertion indeed. In addition, reading together with young children also encourages curiosity, pleasure and fun! Lots of cuddles often go alongside these valuable early reading activities for under-fives. Remember that early reading is not just about reading stories, but also includes many other language-rich activities such as singing, rhyming, music making – rhythm and beat, sounds in the environment and listening activities – which is why I sometimes struggle with the concept of language and/or word gap discourse (discussed further in Chapter 6).

Some early reading activities that we have discussed so far may have surprised you, given that they may not be related specifically to formal reading or writing formats. However, when focused on cognitive development, neuroscientific research explains that where children are encouraged to use their multisensory, physical, emotional, social and cultural experiences and their imagination within play, this enables children's thinking to have greater depth of meaning. Therefore, these early reading experiences are vital in young children's learning and development.

Case Study 2.4: Carpet Rules for Story Time

A practitioner is reading a picture book to a large group of three- and four-year-olds. The practitioner introduces the title, author and what the book is about. She reminds the children about sitting still, crossed-legged and not shouting out – putting hands up to ask a question etc. While reading the story she stops at various points in the book to remind the children about these carpet rules and identifies individual children in her reminders. While she has stopped reading to remind the children about fidgeting, she takes the opportunity to ask the children questions about the characters and the images in the book. The children start chatting to each other and do not respond to any of the questions. Some children continue to move around the carpet. The practitioner continues to read the story until the end and then asks the children some questions at the end of the story. She reminds them to put their hands up to ask a question. A few children respond to the questions at the end of the story, but they often forget to put their hands up.

After the story, the practitioner initiates singing songs – the children are encouraged to choose the songs. All the children join in with singing the songs.

Reflection Points

- What are your thoughts?
- Why do you think the children did not respond to the questions during the story?
- What might you do differently?

Sharing books and telling stories ignites creativity, but perhaps not if there are too many rules to follow. It is important to understand that encouraging and supporting children with their language is also not just about asking questions – meaningful or otherwise – it is about culturally relevant, authentic exchanges within routines, activities and during play. I would suggest that storytelling and sharing stories is not an activity that has any rules attached to it at all, such as putting hands up to ask and answer questions. Our role as practitioners/teachers is to encourage a culture for early reading – making it meaningful and fun, where children are excited and curious and not hindered in this joy by a set of 'rules' or sitting still.

Case Study 2.5: Nursery Rhyme Prop Basket

A practitioner working with two-year-olds has realised that when it is singing time the same children choose the same songs, based upon their own individual language, experiences and comprehension skills. The practitioner decides to make a nursery rhyme prop basket to support all the children with having their own voices and choices heard. He gathers a range of props – a spider, a fish, a bus, teddy bears, a star etc. to represent some of the traditional and well-known rhymes and puts them in the basket – 'nursery rhyme prop basket'.

Reflection Points

- What do you think might happen?
- How do you think the children respond to these props?

The case study highlights that when we use props to support communication, the children can independently choose and associate this visual to their chosen rhyme. For example, a star to sing 'Twinkle, twinkle little star', a bus for 'The wheels on the bus'. This may not be apparent for all the children at first, but most children already associate an action, an object, a visual image etc. with their favourite nursery rhyme or song if they have experience of this. This activity is a good example of an early reading activity.

Review and Rethinking Pedagogy

- How do you gather the child's views about early reading in your setting?
- How have you involved and supported parents, carers, families and the wider community with early reading? How can you develop this further?
- How are you supporting access to early reading resources and experiences within your environment and planning?
- Why is reading to babies and toddlers essential?
- When should you read and share stories with young children, as part of their daily routine?
- Are there any occasions where you might consider that you are too busy to stop and read stories to young children at their request?
- Why is it important to sing nursery rhymes or rhyming songs with young children?
- Are you talking to children about displaying their work?
- How are you considering representation for all children and their families in your early reading pedagogy?
- Make a list of some of the important points you now need to take back to your setting/school.

In Summary

'Early reading is a broad and holistic concept' (Boardman & Levy, 2019, p. 3) which is focused on interaction, engagement and involvement with knowledgeable adults. The holistic nature of early reading recognises all children from birth when immersed in language, communication and social interactions have access to significant new learning to enhance their real-life experiences. Therefore, early reading does not happen by accident and is dependent upon quality interactions in both the home environments and in settings with unlimited access to meaningful activities and resources (Boardman, 2022). As such, a critical part of our early reading discussions involves the fundamental skills of learning to listen, lots of time for talking, music, movement, storytelling and sharing stories, rhythm, rhyme and singing as some examples. The strength of relationships, communication, gesture, signing and language development sit alongside the resources we provide to support early reading, and these are not only focused on print.

This chapter has hopefully set us on our journey into the complexity of what early reading is for under-fives and what this means for us within our pedagogy and provision.

Further Reading to Continue Your Learning

This is an article I wrote in 2022 to support families with their understanding of early reading beginning from birth.

theconversation.com/learning-to-read-starts-earlier-than-you-might-think-five-tips-from-an-expert-171561

This is a contemporary article which revisits the Baby Room Project, supporting baby room practitioners from 2013, with an enhanced focus on why singing and 'babysong' matters for communication.

Young, V., Goouch, K., & Powell, S. 2022. Babysong revisited: communication with babies through song. *British Journal of Music Education, 39,* 273–285.

Here is a journal article which outlines what early reading is for under-threes.

Boardman, K. (2020). 'Too young to read': early years practitioners' perceptions of early reading with under-threes. *International Journal of Early Years Education, 28*(1), 81–96. doi: 10.1080/09669760.2019.1605886

Read more about creating language and literacy-rich environments for under-threes. This Famly article from Soundswell speech therapists Diana McQueen and Jo Williams outlines some key components.

www.famly.co/blog/language-rich-environment-early-years

Utilise the Birth to 5 Matters *non-statutory document readings, references, reports and under-pinning research to support your knowledge and understanding of practice with under-fives.*

Early Education (2021). Birth to 5 Matters: non-statutory guidance for the Early Years Foundation Stage. Early Years Coalition. Early Education.

References

Bearne, E., Clark, C., Johnson, A., Manford, P., Mottram, M., & Wolstencroft, H. (2007). *Reading on screen.* UKLA.

Boardman, K. (2017). 'I know I don't read enough or even pick up a book in the baby room sometimes': early years teacher trainees' perceptions and beliefs about reading with under-threes. Doctoral thesis. University of Sheffield.

Boardman, K. (2019). The incongruities of 'teaching phonics' with two-year olds. *Education 3–13, 47*(7), 842–853. doi: 10.1080/03004279.2019.1622499

Boardman, K. (2022). Where are the children's voices and choices in educational settings' early reading policies? A reflection on early reading provision for under-threes. *European Early Childhood Education Research Journal, 30*(1), 131–146, doi: 10.1080/1350293X.2022.2026437

Boardman, K., & Levy, R. (2019). 'I hadn't realised that whilst the babies and toddlers are sleeping, the other children can't get to the books!' The complexities of 'access' to early reading resources for under-threes. *Early Years, 41*(5), 443–457.

Carrington, V. (2005). *Literacy in the new media age.* UKLA.

Child development Centre (2019). https://www.cdchk.org/parent-tips/the-communication-pyramid/

Cooper, J. (2010). *The early years communication handbook: a practical guide to creating a communication-friendly setting in the early years.* Practical Pre-School.

Ehri, L.C. (2002). Phases of acquisition in learning to read words, and implications for teaching. *British Journal of Educational Psychology: Monograph Series, 2*(1), 7–28.

Finnegan, J. (2016). *Lighting up young brains: how parents, carers and nurseries support children's brain development in the first five years.* Save the Children.

Formosinho, J., & Formosinho, J. (2016). The search for a holistic approach. In J. Formosinho & C. Pascal (Eds.), *Assessment and evaluation for transformation in early childhood* (pp. 93–106). Routledge.

Goodman, K.S. (1996). *On reading.* Heinemann.

Goswami, U. (2015). *Children's cognitive development and learning.* Cambridge Review Trust.

Hulme, C., & Snowling, M.J. (2013). Learning to read: what we know and what we need to understand better. *Child Development Perspectives, 7*(1), 1–5.

Jordan, B. (2010). Co-constructing knowledge: children, teachers and families engaging in a science-rich curriculum. In L. Brooker & S. Edwards (Eds.), *Engaging play* (pp. 97–107). McGraw Hill.

Karmiloff, K., & Karmiloff-Smith, A. (2001). *Pathways to language: from foetus to adolescent.* Harvard University Press.

Knickmeyer, C.R., Gouttard, S., Kang, C., Evans, D., Wilber, K., Smith, K.J., Hamer, M.R., Lin, W., Gerig, G., & Gilmore, H.J. (2008). A structural MRI study of human brain development from birth to 2 years. *Journal of Neuroscience, 28*(47), 12176–12182.

Lally, J.R. (2009). The science and psychology of infant-toddler care. *Zero to Three, 30*(2), 47–53.

Lally, R. (2012). The link between consistent caring interactions with babies, early brain development, and school readiness. Zero to Three. 159 – 163.

Larson, J., & Marsh, J. (2005). *Making literacy real.* Sage.

Law, J., Charlton, J., & Asmussen, K. (2017). *Language as a child wellbeing indicator.* Early Intervention Foundation, Newcastle University.

Levy, R. (2009). Children's perceptions of reading and the use of reading scheme texts. *Cambridge Journal of Education, 39*(3), 361–377.

Levy, R. (2016). A historical reflection on literacy, gender and opportunity: implications for the teaching of literacy in early childhood education. *International Journal of Early Years Education,* 24(3), 279–293.

Levy, R., & Hall, M. (2021). Family literacies: reading with young children. Routledge.

Logan, J.A.R., Justice, L.M., Yumuş, M., & Chaparro-Moreno, L.J. (2019). When children are not read to at home: the million word gap. *Journal of Developmental and Behavioral Pediatrics, 40*(5), 383–386.

Mampe, B., Friederici, A.D., & Christophe, A. (2009). Newborns' cry melody is shaped by their native language. *Current Biology, 19*(23), 1994–1997.

Marsh, J. (2008). Desirable literacies: approaches to language and literacies in the early years. Paul Chapman.

Marsh, J. (2014). *Online and offline play.* In A. Burn & C. Richards (Eds.), Children's games in the new media age (pp. 109–312). Ashgate.

Marsh, J., Plowman, L., Yamada-Rice, D., Bishop, J., & Scott, F. (2016). Digital play: a new classification. *Early Years: An International Research Journal, 36*(3), 242–253.

Moyles, J., Adams, S., & Musgrove, A. (2002). *SPEEL: study of pedagogical effectiveness in early learning.* Research report. DfES.

Neaum, S. (2017). *What comes before phonics?* Learning Matters.

Ofsted (2015a). *Early years inspection handbook.* Ofsted.

Ofsted (2015b). *School inspection handbook.* Ofsted.

Papatheodorou, T., & Potts, D. (2016). Pedagogy of early years. In I. Palaiologou (Ed.), *The Early Years Foundation Stage: theory and practice.* Sage.

Schore, A.N. (2005). Back to basics: attachment, affect regulation, and the developing right brain: linking developmental neuroscience to paediatrics. *Paediatrics in Review, 26*(6), 204–217.

Sénéchal, M. (2006). The effect of family literacy interventions on children's acquisition of reading from kindergarten to grade 3: a meta-analytic review. National Centre for Family Literacy/National Institute for Literacy. RMC Research Corporation.

Smith, V., & Arizpe, E. (2016). Introduction: the fictional portrayal of reading. In E. Arizpe & V. Smith (Eds.), *Children as readers in children's lsssiterature: the power of texts and the importance of reading (pp. xi–xvii).* Routledge.

Street, B. (1984). *Literacy in theory and practice.* Cambridge University Press.

Street, B.V. (2006). Autonomous and ideological models of literacy: approaches from new literacy studies. *Media Anthropology Network,* 124–125. Redefining Literacy as a Social Practice.

Whitehead, M.R. (1996). *The development of language and literacy.* Hodder & Stoughton.

Wyse, D., & Goswami, U. (2008). Synthetic phonics and the teaching of reading. *British Educational Research Journal, 34*(6), 691–710.

3

EARLY READING – WHAT IT IS NOT

Chapter Objectives

This chapter is focused on early reading and what it is not, to support you with your understanding of the complexity of early reading. By the end of this chapter, you will:

- understand that when we talk about early reading, it is not about teaching phonics;
- understand why early reading needs to be separated from the phonics discourse for under-fives;
- consider the voices of professionals about their provision for early reading;
- review some working definitions of early reading;
- reflect on the values, culture and the environment for early reading pedagogy for children from birth.

Early Reading – What it is *Not*

Chapter 2 outlined the focus on early reading in context for under-fives, as part of a literacy-rich early reading environment. We have also started to explore early reading in relation to our own pedagogy with under-fives. This chapter enhances this pedagogical approach and focuses on how the terminology of early reading is very different to the formal teaching of phonics (often used by policy-makers, regulators and various international organisations). This chapter shares experiences from graduate practitioners/ teachers about their early reading provision for under-fives, their approaches and understanding of early reading, which is discrete from the teaching of phonics.

Early Reading is Not 'Just About Teaching Phonics'

Early reading is not about teaching phonics. As such, Gee (2004, p. 13) highlights that: 'children who learn to read successfully do so because for them, learning to read is a cultural and not primarily an instructed process'. Gee (2004) also explains that teaching reading in schools is a decontextualised process for children. This is often where the early reading discourse slots in – the contextualisation of 'later' reading skills. What is meant by this is the 'early' bit of the reading debate is largely linked with the things that come before the actual 'reading', as in the decoding of printed text. The value is then placed on the process of learning to read by teaching phonics, which is often considered in isolation from the wider literacy debate. This book maintains a firm stance that early reading is not about teaching phonics – teaching phonics comes much later in the hierarchy and is a small component of the teaching of reading. Early reading is the most important aspect to focus on to ensure that all children are supported.

Reading and how children learn to read is certainly not a secure concept, given that many researchers and educationalists already have their own perceptions on what reading is. For example, reading is becoming more open to debate, certainly within the 21st century within our interactive online social and cultural societies. In addition, birth cohort studies from Sullivan and Brown (2013) and contemporary research from OECD (2021) clearly outline how reading is vital for children to make effective progress throughout each education phase, thus increasing the focus on reading for policy-makers. When you then factor in the terminology of early reading, this is often questionable, as discussed in Chapter 2. The following underpinning theoretical perspectives are good starting points to consider where early reading fits into the educational reading and wider literacy debate:

- cognitive-psychological;
- linguistic;
- socio-political;
- socio-cultural;
- socio-economic.

Activity 3.1: Consider the Perspectives From Research

Find out what these terms mean and make some notes in your reflective journal or use mind-mapping software to capture your thoughts if you prefer.

What does the research say about how children learn to read and write?
What do you think about these perspectives and how do they fit into your understanding of early reading?

The cognitive-psychological perspective is focused on the traditional structured phonics approach of decoding words for reading or **segmenting** words for spelling, where children learn to read in sequenced stages, positioning early reading as a 'pre-stage'. The psycho-linguistic standpoint considers all language is meaningful and contextual for children within their environments, therefore learning to read cannot be separated from this. Socio-political perspectives link literacy with attainment, gender, culture, politics, social power and cultural capital. For example, governance and the politics of how reading is taught in schools falls under the socio-political perspective – reading is a political concern for wider society (economics). A socio-cultural perspective is influenced by the context in which children learn to read (and write) and considers environmental print and home-literacy practices supporting how children learn to read.

Activity 3.2: Early Reading is Socio-Cultural

Explore what these statements mean within the environment and provision for early reading:

Early reading is socio-cultural and connective for under-fives.

Early reading:

embraces the development from birth of 'readerly curiosity behaviours', such as enjoying and handling texts of all types and **modalities**, reading pictures, following images and making meaning from these interactions. These communications are significant alongside the social and emotional benefits of reading and the profound engagement with music, stories, poetry, rhymes and songs – reading as a social, cultural and consequential activity.

(Boardman, 2021, p. 2)

Does this help with your understanding of early reading for under-fives?

As we have started to explore, early reading is a holistic activity in the early years (Boardman, 2022; Lysaker, 2006), yet often there are narrow government-driven definitions that cause confusion for educationalists. For example, when educationalists, researchers and policy-makers discuss the teaching of reading in schools, the terminology of 'early reading and phonics' is used (DfE, 2021; Rose, 2006; Ofsted, 2017). This focus on print-based letters and sounds – phonics, which usually includes grammar, spelling and punctuation – becomes a measured outcome to be carefully monitored by testing, grouping and national benchmarking: statutory assessment tests (SATS) and Phonics Screening Check (Bradbury, 2018; Bradbury et al., 2021). Some researchers highlight that the assessment data available to us is not favourable, with little increase in attainment over many years (Clark, 2018; Clark & Glazzard, 2018; Wyse & Bradbury, 2022). Likewise, internationally the Progress in International Reading Literacy Study (PIRLS) and Programme for International Student Assessment (PISA) data do not highlight a noteworthy increase in scores with the introduction of systematic synthetic phonics (SSP) in England, despite great investment and subsequent changes to policy development. However, the constant debate about varying approaches to phonics has certainly not helped here. Children need to be taught the alphabetic code consistently and in context by teachers who know the children well.

Activity 3.3: Data and Measurement

What are your thoughts on the data available to measure how well children learn to read?
What do you know about baseline assessments?
How do you think we should 'measure' how children learn to read? Do you think we should be 'measuring' at all?
Think about the children in your setting … what observable behaviours do you see that enables you to make decisions about how best you can support the children in your setting with early reading?
Are you teaching phonics to children in your setting? If so, why? Why not?

Consequently, when we think about this heavy focus on reading attainment, our thinking becomes constricted and takes us on the journey of the school readiness agenda – children need to be ready for school and ready to read and we do this by teaching phonics from as early as possible. Given that starting school is often seen to be synonymous with 'learning to read' (Levy, 2009) and policy frameworks in England have a heavy focus on teaching phonics (SSP), it is not surprising that we forget about the value of early reading for under-fives. Early reading gets lost as the formality of education and 'schooling' takes over. I would argue that early reading is the most vital aspect for under-fives. We do not need to get under-fives ready to read as everything we do with under-fives is early reading within our pedagogy of play when we do this well. We appear to have a domineering policy stance on reading in England, which is vastly different to the play-based approaches advocated internationally. Moreover, if we keep prioritising teaching phonics to children before they have been immersed in the early reading environment and teach phonics *instead of* sharing stories, singing songs, having lots of fun with rhythm and rhyme, the consequences are detrimental. Detrimental in that very young children may not fully engage in reading behaviours as it is not fun or meaningful to them. Teaching phonics is not early reading. I would also argue that this focus on phonics may not appear to be working for many children in England, given the outcomes data we have at hand to review. Chapter 5 will delve deeper into the DfE Phonics Screening Check data and the impact of this data.

In Chapter 2, we reviewed some of the research relating to the way that communication, critical thinking and social interaction (the key literacy skills) are shaped through the experiences babies have in the early years (Kendall-Taylor et al., 2015; Lally, 2011). These experiences are also significant for children attending nursery settings and for many children in their first year of school in their reception year, given that in England children begin formal education at the age of four years. It feels like we are always in a rush in early years – a rush to get ready for the next stage as we use the language of 'next steps' often in early years. Consequently, early reading becomes a product of this school readiness – rushing to learn letter names and their sounds earlier, out of context; rushing to the next stage where children formally learn to read. The introduction of the DfE policy paper, *The reading framework: teaching the foundations of literacy*, in 2021, perpetuates this 'rushing' and again prioritises the teaching of phonics. There are some lovely sections in this policy paper about 'the importance of talk and stories, and the critical links between these, especially the role stories play in developing young children's vocabulary and language' (DfE, 2021, p. 7). There is also an initial introduction to listening, talk, communication, story times, rhyming and poetry. Yet still the focus is on 'fluent and engaged readers at the very earliest stages' (DfE, 2021, p. 4) and pages 38 onwards (out of 113 pages overall) are dedicated to teaching SSP. Remember that the pivotal *Independent review of the teaching of early reading* (Rose, 2006) situated phonics teaching firmly within a language-rich and literacy-rich environment to foster a love of books and reading. Rose (2006, 2009) also included speaking and listening within the discourse of literacy, given that reading and writing is not developed in isolation from communication, interactions and relationships. We do need to consider what Rose meant by language-rich and literacy-rich here and what evidence is used to support.

Reading is not just about reading print-based books, decodable books or reading digital texts (Bonello, 2022; Levy, 2011). The wide range of reading practices I would like to discuss in this book are much more important than the print reading endorsed and measured in education. This chapter is focused on early reading overall, linked to the interactions with families, communities and the practitioners/teachers working with under-fives.

Voices from Professionals in the Field

As a researcher and literacy advocate, I am increasingly concerned that early reading is a concept that is misunderstood by many. This often causes some confusion about the nature of reading, the importance of communication, language, rhyming and book sharing with babies and the role that phonics plays in teaching children to read. Often early years practitioners and the field of early childhood appear to be drawing on the phonics discourse in their provision and pedagogy for under-fives, which, I maintain, is the least important part of holistic literacy and early reading in particular.

The following case studies evolve initially from a research project carried out over five years, from 2017–2021 to explore how graduate early years practitioners/teachers support the early reading development of under-fives. Some of these case studies are based on interview transcript data and reflective zine data. A reflective zine is an empty page booklet that practitioners own and use to write in their reflections related to the research question or it can be a series of papers stapled together with reflections from practice and reflection. The research question is 'how do you support under-fives with early reading?' Other case studies are later contributions from graduate practitioners/teachers and leaders in ECEC settings asked to reflect on what early reading is within their provision for under-fives and to support with a working definition of 'early reading for under-fives'.

Voices from Professionals in the Field About Their Experiences with Under-Threes as Practitioner Case Studies

Case Study 3.1: 'I am Not Really Sure What We Do to Support Early Reading'

I am not really sure what we do to support early reading with our under-threes. We provide books, share stories and sings songs, we do lots of nursery rhymes. We do Jolly Phonics and lots of action rhymes to introduce sounds and letters. We know how important this is for the children.

Case Study 3.2: 'I Know I Don't Read Enough or Even Pick Up a Book in the Baby Room Sometimes'

This is a bit confusing to say exactly what early reading is for under-threes. With our toddlers, we have lots of rhyme and share simple storybooks. It is different with the babies. I know I don't read enough or even pick up a book in the baby room. It is a busy routine – once you have finished one round of feeding, nappy changing, playing, it seems to start all over again. They are not quite ready to read yet – they will do this later in the pre-school room.

Case Study 3.3: 'I'm Always too Busy to Stop and Read'

Story time today … I read *We're going on a bear hunt* and the babies (twelve months) loved it. I encouraged them to stamp through the mud and splash in the water. They concentrated a long time and requested the story again. I left the hard-backed book out for them after lunch. While I was sitting at the table completing an observation, one of our eleven-month-olds brought the book to me to read and when I started to read, he just wanted me to get to the splashing page. Good language 'splosh, sploshy'. He didn't really want me to read it – just to be next to him while he read it. Two of the other babies and some toddlers also came over to share the book. I shared this with his dad at pick-up time and his dad had said they have this book at home and it is his favourite book.

Two things here for me to take on board – one, I should know this about favourite books and if I hadn't sat down, this wouldn't have happened. I'm always busy, standing or moving or doing something. I need to stop and just be there more!

(Boardman, 2017)

Case Study 3.4: 'We Read with Our Toddlers Every Day'

We support our toddlers with early reading by reading with them and to them every day – so we have two story time sessions and lots of reading books one-to-one in between. Our toddlers have favourite books and lots of picture books and we change these over a lot to introduce them to new books. I encourage the team to sit and read when possible, but it is a busy toddler room with lots of creative stuff, outdoor play and sensory play – sometimes the routine does take over.

These case studies highlight some confusion for practitioners/teachers, along with the busyness of the daily routine in their settings. Their understanding of early reading is rooted in books (print) and one practitioner has already introduced phonics into this discussion with under-threes. There is also some wonderful pedagogy and lots of reading to and with children often. It is worth considering that this might be about how individual practitioners/teachers feel about reading themselves and how much of their training has been or was devoted to this focus on early reading and how children learn to read. Nevertheless, it is not surprising that this is confusing, given the lack of a definition for early reading that is understood and in action alongside the intense focus on phonics in educational policy to muddy the waters. Yet, these case studies highlight some key reflection points for practitioners/teachers about their own understanding of reading – 'being ready to read' is a common thread and one that does need to be unravelled.

Activity 3.4: How Do You Support Early Reading?

Think about how you would answer the research question – 'how do you support under-threes with early reading?'

Write your own case study here.

Have the above case studies influenced your own perspectives? You have the benefit of the previous chapter's discussions about early reading. Go back to your thoughts about reading again to see if this has any influence on your response.

Is how you support early reading for under-threes different to under-fives?

Did/does teaching phonics come into your case study?

I assert that early reading is not about teaching phonics to any children under the age of five – it has no meaning or context to children under five, unless rooted in their life experiences. Teaching phonics (SSP) usually begins in reception classes in England for most children, which is considerably different practice to international approaches to teaching reading, where it is embedded in everyday routines and nurtured within play-based pedagogy. Remember that many international settings do not expect children to begin formal education until much later when they are six or seven and these countries usually outperform England in reading attainment (OECD, 2019).

It is essential to recognise that when we discuss activities, such as exploring letters and sounds and phonology within play for under-fives, this is very different to the formality of teaching phonics, and this is perhaps where we get a bit lost in these discussions. Perhaps we need to be clearer about how we define teaching phonics. I propose that any time we formally sit in small groups or large groups to teach the alphabetic code, blending, segmenting, or follow any scheme that encourages this is classified as teaching phonics.

Reflection Point

Think carefully about where exploring letters in our names when writing a child's name, finding letter shapes in sand, water or carrying out a letter-hunt outdoors fit into these discussions.

Voices from Professionals in the Field About Their Understanding of Early Reading with Four- and Five-Year-Olds as Practitioner Case Studies

The following case studies share experiences and practioners' own understanding of early reading pedagogy and provision within a range of settings.

Case Study 3.5 'We Support Early Reading with Teaching Phonics'

We support early reading in pre-school with teaching phonics – we do Jolly Phonics and focus on a letter each week. We use magnetic letters on the carpet and choose the focus from 'Letters and Sounds' document, advised by our school colleagues. Our four-year-olds love this time – we sit on the carpet together and have letter bags and **phoneme** frames. We also encourage our parents to send in objects for our letter bags.

Case Study 3.6 'We Do Lots of Rhyme, Rhythm, Alliteration and Lots of Fun Phonics Games'

We do lots of rhyme, rhythm, **alliteration** with our four-year-olds. We have a daily rhyme and we do this together at carpet time. We have a daily music session which has lots of rhythm and beat – stamping, clapping etc. Each week we do an alliteration activity with small groups. We play lots of fun phonics games at the end of each morning session – based on our letter each week, letter hunt and we do lots of writing in the sand and in the air for letter formation.

Case Study 3.7 'Our Children are not Meeting the Early Learning Goals (ELGs) for Communication, Language and Literacy at the End of Reception'

We have to rethink our provision for early reading because our children are not meeting the ELGs for communication, language and literacy at the end of reception and haven't done for the past three years. We have tried lots of different approaches to support our children's communication and language. We have tried intervention after intervention. In fact, we have probably done every single intervention with them now. I can't decide whether the ELGs are too high, measured incorrectly or the children are beginning from a much lower point than they used to. There doesn't seem to be much point focusing on SSP if the children are not speaking fluently.

Reflection

What are your thoughts on the case studies?

Are some of these scenarios familiar to you?

Any further suggestions for these practitioner/teachers to support the children?

Practitioners/teachers working with four- and five-years-olds appear to be just as confused about early reading and the discourse of teaching phonics as those colleagues working with under-threes, yet do have some understanding of how rhyme, rhythm and music is important. The additional measurement of early learning goals (ELGs) within the Early Years Foundation Stage (EYFS) in England seems to cause some further concerns. The statement from a reception teacher, 'There doesn't seem to be much point focusing on SSP if the children are not speaking fluently', highlights the complexity of the SSP agenda as a top-down imposed agenda for many settings.

Early Reading in Context, Distinct from the Teaching of Phonics in Schools

Most speech and language development resources or literacy interventions (such as Elklan, Wellcomm) begin with attention and listening and end with speech sounds. Therefore, it makes good sense that before we even consider letter sounds, phonology and teaching phonics, we need to be secure about communication, language and talk, including the essence of stories, rhymes and rhythm.

Activity 3.5: Activities and Routines

Think carefully about your daily routine in your setting. Do you provide opportunities for:

- listening
- talking
- rhyming
- singing songs and one-to-one interaction
- rhythm and music
- storytelling
- sharing picture books
- sharing stories
- mark-making
- digital literacy (tablet, TV, podcast, computer, games)
- outdoor literacy?

How much time is allocated for each of them if you do?
Are you embedding early reading in everything that you do?
How do you value all of these aspects in your daily or weekly routine?

The complexity of agreeing on a definition of early reading for practitioners who work with under-fives is often based on a range of much wider issues to consider. These wider issues include:

- Working practitioners who note that they do not have time to sit and look at picture books with individual children, due to the busy routines of the day – cleaning and assessments, for example.
- Practitioners do not understand the complexity of reading or early reading, given their own lack of 'reading for pleasure' as they do not enjoy reading at all or misunderstand what reading is.
- The teaching of reading is something that is done in schools, 'we are not teachers of reading, we are practitioners who focus on child development'.
- It is felt that under-threes are too young to read, based on definitions of print-based reading.
- Pressure to focus on print in curriculum and pedagogy.
- It is assumed that every child has access to early reading experiences in the home environment.
- It is assumed that every child has access to early reading experiences in the setting.

- There is so much to focus on in a typical nursery day and much of the focus is on care routines for under-threes – nappy changing, feeding, dressing, sleeping.
- There is no clear definition of what early reading is to support working practitioners.

Reflection Point

- These are all valid and appropriate reasons – what are your thoughts?
- How do these issues impact on the value of early reading for under-fives?
- Perhaps some of these issues are visible in your setting or settings you have spent time in and you have observed this in practice.

Much of the research about early reading is focused on print and the journey of print for literacy learning. Equally the focus for reading is on phonics – teaching the alphabetic code, which is essential to support readers. Although the printed word, the sounds, the letters and writing words is clearly important for literacy learning, there is much more that needs to happen for young children to understand how letters, sounds and words fit into their worlds – culturally and socially. Early reading is not phonics and needs to be distinct from the teaching of phonics. It is tempting to suggest it is the 'before' stage, but it is not. If we do not acknowledge that early reading is an important stage in its own right, then these 'earlier the better' perceptions of reading by teaching phonics will continue to impact on literacy learning (Larson & Marsh, 2015; Roskos & Christie, 2007; Wohlwend, 2008). In addition, Sharp (2002, p. 16) states that 'children who are taught phonic skills up to three years later [aged eight years] seem to acquire them rapidly, and thereafter perform as well as or better than children with an early start'. The National Foundation for Educational Research (NFER) *School starting age: European policy and recent research* (2002) makes a strong case for considering a much later formality of teaching for children, which includes literacy and learning to read. Suggate (2012) also proposes that those children that do learn to read later on usually catch up with the children who begin to read early. This research highlights that those children taught to read at eight achieve just as well when they reach eleven years as those who are taught systematically from age four or five. Therefore, it does not seem to be logical to be rushing children with their educational learning or teaching phonics early. As previously stated, this is at odds with international provision. This will be explored in further depth in Chapter 5.

A Working Definition of Early Reading for Under-Fives

Now we have explored that early reading is not about teaching phonics, let's remind ourselves of what practitioners/teachers think about early reading. Here are some of their 'working definitions':

Head Teacher

Early reading is language, rhyme and story rich. This also includes poems, songs and rhymes that the children are interested in and that honestly reflect culture, tradition and community.

Nursery Manager (Private Day Nursery)

Early reading is all the foundations of literacy – talk, gesture, song, music, rhyme, rhythm and tuning into sounds for young children.

Nursery Practitioner (Private Day Nursery)

I work with two-year-olds, so early reading for us is stamping, clapping, rhythm, rhyme and lots of story, role play and music. It is important for two-year-olds to have fun with sounds, letters and words – we share a lot of images, storybooks and puppets.

Nursery Practitioner (Nursery Class, Primary School)

I think that we should have a strong focus on these important areas for our early reading definition

- listening and talking
- music, songs and rhyme
- story time, sharing books
- understanding print and the environment

Nursery Practitioner (Infants and Toddlers)

Early reading should be about talk, rhyme, songs, rhythm, music, books and sharing stories. But we also need to have a focus on print, writing and letters and sounds – print in the environment and the community and recognising the meaning of print.

Reception Teacher

Early reading has a focus on developing children's speaking and listening skills within their play, plus reading stories, singing nursery rhymes and counting songs. We need to support children with developing their listening skills – tuning into sounds, sound discrimination and playing lots of games that involve letters and sounds – matching games, for example.

As you can see, it is difficult to pin down a clear definition, which is probably why there isn't one! Practitioners/teachers know that listening, talking and playing is somehow involved and the importance of rhythm and rhyme features for under-fives. These definitions appear to align with Street's (1984) philosophical model of literacy, which highlights that playful and child-centred quality early literacy learning is preferred over formal instruction processes, which is clear to see.

Early reading requires under-fives to have access to, and meaningful playful engagement with, a wide range of multimodal resources. For example, images, picture books, videos, moving images, audio rhymes, raps, poems, musical instruments, storybooks, puppets, printed words, environmental sounds and letters. In addition to access and playful engagement with resources, real-life experiences and collaborative talk, listening and communication needs to be embedded within the everyday routines for children (Boardman, 2022). Early reading is about access, agency, engagement and interactions. As such, we also need to be highly attuned to the ways in which we present authentic representation within our resources and interactions, ensuring that we do not favour whiteness or middle-class norms which may devalue children from different backgrounds or with different lived experiences (Dernikos, 2018, 2020; Kirkland & Jackson, 2009; Stoever, 2016), or include any gender bias. This critical unconscious and conscious bias within interactions, resources and educational policy will also be explored in further chapters, as it is important to consider what we mean by 'middle-class norms' relating to reading and representation.

Activity 3.6: Values, Actions and Culture for Early Reading

Now that we have reviewed what early reading is and what it is not, use the Venn diagram below to think carefully about your values, actions and culture for early reading within your setting.

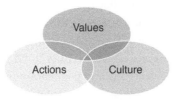

Figure 3.1 What will early reading ideally look like and feel like in your setting?

What is your pedagogical approach to supporting early reading?

Where does teaching phonics fit in, if at all?

How does representation, culture, race, SEND and inequality fit into your diagram? Think about how can you value these aspects and ensure early reading is not tokenistic, false and does not present inaccuracies for young children.

We will return to review this diagram again in later chapters.

It is important to understand the values and the culture you need to create for early reading in your setting, leading to the actions you will need to take to support this pedagogy and provision. For example, do your values include digital technology for under-threes, will the culture you create for young children include lots of talk and signposting to everyday objects, signs, words and pictures in the environment and might your values ensure that reading is fun, has usefulness, providing significant context for their learning. Perhaps, if we read to children, with them and for them and engage in early reading behaviours, children will be interested in what is written within their environment. Remember that reading does not need to be a quiet sitting activity either. Your culture for early reading should also include authentic outdoor learning and involve the home learning environment too. Remember to ensure that there is accurate and relevant representation for all children, families and communities in everything you do with under-fives to support early reading. This is non-negotiable and requires us to radically rethink our pedagogy.

Review and Rethinking Pedagogy

- Discuss early reading provision in your setting with your colleagues.
- How do you feel about explaining what early reading provision is in your setting with parents, carers and families, governors?
- Explain your early reading provision to Ofsted (or any other quality assurance body) – are you clear about what you do with the children and the position that early reading has in your setting?
- How will you convince or persuade a colleague to 'hold off' on formally teaching phonics when you can see that the children are not ready?
- When do you think that children are 'ready' to be formally taught phonics? Find out more about the alphabetic code.
- Think about producing some quick guidelines for early reading provision for all stakeholders. Consider what will you need to include and why.
- Which underpinning theoretical perspectives could you consider explaining where early reading fits into your setting and your community?
- Read and share the DfE policy paper *The reading framework: teaching the foundations of literacy* (DfE, 2021). Make notes about the key messages for you and your setting. If your setting is in Scotland, Wales or an international country – how does this fit into your understanding of provision for early reading with under-fives?
- How do you present authentic representation within your resources and interactions, with all children, ensuring that you do not devalue children of colour?
- How do you present authentic and inclusive representation within your resources and interactions, with all children, ensuring that you do not devalue children with individual SEND needs, backgrounds, individual family circumstances or LGBTQI + communities?

- Think about how exploring letters and sounds and phonology within play is different to the formal teaching of phonics. How do you plan for supporting children's phonological development?
- What is your working definition of early reading? Is it the same as your senior leadership team's?
- Consider when children start their reading journey and plan your environment to support.
- Make a list of some of the important points you now need to take back to your setting/school.

In Summary

Chapter 3 has explored what early reading 'is not' to support our developing knowledge and understanding. It is important to ensure that early reading as a concept is separated from the phonics discourse because if it is not, it means something very different. We have also reviewed voices from professionals and their opinions about provision for early reading, leading to some working definitions of early reading. This chapter has also highlighted that it is important to understand the values and culture you need to create to support early reading in your setting and the actions you will need to take to support this pedagogy and provision in future. Supporting early reading provision is also about carefully considering whether the resources that you provide are representational and inclusive to support equality, race, diversity, inclusion, religion and culture.

Further Reading to Continue Your Learning

This paper highlights how the current DfE and Ofsted policy in the UK is focused on teaching phonics to support children with reading and how this policy is now impacting on provision for under-threes.

Boardman, K. (2020). Occasional paper 12 – What is 'early reading' for under-threes? A reflection on 'conversations' with graduate practitioners in England: a response to Ofsted's 'Early reading' training video. tactyc.org.uk/wp-content/uploads/2020/05/Occ-Paper-12-Karen_Boardman.pdf

This important book explores the unique experiences of young black children during their first year of school and how the environment impacts on their identity. Their stories emphasise through a critical race lens how the children are racialised through everyday interactions and routines.

Houston, G. (2019). Racialisation in early years education: black children's stories from the classroom. Routledge. TACTYC book series.

This article from Cornerstones outlines some suggestions for promoting reading and the reading environment.

How to provide excellent opportunities for early reading: cornerstoneseducation.co.uk

This is a useful booklet from the International Bureau of Education.

Pang, E.S., Muaka, A., Elizabeth B. Bernhardt, E.B., & Kamil, M.L. (2003). *Teaching reading.* IBE.

Read more about representation and becoming an anti-racist educator.

Thomas, A. (2022). Representation matters: becoming an anti-racist educator. Bloomsbury.

References

Boardman, K. (2017). 'I know I don't read enough or even pick up a book in the baby room sometimes': early years teacher trainees' perceptions and beliefs about reading with under-threes. Doctoral thesis. University of Sheffield.

Boardman, K. (2021). Why do early years educators engage with phonics policy directives in their work with under-threes in England? *Policy Futures in Education, 20*(1), 1–18. doi.org/10.1177/14782103211003221

Boardman, K. (2022). Where are the children's voices and choices in educational settings' early reading policies? A reflection on early reading provision for under-threes. *European Early Childhood Education Research Journal, 30*(1), 131–146, doi: 10.1080/1350293X.2022.2026437

Bonello, C. (2022). *Boys, early literacy and children's rights in a postcolonial context a case study from Malta.* Routledge.

Bradbury, A. (2018). Datafied at four: the role of data in the 'schoolification' of early childhood education in England. *Learning, Media and Technology, 44*(5), 1–15.

Bradbury, A., Braun, A., & Quick, L. (2021). Intervention culture, grouping and triage: high stakes tests and practices of division in English primary schools. *British Journal of Sociology of Education, 42*(2), 147–163.

Clark, M.M. (2018). The views of teachers, parents and children on the Phonics Screening Check: the continuing domination of politics over evidence. *Education Journal, 347,* 20–24.

Clark, M.M., & Glazzard, J. (Eds.) (2018). *The Phonics Screening Check 2012–2017: an independent enquiry into the views of head teachers, teachers and parents. Final Report September 2018.* Accessed and downloaded from: newman.ac.uk/knowledge-base/the-phonics-screening-check-2012-2017

Department for Education (DfE) (2021). *The reading framework: teaching the foundations of literacy.* Updated January 2022. DfE.

Dernikos, B.P. (2018). 'It's like you don't want to read it again': exploring affects, trauma and 'willful' literacies. *Journal of Early Childhood Literacy.* doi.org/10.1177/1468798418756187

Dernikos, B.P. (2020). Turning into 'fleshy' frequencies: a posthuman mapping of affect, sound and de/colonised literacies with/in a primary classroom. *Journal of Early Childhood Literacy*, 20(1), 134–157.

Gee, P.J. (2004). *Situated language and learning: a critique of traditional schooling*. Routledge.

Kendall-Taylor, N., Haydon, M., & Fond, M. (2015). *Communicating connections: framing the relationship between social drivers, early adversary and child neglect*. FrameWorks Institute.

Kirkland, D.E., & Jackson, A. (2009). 'We real cool': toward a theory of black masculine literacies. *Reading Research Quarterly*, 44(3), 278–297.

Lally, J.R. (2011). The link between consistent caring interactions with babies, early brain development, and school readiness. In E. Zigler, W.S. Gilliam & W.S. Barnett (Eds.), *The pre-K debates: current controversies and issues* (pp. 159–162). Brookes.

Larson, J., & Marsh, J. (Eds.) (2015). *The Sage handbook of early childhood literacy*. 3rd ed. Sage.

Levy, R. (2009). Children's perceptions of reading and the use of reading scheme texts. *Cambridge Journal of Education*, 39(3), 361–377.

Levy, R. (2011). *Young children reading: at home and at school*. Sage.

Lysaker, J.T. (2006). Young children's readings of wordless picture books: what's 'self' got to do with it? *Journal of Early Childhood Literacy*, 6(1), 33–55.

National Foundation for Educational Research (NFER) (2002). *School starting age: European policy and recent research*. NFER.

Organisation for Economic Co-operation and Development (OECD) (2019). *Society at a glance 2019: OECD Social Indicators*. OECD. doi.org/10.1787/soc_glance-2019-en

Organisation for Economic Co-operation and Development (OECD) (2021). *21st-century readers: developing literacy skills in a digital world*. OECD.

Ofsted (2014). *Getting them reading early: guidance and training for inspectors*. Version 4. Ofsted.

Ofsted (2017). *Bold beginnings: the reception curriculum in a sample of outstanding primary schools*. Ofsted.

Rose, J. (2006). *Independent review of the teaching of early reading: final report*. March. DfES.

Rose, J. (2009). Identifying and Teaching Children and Young People with Dyslexia and Literacy Difficulties. DCSF.

Roskos, K., & Christie, J. (Eds.) (2007). *Play in the context of the new preschool basics in play and literacy in early childhood: research from multiple perspectives*. 2nd ed. Lawrence Erlbaum.

Sharp, C. (2002). *School starting age: European policy and recent research*. NFER. www.nfer.ac.uk/media/1318/44414.pdf

Stoever, J.L. (2016). *The sonic colourline: race and the cultural politics of listening*. New York University Press.

Street, B. (1984). *Literacy in theory and practice*. Cambridge University Press.

Suggate, S. (2012). Children learning to read later catch up to children reading earlier. *Early Childhood Research Quarterly*, 28(1), 33–48.

Sullivan, A., Ketende, S., & Joshi, H. (2013). Social class and inequalities in early cognitive scores. *Sociology*, 47(6), 1187–1206.

Sullivan, A., & Brown, M. (2013). Social inequalities in cognitive scores at age 16: the role of reading. CLS working paper. CLS.

Wohlwend, K. (2008). Play as a literacy of possibilities: expanding meanings in practices, materials, and spaces. *Research Directions: Language Arts, 86*(2), 127–138.

Wyse, D., & Bradbury, A. (2022). Reading wars or reading reconciliation? A critical examination of robust research evidence, curriculum policy and teachers' practices for teaching phonics and reading. *Review of Education, 10*, e3314. doi.org/10.1002/rev3.3314

4

UNDERSTANDING EARLY READING IN A WIDER LITERACY CONTEXT

Chapter Objectives

This chapter will consider early reading within the wider literacy context for under-fives. By the end of this chapter, you will:

- understand early reading within a wider literacy context, which includes outdoor learning and places of interest;
- explore further why it is important for all children to read and write;
- review the pedagogy of storytelling, sharing stories with young children and mark-making.

Understanding Early Reading in a Wider Literacy Context

Chapter 3 focused on some of the terminology surrounding early reading, which always seems to be associated with the teaching of SSP and is then often difficult to separate for educators. We have also appraised and reflected on the shared experiences from graduate practitioners/teachers about early reading with under-fives and their own approaches and understanding of early reading pedagogy. This chapter aims to encourage and support your understanding of early reading within the broader definition of literacy. It is important at this point to clarify literacy in context for under-fives; why it is vital for young children to be able to read and write as an outcome for lifelong learning and what literacy pedagogy is for under-fives.

One of the many uncomfortable global debates for the field of ECEC and education provision itself is when to begin the formality of reading and writing – uncomfortable in that, when early years practitioners, educators and literacy advocates think about literacy it does not begin with the skills of decoding print (reading), writing words, writing for comprehension, spelling, grammar or punctuation. This 'outcome' focus is expertly steered by government policy-makers. Literacy as a contemporary debate begins from birth and is not outcome focused. As such, we then get into another ambiguous discussion about the 'preparation' pre-stage of literacy – when this happens and how this supports the outcomes of reading and writing. I suggest that the terminology of early reading is just this. It is not preparation for anything that comes later, it is not the pre-stage. It is 'early reading' in its own right, which we have previously outlined includes language exploration, identifying images and sharing stories, making music, rhythm, rhyme and any forms of mark-making – not the before stage of anything. 'I use the terminology of "early reading" to refer to reading that happens at the very begin- ning of life, but this terminology does not presume that there is a "pre-reading" stage and then an "actual" reading stage. Early reading is "reading"' (Boardman, 2017, p. 12). Early reading includes communication, listening, developing language involving real connections and interactions. Goouch (2014) proposes that babies' 'language develop- ment is an active and interactive process which includes attachment and attunement, communication and contingency from a very early age' (p. 5). Similarly, Blythe (2011) argues that 'communication begins before birth and thus, babies are already born with an innate desire to communicate' (p. 38). In addition, Elkin (2014) suggests that edu- cationalists are now 'very aware that babies are active listeners and learners from their earliest moments' (p. 43). Therefore, early reading begins from birth.

In order to be considerate of everyone's views and to carefully position this book, I also use the term 'early literacy', but this is not meant to be a preparation stage with the use of 'early' either. This is an important factor in all discussions with graduate practi- tioners, leaders and teachers working in early years settings. The terminology of 'early' imparts value and recognition to the early childhood education and care (ECEC) field and is focused on under-fives. It is hoped that this chapter will contextualise further these debates and lead to some confidence in using early reading as key terminology for contemporary literacy, with value and meaning.

Activity 4.1: Reflecting on Early Literacy

Go back to your reflective journal and think about what literacy and early reading means to you now you have read previous chapters. A good starting point is to think about the person you are in your own home, the person you are with your peers and then also as a professional at work:

Where is your place in a literate society? Where do you fit in to society today?
Is reading important to you in your life? Why? If not, why not?
Is writing important to you? How do you generally write to share information?
What are your thoughts on 'literacy', society, your world, your own community, and culture?

Perhaps you do not consider yourself a reader if you do not read traditional books or fiction novels. Perhaps you read for information, non-fiction books. When you read stories, poems and plays (fiction) you are encouraged to use your imagination. Reading reference pages of the internet, reference books, biographies, autobiographies, newspapers, adverts, brochures (non-fiction) is often about facts, people or events. Both of these are equally important when we think about 'reading' in its wider sense. Remember that reading print-based text is just one highly limited definition of what reading is. Hold that thought and we will return to your own literacy experiences and their impact on pedagogy in later chapters.

Why is it Important for Young Children to Read?

The Scottish *Curriculum for excellence* (Education Scotland, 2016) defines literacy as the set of skills which allows an individual to engage fully in society and in their own learning, through the many different forms of language and a range of texts, which society values and finds useful. In addition, Reid (2003, p. 19) advocates that: 'reading is the extraction of meaning from print – literacy is much wider, this involves the appreciation of the literate culture, the conversations of society and the purposes and the responsibility placed on the use of literacy by society'.

It appears that it is difficult to separate literacy into component parts, given that these relate to and include family, community, society, experiences, language and culture. Freire (2004) advocates that literacy is a tool for reading both the word and the world.

Reflection Points

- Explore what you think Freire means here by 'reading both the word and the world'.
- Think about how you might explain literacy as a concept for your own pedagogy and within your own world.

Research reports from the BookTrust (www.booktrust.org.uk/what-we-do/impact-and-research/Research/) and the National Literacy Trust outline a wide range of benefits of reading which support young children and their holistic development. These include:

- social and emotional interactions/relationships between adults and children;
- supporting children with a wider world view, new knowledge they would not have otherwise known;
- offering key sources of information for children, including knowing how to access support for those who may find themselves in challenging circumstances;
- cognitive development – new knowledge, deeper understanding of concepts, to make sense of their place in their own community;
- developing empathy and understanding their own and others' emotions;

- deeper knowledge and understanding of a world view, culture, places, people, events, history, new concepts;
- nurturing well-being, building relationships and confidence;
- regular, shared activities, reassurance, bonding;
- improved concentration, creativity and imagination;
- access to language not often present in talk or communication;
- encouraging a love of reading – fun, enjoyment, meaning.

Activity 4.2: Benefits of Reading

Can you add five more benefits to this list above?

You may have included suggestions that are linked to a greater/larger vocabulary, enhanced academic achievements, fun, enjoyment and further social, emotional, physical or cognitive interactions. Often early years practitioners/teachers find it difficult to explain the benefits of reading for under-threes, given a perceived lack of observable behaviour. This could also be for many valid reasons, but one of the reasons, I would like us to focus on, in particular, is how we explain the value of early reading in the wider literacy context to each other, parents, carers, families and communities – how we explain early reading without it becoming preparation for later reading.

Activity 4.3: Top Ten Benefits of Reading

Organise your thoughts and some further suggestions from your reflections into your 'top ten' list of the benefits of reading. This could be something that you create, enhance and share with the parents, carers, families (PCF) and your local community to support their understanding of the importance of reading.

Now, focus on under-threes and think carefully about how we would adapt/enhance these benefits to explain the value of early reading for under-threes.

You could create a fun infographic about what early reading is for under-threes or just focus on the benefits of reading, sharing books for babies, sharing songs and rhymes.

It is important for young children to engage in reading relating to all the benefits we have reflected upon so far. It is also vital that we put reading in the wider literacy context to support our understanding and in an international context. Currently, the *Progress in International Reading Literacy Study* (PIRLS) definition of reading literacy is:

Reading literacy is the ability to understand and use those written language forms required by society and/or valued by the individual. Readers can construct meaning from texts in a variety of forms. They read to learn, to participate in communities of readers in school and everyday life, and for enjoyment.

(IEA, 2021, p. 6)

In addition, the *PIRLS 2021 Assessment frameworks* (Mullis & Martin, 2021, p. 1) suggests the frameworks are 'based on a broad notion of what the ability to read means', which includes reading for pleasure,

allowing us to experience different worlds, other cultures, and a host of new ideas. It also encompasses reflecting on written texts and other sources of information as tools for attaining individual and societal goals, also known as 'reading to do' ... This view is increasingly relevant in today's society, where greater emphasis continues to be placed on students' ability to use the information they gain from reading ... Emphasis is shifting from demonstrating fluency and basic comprehension to demonstrating the ability to apply what is understood or comprehended to new situations or projects.

(p. 1)

The PIRLS framework for assessing reading achievement is updated each year and carefully considers further advances in contemporary digital literacies, which is critical to acknowledge. The Programme for International Student Assessment (PISA), which is a study of the academic achievements of fifteen-year-olds, is led by the OECD. This data often contributes to future policy recommendations, particularly relating to those socially disadvantaged – 'closing the gap' **ideology**. The OECD indicators relating to disadvantage are measured from data sources on parental education (highest parental occupation), household income, wealth and possessions, which also includes access to books at home. However, Banerjee and Eryilmaz (2022) suggest that we cannot rely on these measures, given the complexity of individuals' and countries' socio-economic status; this appears to be particularly pertinent when literacy and access to books is the sole focus.

Perhaps you also included 'developing listening skills' as a further benefit of reading/sharing stories in your earlier list. We already know that storytelling and/or sharing stories is crucial to developing listening skills, which is also a key component of early reading for under-fives.

Table 4.1 Developing listening skills with sharing stories and storytelling

Sharing stories/books	Storytelling
Adult can make some eye contact	Adult is able to make consistent eye contact
Adult can use some gestures, body language to capture attention	Adult is able to make good use of gestures, body language and maintain attention/interest

Sharing stories/books	Storytelling
Adult can use interesting facial expressions, vocal adaptations to capture further engagement in the storybook	Adult is able to use and model interesting facial expressions, vocal adaptations to capture further engagement in the story
Adult can invite participation at key points	Adult can invite participation throughout the story, without being distracted by the book
Adult is reliant on their choice of story book for developing further language opportunities	Adult is able to use repetitive language and introduce enhanced language patterns of rhyme, rhythm, alliteration, throughout the story. Adult is able to use gesture and sign language, where appropriate
Adult can develop auditory memory, attention and develop further communication skills after the story or interrupt the story	Adult can initiate and enhance auditory memory, attention and develop further communication skills
	Everyone can have extended fun with developing new endings for the story, using props, puppets, soft toys, story sacks, images, artefacts, familiar objects

- Review the table above and consider the points made – do you agree?
- Can you add anything further?
- Think about your own experiences of sharing storybooks and storytelling with young children.
- Complete a similar table for 'developing language skills' while sharing stories and storytelling. You may find this a useful exercise to complete in your setting.

Storytelling is an influential way to develop and enhance children's listening, speaking and communication skills. It is also a great way to develop and extend speech, vocabulary, the pattern of stories, characters and events. For example, stories have a beginning, middle and ending with characters, settings and interesting events. It is significant to note that researchers, including Bourdieu et al. (1994), argue that sharing stories is a particularly important factor for enhanced vocabulary development for very young children, given the increased potential for new and interesting vocabulary introduced within books (Cunningham & Stanovich, 1998). Bourdieu also suggests that cultural resources matter more than material resources for cognitive outcomes, linked to reading – interactions, social relationships, community, role models. As such, it is crucial to consider value and representation in our storytelling, reading and sharing stories for all children within the choices we make about role models or characters within these stories. Thomas (2022) highlights that 'when Black, Asian and racially minoritised children have role models who look like them, they are more likely to feel a sense of belonging' and therefore able to 'visualise themselves in different roles' (p. 106). This also includes and equally applies to inclusion, disability and gender identity (for example, lesbian, gay, bisexual, transgender, queer or questioning, LGBTQI+).

Activity 4.4: Sharing Stories and Storytelling

Using Table 4.1, think about how sharing stories and storytelling develops communication, speaking and language skills for children under five.

Is there a notable difference between sharing a story and telling a story? Why?
Think about Bourdieu's view of cultural resources for early reading – what does he mean and how does this link to your own understanding of early reading?
Think about how you choose storybooks and picture books. Have you carefully considered positive representation within the characters, images?

It is absolutely essential to ensure that you share stories, using books, images, picture books and tell stories often during the nursery and school day, in both large and small groups. In addition to this, make time to read with individual children and read aloud in small or large groups. Most literacy advocates recommend that children in nursery or school should be involved in stories, reading aloud and storytelling activities at least three times a day. I would urge all early years professionals to follow the advice of Palmer and Bayley (2013) and read aloud with children five times a day! I would also suggest that we read outdoors to children as often as we can and encourage children to do this also – after all you can read, sing or rhyme anywhere.

Let's consider the early years practitioner's/teacher's thoughts about how often, when and why they share stories with under-fives:

Nursery Practitioner (Pre-School Room)

I try to share a picture book one-to-one with all my key children every day. I have eight key children, so it is possible – it does depend though on what else we plan to do. We read a story at story time at the end of the morning session and the afternoon session and we have a rhyme time during the day. I think it is really important to read stories to pre-school children to support their early reading development.

Reception Teacher

We have three story time sessions in our daily routine and our children just love this – a morning story, just before lunch and at the end of the day. There are 28 children in my class, so it is difficult to read with them on a one-to-one basis. I know all the advice out there is to read on a one-to-one basis, small group and whole group to engage children in reading.

However, we do a lot of listening games, talking and our continuous provision environment has books everywhere!

Nursery Practitioner (Baby Room)

We don't have a set story time with our babies – we look at picture books together perhaps just before lunch or after lunch to help with settling for sleep. Babies have access to books – hard-backed on the carpet area and we do have cloth books in cots. I have tried to do a story time with nine-month-olds – but they like to look at the books themselves mainly.

Nursery Manager (Private Day Nursery)

We encourage sharing stories – reading or telling throughout the day. It is really important to us that we do share stories with each room – babies and toddlers have one-to-one stories. Our pre-school enjoy story time at the end of the morning, before lunch. This helps to create a calm, relaxed atmosphere and at the end of the day too.

Activity 4.5: How Often Do We Read with Children

Write your own case study about how often, when and why you share stories with under-fives in your setting or your experience.

> Think carefully about how often this happens and when – why is this important?
> If you are not sharing stories more than once in your typical day, what else are you doing to encourage early reading in the wider literacy context?
> Do you read outdoors?
> Go back to your list of the benefits of reading – can you add anything further?

You may find it interesting that practitioners/teachers referred to reading as 'looking at picture books' and also as a quiet activity. As we have previously determined, sharing stories is only one aspect of our early reading provision within the wider literacy context. Remember that music, movement, rhythm and rhyme are also important and, as such, we cannot stress enough about talk, gesture, communication and language for early reading. In addition, early reading does not need to be quiet or inactive.

Many children from birth now have a digital footprint of their own, given that digital media influences how we live and sometimes how we learn. A digital footprint refers to the path of data left while using digital media from the information an individual submits online. Families might register their babies' data for support, for gifts, shopping and also use platforms to share their achievements (Facebook, Twitter, Instagram, Tik-Tok). For some very young children, digital media and television already influences how young children develop their early talk and understanding of literacy, as this is often a medium for how families support their learning and well-being. Traditional literacy in today's society is a very different concept to what it is for young children – particularly for under-fives. Think about how often you use a pen and paper, for example. You might be more likely to type into your phone or tablet. How often do you visit a library or purchase books – perhaps you prefer to download from a kindle or website.

Reflection Points

- Think about how society has changed relating to literacy. Can you think of some examples of how it might be a different environment for young children in nursery compared to older children in the community?
- Discuss digital footprints for young children and make some notes about your thoughts to take back to your setting.
- Think about how television as a medium might influence learning for children.

Text, symbols, imagery and technology are everywhere within the literacy community environment. Literacy is often captured in print with a variety of texts alongside imagery everywhere on a wide variety of screens (phones, tablets, advertising boards, signs etc.). In addition, text is constantly on electronic displays (shops, outdoor spaces, toys, resources, cars, trains, buses, aeroplanes, QR codes etc.). Consequently, Smith and Arizpe (2016) suggest that young children, families and communities must see literacy today as an inseparable function of everyday life, given the wide range of electronic words and images carried everywhere. As such, literacy – reading and writing – is key to communication, and this appears everywhere in our world. Therefore, early reading is all about communication, language, talking, interactions, relationships and meaning-making.

However, it is also important to remember that the focus on reading and traditional literacies is still rooted in the printed word in our ECEC settings and schools. Marsh et al. (2015) highlighted in their paper 'Play and creativity in young children's use of apps' that approximately a third of under-fives own their own tablet at home. I wonder if this is replicated in our ECEC settings, valued, or encouraged.

Additionally, it appears that children's literature has not yet caught up with today's communities. CLPE (2022) highlights that only 15 per cent of children's books feature characters who are black, Asian or minority ethnic characters/communities in its *Reflecting Realities survey of ethnic representation within UK children's literature 2017–2021*. The findings also note that only 7 per cent of fiction titles published in 2020 featured characters of colour. Although there is improvement from previous years, this is significant to note.

Reflection Points

Think about the *Reflecting Realities* (CLPE, 2022) study findings above.

Think about the messages this data is suggesting for UK children's literature.

Think about how important representation is for children under five.

It is so important for young children to read in whatever form they wish to – digital or print. It is also vital that children engage in reading experiences that support their cultural worlds – rhyme, rap, poetry, all forms of music-making. As we have already discussed, it is equally important to ensure that images and experiences reflect the children, families and communities who live in our world.

Let's consider how we can support literacy when we visit places of interest and what these valuable cultural experiences offer young children. Think about visiting:

- art galleries
- museums
- libraries
- zoos
- aquariums
- theme parks.

Art galleries, museums and zoos offer a wealth of literacy experiences for under-fives. Young children will see and sometimes be able to touch new objects, artefacts, paintings and drawings and can take part in QR code activities, digital screen tasks, treasure trails and listening pods, to name a few. Most art galleries and museums have dedicated play spaces for under-threes to explore and investigate water, paint, mud, bubble machines, sensory play, machinery etc. Many art galleries and museums also have stay and play sessions for parents, carers and families. Equally, local libraries offer similar early reading experiences, plus storytelling sessions or rhyme sessions. My local museum offers book-making sessions with nursery groups and reception classes and 'rapping rhyme time' slots for under-threes. MacRae (2007) reflects on a collaborative project between an art gallery and a university with the purpose of encouraging very young children and their families to engage in exploration of the art gallery. Sessions such as 'Exploring with Fingers' (p. 163) highlighted that museums must begin to offer more tactile experiences for very young children, with examples of 'where children encounter paintings, telling stories about them is one way to imagine them, but so is having things represented in the picture to look at and handle' (p. 168). Museums and art galleries can and do offer a vast range of tactile literacy experiences, where talk and exploration are encouraged – not just based on arts education. MacRae discusses the ways that museum visits can connect people, families, places and culture – powerful early reading narratives. Are you making the most of your local places of interest?

Reflection Point

If you are unable to take nursery/reception children on outings, consider bringing some of these experiences into your setting. Consider contacting libraries, museums and art galleries to see how you can connect.

Outdoor Literacy Experiences

Outdoor literacy experiences can often be overlooked or forgiveably, not purposefully planned for outdoors. For example, the premise of outdoors, Forest School, Udeskole approaches,* Beach School and local nature reserves are not often considered early reading or literacy experiences and are associated with freedom, nature and the natural physical world, for very good reasons. Indeed, the features of Forest School include regular, long-term access to freely roam and explore the natural outdoors (Knight, 2016). However, when we have true Forest School settings that allow children to spend all or most of their time outdoors, it feels reasonable to consider where early reading and literacy might fit in. There are a wide range of early reading experiences already in place for many settings, engaging in Forest School, such as:

- use of 'talking and thinking floorbooks' to document children's ideas and learning;
- nature craft-making activities;
- outdoor cookery;
- 'smell pots', perfume-making;
- sensory story walks;
- journey sticks;
- nature trail – following pathways and patterns;
- linking trees and story-making (Waters, 2011);
- tree climbing;
- mud mark-making, mud faces;
- wood name tags, necklaces, crown-making, bracelets;
- earth walks (focused on sensory experiences);
- leaf art, wild weaving, natural art;
- den-making, bridge-making;
- natural musical instruments and music-making;
- self-portraits and mythical characters to begin storytelling;
- using tools, bushcraft.

These ideas are just some of the activities I have carried out as a Forest School lead. There will be many more.

There are also many opportunities for singing, rhyming, chanting and reflecting in the forest.

---

* Udeskole is a Scandinavian curriculum-based approach where learning occurs outdoors in both natural and cultural settings, focusing on natural environments – it is 'outdoor school'. It is not the same as Forest School or Beach School, as they all have individual principles.

There is much to be said about the informal'ness' of learning outdoors, which draws out deeper knowledge, builds confidence and 'feeds us spirituality, emotionally' (Barnes, 2007, p. 92). This is the complete opposite, of course, of 'receiving knowledge' indoors.

Activity 4.6: Outdoors for Literacy

Using the list of early reading engagement opportunities at Forest schools above, explore these early reading opportunities for young children outdoors. Reflect further on your understanding of early reading.

Can you introduce some of these ideas to your outdoor areas if you don't already have a Forest School experience in place?

Now think about Beach School – what kinds of experiences might this approach offer to under-fives to support early reading?

Find out more about Udeskole 'outdoor school' and consider how being outdoors promotes academic well-being.

Using the natural environment is powerful to support literacy – why is this important?

Beach School follows similar principles of Forest School and utilises the coast as the platform for new learning experiences – the opportunity to explore their natural surroundings.

Aside from the previous outdoor school approaches, your own settings will have outdoor spaces to enable you to plan for early reading experiences outdoors. You might wish to consider creating an outdoor space to encourage reflection, language and listening outdoors. For example:

- having a picnic blanket, a comfortable seating area, carpet and some outdoor cushions on the ground so that you can tell stories or sing songs outdoors;
- hanging sheets from trees or draped over branches;
- creating a natural music-making space – hanging a range of natural materials over a fence, on a stand or on the floor;
- creating a series of sensory props – natural materials, twigs, flowers, shells and so on;
- using torches and battery-powered lanterns for shadow-making.

Why is it Important for Young Children to Write?

Reading and writing go hand to hand. As such, it is important to provide many writing and mark-making opportunities alongside early reading experiences. Significantly, very young children often explore and develop their writing through play (Smith and Vincent 2022).

Writing is also all about communicating, language, talking, interacting, making meaning and, 'most importantly', 'language changes thinking' (Stewart & Moylett, 2022, p. 115). For under-fives, mark-making is writing. It is important for children to write for all the same reasons it is for them to read – to be able to navigate their place in their world and represent themselves. However, the formality of writing is not just the end product for under-fives. It is essential to immerse children in experiences involving malleable materials, sensory experiences, large physical movements, finger-play rhymes and songs as well as painting and drawing, using scissors and plenty of other writing resources. Try to leave the formality of requesting that children write letters and words until at least Year 1 when children are six years old if you can, unless they want to. I do appreciate that this is problematic!

Reflection Point

Think about all the ways in which you use/record/access/read or write information in your typical day. Start with as soon as you wake up … it is probably a very long list!

Your list will include a variety of ways in which you need to know how to read and write to get through your day. Perhaps some of these will also apply to young children?

Case Study 4.1: Writing is Mark-Making

A fifteen-month-old child is using crayons and paper to make marks, using curved lines and dots, choosing different colours and holding the crayons in lots of different positions to make marks. Outdoors, on the floor, on the wall and a chalkboard surface the same child uses chalks to dot and make large marks, using up all the space on the chalkboard. In the water tray and sand tray the child makes marks with a variety of resources – cars in the sand, sticks, squeezy bottles. The intent to make marks is clear. Their mark-making includes large movements and small movements.

Very young children write – not only by producing the shapes of letters and words, but by making marks. These marks have meaning and, although seemingly random, the intent is clear. When children see writing in their environment and have writing modelled to them and with them in a variety of ways, they will continue to make marks and write. It is fascinating observing children making meaning from their mark-making and how they use the space and materials provided. In my experience all materials are writing materials.

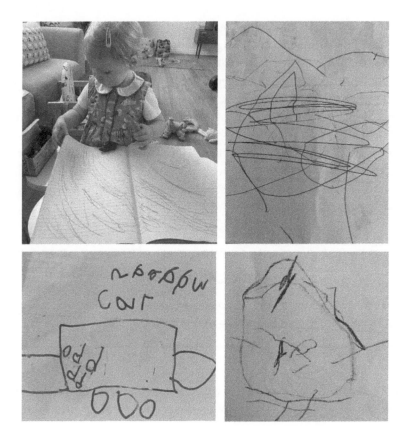

Reflection Points

Let's think about scaffolding children's writing.

Try to resist the urge to use dots to form outlines of the shape of letters to encourage writing and particularly when children are writing their names – this is not a useful scaffold, and it may suggest to young children that they have to write in a certain way and that their way of writing/mark-making is invalid. My own child was taught in nursery to write his name with a scaffold of dots and whenever he wrote his name, he wrote his name and then added dots over the top!

Remember that writing is what the child intends and is often not as random as you think. Writing and mark-making are very different processes to the formality of 'handwriting'.

Consider how you support children's writing in your setting.

Literacy Provision for Under-Threes

It is widely acknowledged within ECEC literature and research that babies and toddlers are expert learners from birth (DfE, 2014; Moylett, 2022). Indeed, Gopnik et al. (1999) suggest that babies and toddlers are 'mini-scientists, already primed to explore, investigate and explain their word' (p. 17). Researchers are also in agreement that literacy development begins from birth and continues throughout these early childhood years (Morrow & Dougherty, 2011; Stewart & Moylett, 2022; Wolf, 2008). We have already highlighted how babies and young children explore and engage in those early experiences and interactions with literacy materials such as sounds, pictures, books, paper and mark-making resources and, more recently, with digital resources such as tablets and computers, alongside adults' communications and engagement. This understanding that literacy development begins from birth complements contemporary research that supports the criticality of early experiences, provision and interactions in shaping early brain development (Conkbayir, 2022; Finnegan, 2016; Gros-Louis et al., 2016). In addition, we have already discussed in earlier chapters how babies are learning the processes and patterns of language from birth (Blythe, 2011). Hence, language and literacy provision for under-threes is inextricably linked to interactions, routines and significant adults. Pahl and Allan (2011) highlight that their research with nursery children 'led to an understanding of literacy as connective and linked to emotional and sensory experiences' (p. 212). Therefore, it is essential in shaping very young children's experiences; their learning and development (Kuhl et al., 2006) and reminds us again about providing quality interactions. Byrnes and Wasik (2009) suggest that when significant adults share 'language patterns and the rhythm of stories', songs and rhymes, these 'shared conversations also support the working memory' (p. 205), which, as we are already aware from previous chapters, is an essential element in supporting early reading and wider literacy development and writing.

Research into the beginnings of communication and the development of language considers all aspects, such as baby signing (Vallotton, 2009, 2011) and bilinguialsim. Many studies place the value of talking, interacting and communicating through play as central to the wider literacy context. In addition, the findings from Powell et al.'s (2013, p. 15) Froebel Trust Baby Room Project highlight how singing songs and rhymes often with babies promotes 'intimacy, connectedness' and shapes babies' educational and emotional growth in literacy – powerful learning!

Nursery Children and Their Literacy Learning

Wood (2013) suggests that literacy within playful pedagogies is now more clearly established within research. As such, the associations between children's play and significant literacy learning have also been previously documented by Paley (2004), Nutbrown (1999) and Hall and Robinson (2003). Hence, nursery children's knowledge about language, language patterns, sounds and words can be developed through playful and imaginative interactions with knowledgeable adults, both at home and in settings (Smith & Vincent 2022). Purposeful activities such as singing nursery rhymes, songs, raps, music-making and focusing on alliteration patterns in songs, rhymes and stories supports nursery children with their early reading development (Goouch & Lambirth, 2013; Whitehead, 2009, 2010). Children naturally attune to the beating of a rhythm and sense of structure when immersed in a playful environment that encourages and promotes singing, music-making, nursery rhymes, finger-play songs and sharing stories often. This learning will be explored further in later chapters.

Review and Rethinking Pedagogy

- Create an action plan to support literacy provision for under-fives – think about the things you might not yet do and the things you would like to put into practice. Also think about the wonderful stuff that you already do to support literacy.
- How will you build in representation, culture and communities?
- How will you ensure that you share your ideas with all stakeholders?
- How does singing, rhyme and rhythm fit into your early reading provision? How often?
- Remember to include early reading and writing – consider carefully what writing is for very young children.
- Think about some things you may need to discuss back at your setting to support literacy in context.

In Summary

To summarise, I have used the term 'early literacy' to refer to language, communication, reading and writing, which are based upon current theoretical perspectives of emergent literacy and social practice perspectives. Much of the international literature suggests that it is essential that teacher/practitioners create a literacy-rich, reciprocal environment for young children and promote language and literacy within their everyday practice and provision, as these early literacy behaviours shape early reading development (Pan et al., 2005). Wolf (2008) indicates that these high-quality literacy experiences (such as talk, language and communication, enjoyment of books, positive interactions, and social experiences with wider literacy materials) will consequently support early reading and writing skills and begin to nurture an engagement with and an impactful love of reading and writing.

Further Reading to Continue Your Learning

Paulo Freire's seminal work explains the socio-cultural approaches to literacy.

Freire, P., & Macedo, D. (1987). *Literacy: reading the word and the world.* Bergin & Garvey.

This book presents some interesting concepts and theories about children and their families exploring museums and places of heritage, which is relevant for all ECEC professionals.

Hackett, A., Holmes, R., & MacRae, C. (Eds.) (2020). *Working with young children in museums: weaving theory and practice.* Routledge.

Read more about EYFS approaches to mark-making and writing from Penny Tassoni, writing for Early Education in 2022.

early-education.org.uk/making-their-mark-childrens-early-writing/

@teach_outdoors is an informative Twitter site to support professionals with ideas and connections for teaching and planning experiences outdoors. It is also useful to connect to international networks for Forest School and Outdoor Learning as well as national organisations.

www.outdoor-learning.org/

Read more about the unheard voices of boys who feel demotivated by the formality and structured approach to reading in Malta.

Bonello, C. (2022). Boys, early literacy and children's rights in a postcolonial context a case study from Malta. Routledge.

References

Banerjee, P.A., & Eryilmaz, N. (2022). Can we really trust socioeconomic measures used in PISA tests? BERA Blog Post 5 September. British Educational Research Association.

Barnes, S. (2007). *How to be wild.* Short Books.

Blythe, S.G. (2011). *The genius of natural childhood: secrets of thriving children.* Hawthorn Press.

Boardman, K. (2017). 'I know I don't read enough or even pick up a book in the baby room sometimes': early years teacher trainees' perceptions and beliefs about reading with under-threes. Doctoral thesis. University of Sheffield.

Bourdieu, P., Passeron, J.-C., & Saint-Martin, M. (1994). *Academic discourse.* Polity Press.

Byrnes, J.P., & Wasik, B.A. (2009). *Language and literacy development: what educators need to know.* Guilford Press.

Centre for Literacy in Primary Education (CLPE) (2022). *Reflecting Realities survey of ethnic representation within UK children's literature 2017–2021.* CLPE.

Conkbayir, M. (2022). *Early childhood and neuroscience: theory, research and implications for practice.* Bloomsbury.

Cunningham, A.E., & Stanovich, K.E. (1998) What reading does for the mind. *American Educator, 22*(1–2), 8–15.

Department for Education (DfE) (2014a). *Graduate leaders in early years. early years teachers.* DfE. www.education.gov.uk/childrenandyoungpeople/earlylearningand childcare/h00230355/graduate-early-years-leadership/early-years-teachers

Department for Education (DfE) (2014b). *Improving the quality and range of education and childcare from birth to 5 years.* DfE.

Education Scotland (2016). *Curriculum for excellence: statement for practitioners.* August. Education Scotland.

Elkin, J. (2014). Babies need books in the critical early years of life. *New Review of Children's Literature and Librarianship, 20*(1), 40–63.

Finnegan, J. (2016). *Lighting up young brains: how parents, carers and nurseries support children's brain development in the first five years*. Save the Children.

Freire, P. (2004). *Pedagogy of hope* (new ed.). Continuum.

Goouch, K. (2014). Baby rooms. In V. Bower (Ed.), *Developing early literacy 0–8: from theory to practice*. Sage.

Goouch, K., & Lambirth, A. (2013). *Teaching early reading and phonics. creative approaches to early literacy*. 2nd ed. Sage.

Gopnik, A., Meltzoff, A., & Kuhl, P. (1999). *How babies think*. Weidenfeld & Nicholson.

Gros-Louis, J., West, M.J., & King, A.P. (2016). The influence of interactive context on prelinguistic vocalisations and maternal responses. *Language Learning and Development, 12*(3), 280–294.

Hall, N., & Robinson, A. (2003). *Exploring writing and play in the early years*. Fulton.

International Study Centre (IEA) (2021). *Progress in International Reading Literacy Study*. PIRLS.

Knight, S. (2016). *Forest School in practice: for all ages*. Sage.

Kuhl, P., Stevens, E., Hayashi, A., Deguchis, T., Kiritani, S., & Iverson, P. (2006). Infants show a facilitation effect for native language phonetic perception between 6 and 12 months. *Developmental Science, 9*(2), 13–21.

MacRae, C. (2007). Using sense to make sense of art: young children in art galleries. *Early Years, 27*(2), 159–170. doi: 10.1080/09575140701425290

Marsh, J., Plowman, L., Yamada-Rice, D., Bishop, J., Lahmar, J., Scott, F., Davenport, A., Davis, S., French, K., Piras, M., Thornhill, S., Robinson, P., & Winter, P. (2015). Play and creativity in young children's use of apps. *British Journal of Educational Technology, 49*(5), 870–882. doi.org/10.1111/bjet.12622

Morrow, L., & Dougherty, S. (2011). Early literacy development: merging perspectives that influence practice. *Journal of Reading Education, 36*(3), 5–11.

Moylett, H. (Ed.) (2022). *Characteristics of effective early learning: helping young children become learners for life*. 2nd ed. Open University.

Mullis, I.V.S., & Martin, M. (Eds.) (2021). *PIRLS 2021 Assessment frameworks*. IEA.

Nutbrown, C. (1999). *Threads of thinking: young children learning and the role of early education*. Paul Chapman.

Pahl, K., & Allan, C. (2011). I don't know what literacy is: uncovering hidden literacies in a community library using ecological and participatory research methodologies with children. *Journal of Early Childhood Literacy, 11*(2), 190.

Paley, V. (2004). *A child's work: the importance of fantasy play*. University of Chicago Press.

Palmer, S., & Bayley, R. (2013). *Foundations of literacy: a balanced approach to language, listening and literacy skills in the early years*. 4th ed. Featherstone.

Pan, B.A., Rowe, M.L., Singer, J.D., & Snow, C.E. (2005). Maternal correlates of growth in toddler vocabulary production in low-income families. Child Development, *76*, 763–782.

Powell, S., Goouch, K., & Werth, L. (2013). Seeking Froebel's mother songs in daycare for babies. TACTYC occasional paper. TACTYC Annual Research Conference.

Reid, G. (2003). *Dyslexia: a practitioner's handbook*. Wiley-Blackwell.

Smith, V., & Arizpe, E. (2016). Introduction: the fictional portrayal of reading. In E. Arizpe & V. Smith (Eds.), *Children as readers in children's literature: the power of texts and the importance of reading*. Routledge.

Smith, K and Vincent, K. (2022). Supporting early literacies through play. London: Sage.

Stewart, N., & Moylett, H. (2022). Interaction and talking for learning and thinking. In H. Moylet (Ed.), *Characteristics of effective early learning: helping young children become learners for life* (pp. 115–129). 2nd ed. Open University.

Thomas, A. (2022). *Representation matters: becoming an anti-racist educator*. Bloomsbury.

Vallotton, C. (2009). Do infants influence their quality of care? Infants' communicative gestures predict caregivers' responsiveness. *Infant Behavior and Development, 32,* 351–365.

Vallotton, C. (2011). Sentences and conversations before speech? Gestures of preverbal children reveal cognitive and social skills that do not wait for words. In G. Stam & M. Ishino (Eds.), *Integrating gesture: the interdisciplinary nature of gesture* (pp. 105–120). John Benjamins.

Waters, P. (2011). *Learning with nature: embedding outdoor practice*. Sage.

Whitehead, M. (2009). *Supporting language and literacy development in the early years*. 2nd ed. Open University Press/McGraw-Hill.

Whitehead, M. (2010). *Language and literacy in the early years 0–7*. Sage.

Wolf, M. (2008). *Proust and the squid: the story and science of the reading brain*. Icon.

Wood, E. (2013). *Play, learning and the early childhood curriculum*. 3rd ed. Sage.

5

EARLY READING AND PHONICS: SYSTEMATIC SYNTHETIC PHONICS

Chapter Objectives

This chapter will consider the national and international policy debates about teaching phonics within the broader literacy remit. By the end of this chapter, you will:

- understand where the teaching of systematic synthetic phonics (SSP) 'fits into' the early reading and phonics debate nationally and internationally;
- consider the complexity of school readiness and top-down approaches from policy-makers, associated with measurement and attainment in reading;
- understand the position of the DfE Phonics Screening Check and the implications for children, practitioners and teachers;
- review SSP policy and pedagogy for under-fives.

Early Reading and Phonics

This chapter outlines what the local and international policy stance is for teaching phonics and supports the reader with their understanding of the idea that phonics teaching is a small part of a much wider debate to enable children to be lifelong readers. This is a significant chapter to support you with why you need to understand how and where the teaching of systematic synthetic phonics (SSP) 'fits into' the early reading and phonics debate. It is hoped that you will reflect and respond to this chapter and be empowered to counteract the constant steer to focus on teaching phonics when this is just not appropriate pedagogy for under-threes. When we discuss pedagogy and provision for under-fives, formal SSP teaching has no place in our nursery settings – yet there is a vital place for early reading.

It is widely accepted that learning to read is highly complex, involving the 'process of making sense of many different signs, symbols and codes' (Wyse & Goswami, 2008, p. 706), while using the social and cultural contexts of these varied experiences to make meaning. Wyse and Goswami (2008) also highlight that learning to read is 'one of the most complex achievements of the human brain' (p. 706), which is conceivably why there is the breadth and depth of research, policy and governance attempting to under-stand and identify how children learn to read. In addition, Wyse and Bradbury (2021) suggest that given the nature of reading and its association with educational attain-ment, reading is the key measurement for education overall, with high accountability stakes for England and across society. This chapter seeks to inform and position these high stakes with the children at the heart, rather than the policy-makers. It appears that accountability for reading in England is focused specifically on the teaching of SSP, which some might consider to be misplaced. Wyse and Bradbury (2021, p. 13) also propose that 'England's national curriculum has more emphasis on phonics teaching than any other', the other curricula in their study being Canada, Alberia, Ontario and Quebec, Ireland, New Zealand, Australia and USA. I would also argue that the emphasis on SSP is present in the *Statutory framework for the Early Years Foundation Stage* (DfE, 2014) for under-fives. Therefore, this political stance from England is not aligned with interna-tional contemporary debates about literacy and/or the teaching of phonics, and as Wyse and Bradbury (2021, p. 1) suggest 'England represents an outlier.'

Why Do We Teach Reading Focused on Phonics?

Phonics is one specific approach to teaching reading, which is focused on letter–sound correspondence. This means that children are taught how the letter names (graphemes) are linked to the sounds (phonemes) and how to join (blend) the sounds together into words. Phonics is aligned with how the alphabetic code works and how this is applied in reading and spelling. The alphabetic code is the relationship between individual letters of the alphabet (or groups of letters) and the smallest units of sounds in spoken language – letter–sound correspondences. The alphabet consists of 26 letters and the alphabetic code is how these 26 letters represent 44 (or smore) sounds. There are many versions of the alphabetic code in existence from dedicated phonics SSP schemes, such as Phonics Interna-tional, Read, Write Inc., Monster Phonics and so on. These schemes are DfE validated and approved and operate in similar ways to support the discrete whole-class or small-group systematic teaching – beginning with the simple to complex synthetic phonics approaches.

Decades of research into how children learn to read suggests that this is still very much a contested space in that there is some agreement on phonics as an approach to support reading, but perhaps not SSP as such a prescriptive approach. Kelly and Phil-lips (2011) suggest that 'reading involves the two main skills of the ability to decode graphemes (printed symbols, letters) into phonemes (sounds) and comprehension skills – extracting meaning from those words' (p. 54). Similarly, Turbill (2001) advocates that learning to read is all about 'learning to break the code of print' (p. 274), as do Roul-stone et al. (2011), proposing that reading involves cracking the printed code, with the knowledge that this code involves understanding the sounds (phonemes) that make the words, beginning or ending sounds and rhyme. As such, many researchers are already in agreement that teaching phonics is important for young children, when centred on reading as print based. In contrast, various contemporary studies of reading acknowledge 'the many modes of literacy, which include visual, information, emotional, digital technologies and multimodal texts' (Simpson, 2013, p. 16). Essentially, other contemporary research also aligns the development of reading with communication, speech, language and confidence in understanding the world and is not just based on the printed word (Clark, 2017; Finnegan, 2016; Hulme & Snowling, 2013; Preece & Levy, 2020).

If we go back to the earlier chapters of this book, we have already reviewed our understanding of early reading and how this involves a great deal of talking, listening and communicating which is not necessarily linked to the printed word. We also need to remember that reading behaviours, feelings and emotions are being nurtured (or not) when we focus our attention on early reading rather than the teaching of phonics. Claxton and Carr (2004) propose that the behaviours and feelings surrounding reading are already developing from birth during this early learning process and in context for very young children. Context is the crucial component of the argument for many researchers against teaching SSP as the only approach to teach reading. Yet, this is where the policy is firmly rooted in English schools.

Activity 5.1: Reflection on Policy

Why do you think that the National Curriculum in England has more emphasis on phonics teaching than many other national and international comparisons?

Think about the rationale for an increased emphasis on phonics in Development Matters (DfE, 2020) and the EYFS (DfE, 2014), when we know that the age range for these frameworks is birth to five years.

What do you already know about teaching phonics? And teaching SSP specifically?

Find out more information about the alphabetic code – what does this mean and how will you explain this to a colleague or a parent/carer?

Why do you think England is not aligned with any other country when it comes to the reading debate? Where do Scotland, Ireland, Northern Ireland and Wales fit into the SSP mandate?

The Policy Stance on Systematic Synthetic Phonics (SSP)

The contentious debate of teaching phonics has led to a particular viewpoint, beginning in England with the *Independent review of the teaching of early reading* in 2006. Rose (2006) highlighted that an investment in SSP training as the prime approach would support young children's abilities to develop as lifelong readers. The remit for the Rose Review examined:

- 'what best practice should be expected in the teaching of early reading and synthetic phonics';
- how this relates to the development of curriculum frameworks (birth to five and National Literacy Strategy);

- 'what range of provision best supports children with significant literacy difficulties and enables them to catch up with their peers, and the relationship of such targeted intervention programmes with synthetic phonics teaching';
- leadership and management in schools to support best practice;
- value for money and cost effectiveness.

(Rose, 2006, p. 7)

Previous to the Rose Review (2006), practitioners/teachers were utilising a range of teaching methods to support children, which included analytical phonics/whole-word approaches and/or a mix of methods. The analytical teaching method relies upon children learning to recognise words instantly from memory, without requiring them to sound letters out, say the sounds in the order they appear or decode them – often using sight word flashcards. Some researchers have suggested that SSP can be supplemented by analytical techniques when children are faced with non-decodable words, such as 'was' or 'are', as a mixed methods approach (Cameron, 2001; Ehri et al., 2001). Consequently, with research evidence (sometimes contested) gathered from 2010, the UK government has embedded the approach of teaching SSP as the prime approach to teaching reading across all schools in England. However, this focus on one particular approach (SSP) does not recognise that very young children already have social and cultural experiences from birth, involving reading activities in their cultural home environments within the broader definition of reading, previously discussed in Chapters 1 and 4. For example, Erhi et al. (2001) advocate that phonics is just one element of promoting reading development, which needs to be embedded within a rich literacy curriculum. This appears to be the key area of tension from a review of the literature and research relating to the teaching of SSP. Other issues that arise with teaching SSP are that it is a narrow and prescriptive focus, and the expected fast pace of all the SSP scheme approaches do not align within the context and experiences of reading for many children. Researchers, such as Johnson and Watson (2005), Goswami (2015) and Torgeson et al. (2006) advocate that phonics teaching is important for reading development, but it is often not the whole story. This is also the argument that I make within the early reading debate – yes, teaching SSP is important, but not the only approach as all children are individuals and children learn in a variety of ways. Young children need to understand language patterns, letters and sounds and the letters of the alphabet which hold meaning and context for individual children before we even consider teaching SSP.

Nevertheless, the teaching of SSP is now a priority for all schools, teachers and trainee teachers (DfE Phonics Screening Check, 2012 onwards; Ofsted, 2014, 2016, 2022) and has also been embedded within the *Early Years Foundation Stage Curriculum* (DfE, 2014, 2020) and *National Curriculum* (DfE, 2014) in England. The *Early Years Foundation Stage Statutory Framework* (DfE, 2017, 2021) ELGs feature the prominence of SSP for literacy, reading and writing, which is unique among international pre-school curriculum pedagogical approaches. It is interesting to highlight that the Rose Review (2006) suggested that 'for most children, high quality, systematic phonic work should start by the age of five' (p. 29), yet this is not the case in many nursery and/or reception classrooms. Given that most early reading research is aimed at children in schools (aged four or five years and above), and places phonics at the heart of the teaching, there is little or no literature on what teaching reading with under-fives looks like if it is not teaching phonics. It is, therefore, no surprise that the phonics debate intrudes on curriculum pedagogy and provision with under-fives. To illustrate, the early childhood workforce (and their families and communities) is subject to a wide range of policy documents focused only on SSP as the principal approach to teaching reading. This then leads to an increasing emphasis on outcomes: the 'standards agenda' described by Roberts-Holmes and Bradbury (2016), which is a feature in many early years settings. Settings, then start to plan interventions and their teaching approaches based on SSP grouping, sometimes from as young as three years old (Bradbury, 2018a, 2018b; Bradbury & Roberts-Holmes, 2017). This can also be described as 'schoolification' of the early years sector (Moss, 2014; Roberts-Holmes, 2015; Vannebo & Gotvassli, 2017), which is at odds with many international approaches to ECEC.

Figure 5.1 is a chart that I produced in 2017 to present the policy directives and wider sources of information that influence and undoubtedly impact on pedagogy and early

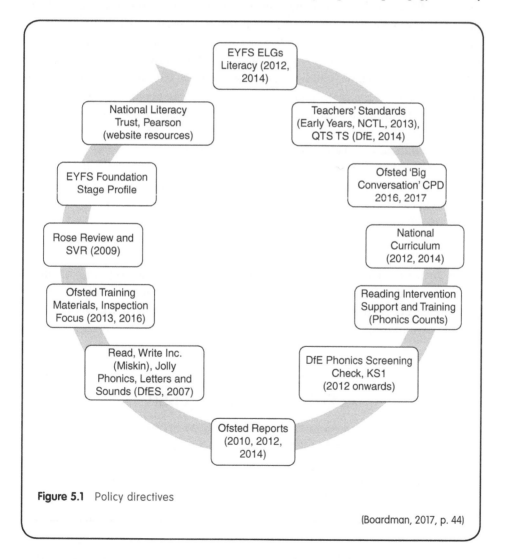

Figure 5.1 Policy directives

(Boardman, 2017, p. 44)

years provision. I suggested in 2017 (Boardman, 2017, p. 44) that these policy directives lead to an 'intense, unnecessary focus' on teaching phonics (SSP) in nurseries with
under-threes, three- and four-year-olds and in reception classes in England.

Activity 5.2: Review of the Policy Directives

What are your thoughts on this diagram?

Do you think that any of these sources have or do influence your provision, or your pedagogy?

Think about anything else you can add to this diagram to update it for 2023 and beyond.

For example, ELGs were updated in 2021 and the focus on phonic outcomes is still present.

How do you think these sources of information influence parents, carers and families and
consequently impact on pedagogy for under-fives?

To update this diagram, you may have suggested that all these boxes would still be in
place with new updates for 2022, 2023 in each box. It would also include the *The reading
framework: teaching the foundations of literacy* (DfE, 2021). This framework is new guidance for schools to meet existing expectations for teaching early reading; it was updated
in January 2022. Therefore, nothing has changed – it is the same intense focus on teaching SSP and the same top-down approach for very young children to be ready for school.
This is also evident in the DfE (2011) policy *Supporting families in the foundation years*:

> the government has made clear its view that teaching in the early years
> should be focused on improving children's 'school readiness', guiding the
> development of children's cognitive, behavioural, physical and emotional
> capabilities, so that children can take full advantage of the learning
> opportunities available to them in school.
>
> (DfE, 2011, p. 62)

This is further evidence that early years is regarded as the preparatory stage of education, with no value as a pivotal stage of development, which is in stark contrast to many
international perspectives on ECEC. This concept can also be applied to literacy – young
children need to be 'ready' for school – everything we do in nursery is preparation for
reading.

Activity 5.3: Teaching SSP

Think carefully about where SSP fits into your pedagogy. What influences this approach?

Do you feel pressure to teach SSP from leaders, parents, carers, families (PCF) and communities? Where is this coming from?

Think about how you are communicating and sharing information about what you do in your
setting to support early reading for under-fives to PCF – could this be enhanced in any way?

DfE Phonics Screening Check

The Department for Education introduced the Phonics Screening Check (PSC) in 2012. The PSC is designed to check the standard of phonic knowledge achieved by each child at one point in their learning and development. Children are expected to take part in the Phonics Screening Check at the end of Year 1, when they are typically aged six. Children who do not meet the expected standard at this point can retake the check again at the end of Year 2. The PSC was intended to be a light touch annual diagnostic assessment, taking place in June each year. The PSC consists of 40 words – twenty real and twenty pseudo (not real) words – which the child is required to read out loud to the teacher. The pass mark is 32 out of 40. The PSC assessments are expected to be finalised by schools by the end of June and submitted to the DfE by late July. The results are collated by the local authority and submitted to the DfE (guidelines are issued each year by the DfE). The DfE then publishes the results at national, regional, local authority and local authority district level. These statistics are scrutinised by the DfE, school governors and, of course, Ofsted, as a regulatory body. In 2022, this data was published in early October. The 2022 data was not favourable at all. The DfE (2022) presents the headlines that:

Attainment in the phonics screening check has decreased compared to 2019.

75% of pupils met the expected standard in the phonics screening check in year 1, down from 82% in 2019.

87% of pupils met the expected standard in the phonics screening check by the end of year 2, down from 91% in 2019.

Attainment at key stage 1 has decreased in all subjects compared to 2019.

67% of pupils met the expected standard in reading, down from 75% in 2019.

(DfE, 2022)

Notably, there really isn't any great improvement from 2012 onwards. Data from 2018 highlights that 82 per cent of children met the expected standard in the Phonics Screening Check in Year 1, a 1 percentage point increase from 2017. By the end of Year 2, 92 per cent met the standard, the same proportion as in 2017. The 2016 and 2017 results are broadly similar. Therefore, it could be suggested that after a series of intense SSP focus initiatives from 2010 onwards and PSC data from 2012 onwards, there has not been any significant improvement in attainment for children the UK. Significantly, post phonics directives 2016 and 2021/22 do not show much improvement than pre-phonics directives in 2001 or 2006. Clark and Glazzard (2018) propose, in their independent enquiry, The Phonics Screening Check 2012–2017: an independent enquiry into the views of head teachers, teachers and parents (p. 2), that the PSC does not tell teachers anything they did not already know. In addition, the implications from this enquiry suggest that the views expressed by teachers and head teachers 'indicate that the government should seriously consider either discontinuing the check or at least making it voluntary' and concerns were also raised about 'the prescriptive method of SSP to teaching reading'.

This survey was completed by 230 head teachers, 1,348 teachers and also 419 parents/carers.

In reality, there are no comparisons internationally to this PSC attainment data or its usage, given that other countries do not request, mandate or collate this data at this early stage in children's learning. The key question here is why – what does this practice/data tell us and what do we do with this practice/data to support and encourage children to read? Consequently, England's PISA reading scores are essentially unchanged from 2006. This data suggests that this approach may not be working for some children, and we do not know if having this SSP knowledge leads to children reading better, sooner or having stronger comprehension, fluency, engagement, or any further enjoyment of reading, or if they will develop better skills for lifelong reading.

For many educationalists and policy-makers, early reading is the beginning and SSP is the end. Yet, SSP cannot be the end – reading is about context, meaning, comprehension, fluency as well as understanding the culture and our place within this culture. These are just some elements of literacy, which also include critical literacy and disciplinary literacy. We do need to strongly encourage young children to think, question and not just accept everything they read, especially in today's society of social media.

Here are some thoughts for you to consider from reception and Key Stage 1 teachers about teaching SSP and the DfE PSC:

Case Study 5.1: 'We end up Teaching to the Test' (Experienced KS1 Teacher)

My greatest worry is that while I am worrying about the results of the Phonics Screening Check, I am putting pressure on the children that does not need to be there. Perhaps I am missing out more important learning – language, vocabulary, context? I worry about the results, we end up teaching to the test – nonsense words in particular and then I remember that these children are five and six years old. Is this what reading is for them? I don't think so, but it is the remit that I am given.

Case Study 5.2: 'We Can Plug the Gaps and Be Better at Teaching SSP' (Experienced KS1 Teacher)

I am totally behind and on board with SSP – it is the right approach for all of our children and particularly struggling readers. We use the Phonics Screening Check to target our interventions – we can plug the gaps and be better at teaching SSP. We focus on the sounds the children do not know and make them real, meaningful, more personalised for the children. We have adapted our teaching to support the PSC results. We also have lots of fun – I do believe it is the right thing to do. Targeted interventions are working for many of our children.

Case Study 5.3: 'I Know I Have to Get Them to that End Point of Phonics Screening Check' (Experienced Reception Teacher and Senior Leader)

Teaching reading is complex and this is widely accepted. Our Literacy Policy is grounded in what it means to be a reader for all our children. Yet, I know I have to get my reception children to that end point of the PSC in preparation for Y1, which goes by so quickly. So, we end up teaching SSP early on in reception, when some children do not know the letter names of the alphabet yet and some children are still not confident to talk. I struggle to see the relevance sometimes, but then the children really blossom and do so well. My only wish is that we slow it down – slow down the pace of teaching SSP a bit.

Reflection Points

What are your thoughts on these three case studies? What do they tell you about the value of reading, the value of the PSC?

Pull out the key themes from these experiences and discuss them in your setting.

The DfE Phonics Screening Check and the mandate of teaching SSP, alongside statutory assessment tests (SATs), are prime examples of narrowing the literacy curriculum for young children and, as such, often end up reproducing inequalities. Inequalities of experiences, access and context. Indeed, Houston (2019, p. 107) outlines that 'phonics teaching can also **marginalise** children's home languages and dialects as assessments standardise articulation of the English language', leading to a presumption of 'hierarchical cultural uniformity, negatively reinforcing ideas of otherness based on intersections of race, class and national identity'. If you analyse the data from the DfE PSC attainment, it is clear that there are inequalities across all the domains of race, gender, SEND, children in receipt of free school meals (FSM, classed as disadvantaged children), children born earlier in the academic year, ethnicity and sometimes EAL (which is less so). Previous chapters have outlined that much of the research suggests that very young children learn to read and write through play in meaningful contexts within their real-life experiences. Let's think about the variety of ways that children learn to read and are interested in reading, other than just concentrating on teaching SSP.

Reflection Points

Consider how you learned how to read. Think about the strategies you used.

Think about what the research says about how children learn to read.

Consider why SSP attainment needs to be measured.

Is There a Place for Teaching Phonics with Under-Fives?

Fisher (2011) suggests that play does not teach phonics or phonological awareness. To a certain extent, I do agree that some small-group or whole-class discrete teaching is necessary to teach phonics, but not until children are at least in their second term in reception class or even later. Once the children have the fundamental principles of early reading and understand the letter names, shape and the corresponding sound(s), teaching phonics will support children in their reading and writing development, as long as this is within the context of their learning. Crucially, phonics needs to be taught within the broader literacy curriculum to hold meaning and context for young children and through activities which include:

- stories and storytelling, oral and picture books;
- story sequencing, making predictions, changing the story and the characters;
- visualisation – being able to picture/image the story, the setting and the characters (Agosto, 2016);
- comprehension – asking and answering questions about stories, words and ideas;
- connectivity – making personal connections to their own life experiences;
- talk and more talk – choosing favourite characters, retelling the story or adding more thought to a poem/rhyme;
- role play – retell and act out the story, idea, poem in their play;
- writing, retelling events, making books, connecting to books and other similar events;
- playfulness within literacy – making up new rhymes, changing words in rhymes, poems, having fun with characters;
- response writing, response drawing to story stimili (Agosto, 2016);
- joy, awe and wonder about new events, happenings – have fun and have 'adventures' in play.

(Bottrill & Cook, 2022)

There is no place for teaching SSP in nursery or pre-school. It does not hold any meaning or relevance for young children. I understand this is a bold statement to make, yet I make it often and will continue to do so. You may wish to disagree – this is part of your own critical literacy. Evangelou et al. (2009) review the literature on when it might be best to start teaching phonics and suggest that the many variations that influence young children's learning and development (home learning environments, ages of children beginning reception classes, cultural and socio-economic factors) lead the authors to the conclusion that personalisation is the only approach to consider and not before young children are secure with language, vocabulary and letter knowledge. This is where early reading is positioned and needs to be separated from the teaching of phonics.

The following image has been created by a group of like-minded trainee teachers, with experience in the field of early childhood. The principles of this iceberg infographic are to highlight the complexity of early reading and teaching SSP for all professionals and enable this to become a starting point for discussions in settings and schools. We decided to present clear visuals relating to the vital experiences that sit underneath the tip of the iceberg and acknowledge the influences from outside the iceberg. As you can see, this also becomes increasingly complicated.

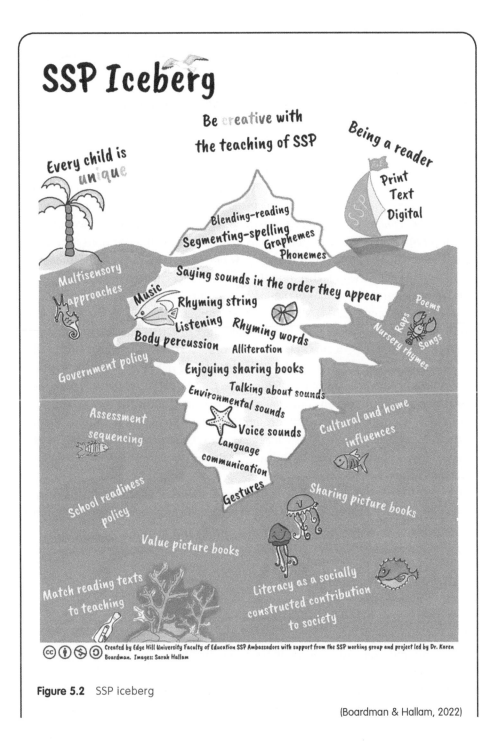

Figure 5.2 SSP iceberg

(Boardman & Hallam, 2022)

Reflection Points

- Review the infographic – what would you change, move, include, remove?
- Think about how this infographic can be used in your own setting or consider creating your own for your setting and share with all stakeholders, including PCF. At the very least it would support some interesting discussions.

Context, Comprehension and Meaningful Experiences

Let's review the premise that children cannot learn phonological knowledge through play.

There seems to be a significant movement to eliminate play pedagogy in many reception and Key Stage 1 classrooms (Ofsted, 2018) and this is also impacting on pre-school nursery settings. Ofsted's (2018) *Reception curriculum in good and outstanding primary schools: bold beginnings* report relied heavily on examples of teacher-led activities and less on play-based pedagogy, with the focus instead on early interventions for reading, writing and mathematics. Yet this narrow view of literacy will undoubtably undermine the social and cultural worlds that form the basis of young children's experiences. Many ECEC researchers maintain that children learn best through play (Broadhead et al., 2010; Bruce, 2011; Nutbrown, 2011; Marsh, 2010; Moyles, 2015; Rogers, 2011; Pascal et al., 2017). As highlighted previously, this is established research, knowledge and understanding across the ECEC sector – play-based learning is advocated consistently. In addition, we must not forget that every child is entitled to the right to play, under Article 31, United Nations Conventions of the Rights of the Child (UNCRC 1989). What we mean here is that play is not merely a mechanism to pass time, but is the way that children learn and develop – it is important for communication, expression, combining thought and action, satisfaction and a sense of achievement. Undisputedly, play supports children to develop physically, cognitively, emotionally and socially, which includes literacy development.

Literacy, learning to read and write, requires context, understanding (comprehension) and meaningful experiences. In order to support literacy development with under-fives we need to be constantly thinking about how we can:

- build, nurture and establish effective relationships to foster communication, language, talk and more talk;
- build, nurture and establish effective relationships to support children's engagement in singing, music, rhyme and finger play;
- foster young children's curiosity and provide plenty of opportunities for hands-on learning and exploration, access to resources, quality reading and writing materials;
- immerse children in experiences that are real and interesting, representative of their own world, their own life experiences;

- embed learner autonomy and collaboration – consider the whole-child approach to reading and writing – what do the children want to do, what is interesting to them?

Activity 5.4: Context and Meaningful Experiences

Think about 'context, comprehension and meaningful experiences' for very young children.

How do you provide the context for children to enable them to learn to read? How does context relate to the resources and reading materials you choose?

Context could mean the environment you provide, the framework you have in place, the setting, the background of the children, the circumstances and situation of the families and communities.

Think about the meaningful experiences that you provide for very young children to support them with reading. Representation matters and is not just focused on images, characters or storylines. Can you think of contexts that are relevant and meaningful for all young children? For example, single parent families, families with SEND, individual children with SEND, travelling or Gypsy Roma communities, refugees. Think also about other scenarios and think carefully about all the children in your setting.

When teaching SSP (if you currently do) how do you embed meaningful experiences in your SSP teaching?

International Perspectives on Early Reading and Phonics

First, literacy is not the same across cultures and society. Reading and writing have many different meanings in many different cultures and societies, with some significant differences. For example, reading might be considered an important leisure activity that takes time to acquire and develop but is time that cannot be afforded in some households where the focus is on water, food, or homemaking. For other households, reading and writing may be the highest priority. We are back to our earlier context discussion again here.

Literacy is a key priority for international governments and policy-makers, as outlined in Chapters 1 and 2. However, teaching phonics, SSP in particular, appears to be less of a priority within the international contexts of early childhood. Many international countries have a stronger emphasis on play, creativity, art, music and collaboration for young children and for a longer timeframe, rather than the formal teaching of a skills-based curriculum. In England, children often start school aged four years old and may have already been in a nursery setting which has included the formality of circle time activities, sitting still, holding pens and having more formal expectations in daily routines, etc. from three years old. Although children in Wales and Scotland may begin school at age four or five years, the curriculum framework is based on play, creativity and child development, and has fewer formal reading and writing expectations. The centrality of play is evident in the variation of formal school starting ages internationally. Many international countries have a much later formal school starting age of six or seven and also have a more relaxed approach to supporting children with their reading and writing: relaxed in that it is not mandated, measured or externally assessed. Many international approaches support the argument that reading and literacy ought to be fostered, not forced. For example, in China, the Stone Soup Happy Reading Alliance (SSHRA) is a programme that promotes fostering a love of reading – reading has emotional and personal benefits for all children – not on a prescriptive approach to teaching reading. Scandinavian countries have a philosophy of creativity, art, music, outdoors and the natural world – led by the children's interests. Many international approaches for early childhood are moving educational objectives away from simply knowing information, as indicated by tests, and more towards holistic thinking, learning to learn in real-life contexts. It is important to point out that the context is very different internationally for many reasons – variations in funding of early childhood, the values of early childhood and training and qualifications of ECEC staff to name a few. Some direct comparisons are therefore problematic.

Review and Rethinking Pedagogy

- Review and refresh your knowledge on teaching phonics and SSP. Discuss this thinking and the underpinning research with your peers and colleagues in your setting. Has your thinking changed? If so, how and in what way?
- Is there a place for teaching phonics (SSP) in your setting?
- Consider the Independent review of teaching reading (Rose, 2006) and the remit of 'cost effectiveness and value for money' linked to what the DfE Phonics Screening Check and PISA data tells us about SSP and children's reading attainment from 2010 onwards. Think about the many SSP schemes written over the years – who has benefited and why?
- How can/should we be measuring reading attainment? Who decides that it is important to measure at age six?
- Does it matter if children learn to read later on, at perhaps age eight or nine?
- What do you think about SSP as the prime focus for teaching reading? You can choose to teach SSP and follow that scheme in Reception onwards and you can also support with incidental SSP teaching.
- Using the SSP iceberg, have you made any changes to this infographic? How can you use this to support your pedagogy?
- How do you consider and embed the culture of the children, families and communities in your early reading and SSP policy/procedure?
- Review the DfE validated list of SSP programmes and make some notes about these, the process and the criteria used.
- www.gov.uk/government/publications/choosing-a-phonics-teac hing-programme/list-of-phonics-teaching-programmes
- Do some more reading about international approaches to teaching young children to read to support your knowledge and understanding.

In Summary

Chapter 5 has reviewed the policy stance on teaching systematic synthetic phonics (SSP) in England and has offered an approach that phonics teaching is a small part of the much wider literacy debate to enable children to become lifelong readers. This chapter maintains that it is important to ensure that early reading as a concept is separated from the SSP discourse, given that SSP is not developmentally appropriate for most children under the age of five. We have also reviewed the measurement of attainment in reading – DfE Phonics Screening Check in England and the international PISA results – to situate this discussion on SSP, the background and the accountability agenda of SSP.

Further Reading to Continue Your Learning

It is important to have my perspective on early reading and phonics, so that you are able to critique and question this for yourself alongside this chapter, so I have included some of my journal articles here as further reading also.

Boardman, K. (2019). The incongruities of 'teaching phonics' with two-year olds. *Education 3–13, 47*(7), 842–853. doi: 10.1080/03004279.2019.1622499

Boardman, K. (2022). Why do early years educators engage with phonics policy directives in their work with under-threes in England? *Policy Futures in Education, 20*(1), 1–18. doi.org/10.1177/14782103211003221

The DfE Reading framework *in England outlines the foundations of literacy from their perspective and links to the SSP as a prime method to teach reading. It is useful reading, particularly the Simple View of Reading conceptual model and rationale, which is essential knowledge.*

Department for Education (DfE) (2021). *The reading framework: teaching the foundations of literacy.* Updated January 2022. DfE.

Section 1: The importance of reading and a conceptual model. publishing.service.gov.uk

Here is the list of validated systematic synthetic phonics (SSP) programmes in England. This may be updated often.

https://www.gov.uk/government/publications/choosing-a-phonics-teaching-programme

It is useful to read more about phonics and the research used to justify the policy stance in England.

https://educationendowmentfoundation.org.uk/education-evidence/teaching-learning-toolkit/phonics

To support your understanding of the complex alphabetic code, I recommend reading more about Phonics International by Debbie Hepplewhite. There are many free resources to support your understanding of teaching SSP. These are freely available to everyone online. Debbie is a pioneer in this field.

Phonics International: an online systematic synthetic phonics programme
http://www.phonicsinternational.com/Training_illustrated_The%20English%20 Alphabetic%20Code.pdf

References

Agosto, D.E. (2016). Why storytelling matters: unveiling the literacy benefits of storytelling. *Children and Libraries*, 21–26.

Boardman, K. (2017). 'I know I don't read enough or even pick up a book in the baby room sometimes': early years teacher trainees' perceptions and beliefs about reading with under-threes. Doctoral thesis. University of Sheffield.

Boardman, K., & Hallam, S. (2022). *Systematic synthetic phonics (SSP) iceberg*. Edge Hill University.

Bottrill, G., & Cook, S. (2022). *Love letters to play*. Sage.

Bradbury, A. (2018a). The impact of the Phonics Screening Check on grouping by ability: a 'necessary evil' amid the policy storm. *British Educational Research Journal*, 44(4), 539–556. doi:10.1002/berj.3449

Bradbury, A. (2018b). *Datafied at 4: the role of data in the schoolification of early childhood education in England*. Learning Media and Technology.

Bradbury, A., & Roberts-Holmes, G. (2017). *Grouping in early years and key stage 1: a 'necessary evil'?* National Education Union.

Broadhead, P., Howard, J., & Wood, E. (2010). *Play and learning in the early years: from research to practice*. Sage.

Bruce, T. (2011). *Learning through play: for babies, toddlers and young children*. Hodder Education.

Cameron, L. (2001). *Teaching languages to young learners*. Cambridge University Press.

Clark, M.M. (2017). Reading the evidence: synthetic phonics and literacy learning. *Education Journal*, *316*, 1–7.

Clark, M.M., & Glazzard, J. (2018). The Phonics Screening Check 2012–2017: an independent enquiry into the views of head teachers, teachers and parents. *Primary and Childhood Education*. Newman University.

Claxton, G., & Carr, M. (2004). A framework for teaching learning: the dynamics of disposition. *Early Years*, 24(1), 87–97.

Department for Education (DfE) (2011). Supporting *families in the foundation years*. DfE and DoH.

Department for Education (DfE) (2014). *Statutory framework for the Early Years Foundation Stage*. Updated 2021. DfE.

Department for Education (DfE) (2017). *Statutory framework for the Early Years Foundation Stage*. DfE.

Department for Education (DfE) (2020). *Development Matters: non-statutory curriculum guidance for the Early Years Foundation Stage*. Revised July 2021. DfE.

Department for Education (DfE) (2022). *National phonics data*. DfE/National Statistics.

Ehri, L., Nunes, S.R., Stahl, S.A., & Willows, D.M. (2001). Systematic phonics instruction helps students learn to read: evidence from the National Reading Panel's meta-analysis. *Review of Education, 71*(3), 393–447.

Evangelou, M., Sylva, K., Kyriacou, M., Wild, M., & Glenny, G. (2009). *Early years learning and development literature review*. Research Report DCSF-RR176. DSCF. dera. ioe.ac.uk/11382/2/DCSF-RR176.pdf

Finnegan, J. (2016). *Lighting up young brains: how parents, carers and nurseries support children's brain development in the first five years*. Save the Children.

Fisher, J. (2011). Building on the Early Years Foundation Stage: developing good practice for transition into Key Stage 1. *Early Years, 31*(1), 31–42. doi: 10.1080/09575146.2010.512557

Goswami, U. (2015). *Children's cognitive development and learning*. Cambridge Review Trust.

Houston, G. (2019). *Racialisation in early years education: black children's stories from the classroom*. Routledge. TACTYC Book Series.

Hulme, C., & Snowling, M.J. (2013). Learning to read: what we know and what we need to understand better. *Child Development Perspectives, 7*(1), 1–5.

Johnson, R., & Watson, J. (2005). *The effects of synthetic phonics teaching on reading and spelling attainment*. Scottish Executive Department. www.scotland.gov.uk

Kelly, K., & Phillips, S. (2011). *Teaching literacy to learners with dyslexia. a multisensory approach*. Oxford.

Marsh, J. (2010). Young children's play in online virtual worlds. *Journal of Early Childhood Research, 8*(1), 23–39.

Moss, P. (2014). *Transformative change and real utopias in early childhood education: a story of democracy, experimentation and potentiality*. Routledge.

Moyles, J. (Ed.) (2015). *The excellence of play*. 4th ed. Open University Press.

Nutbrown, C. (2011). *Threads of thinking: schemas and young children's learning*. 4th ed. Sage.

Office for Standards in Education, Children's Services and Skills (Ofsted) (2004) Reading for purpose and pleasure: an evaluation of the teaching of reading in primary schools.

Ofsted (2014). *Are you Ready? Good practice in School readiness*. London: Ofsted.

Office for Standards in Education, Children's Services and Skills (Ofsted) (2014). 'Getting Them Reading Early': Guidance and Training for Inspectors. Version 4. London: Office for Standards inEducation, Children's Services and Skills. Available at: https://assets.publishing.service.gov.uk/government/uploads/system/uploads/attachment_data/file/379490/Getting_20them_20reading_20early.pdf (accessed March 2015).

Office for Standards in Education, Children's Services and Skills (Ofsted) (2017). Bold Beginnings: The Reception Curriculum in a Sample of Good and Outstanding Primary Schools. London: Office for Standards in Education, Children's Services and Skills.

Office for Standards in Education, Children's Services and Skills (Ofsted) (2018). Reception curriculum in good and outstanding primary schools: bold beginnings. Ofsted.

Office for Standards in Education, Children's Services and Skills (Ofsted) (2022). Now the whole school is reading': supporting struggling readers in secondary school. Ofsted.

Pascal, C., Bertram, T., & Cole-Albäck, A. (2017). *The Hundred Review: what research tells us about effective pedagogic practice and children's outcomes in the reception year*. CREC. earlyexcellence.com/wp-content/uploads/2017/05/10_100-Review_CREC_March_2017.pdf

Preece, J., & Levy, R.A. (2020). Understanding the barriers and motivations to shared reading with young children: the role of enjoyment and feedback. *Journal of Early Childhood Literacy, 20*(4), 631–654.

Roberts-Holmes, G. (2015). The 'datafication' of early years pedagogy: if the teaching is good, the data should be good and if there's bad teaching, there is bad data. *Journal of Education Policy, 30*(3), 302–315.

Roberts-Holmes, G., & Bradbury, A. (2016). Governance, accountability and the datafication of early years education in England. *British Educational Research Journal, 42*(4), 600–613.

Rogers, S. (Ed.) (2011). *Rethinking play and pedagogy in early childhood education. concepts, contexts and cultures*. Routledge.

Rose, J. (2006). Independent review of the teaching of early reading: final report. March. DfES.

Roulstone, S., Law, J., Rush, R., Clegg, J., & Peters, T. (2011). *Investigating the role of language in children's early educational outcomes*. Project Report. DfE.

Simpson, D. (2013). What's new about new literacies? In J. Metcalfe, D. Simpson, I. Todd & M. Toyn (Eds.), *Thinking through new literacies for primary and early years* (pp. 5–21). Learning Matters/Sage.

Torgeson, C., Brooks, G., & Hall, J. (2006). *A systematic review of the research literature on the use of phonics in the teaching of reading and spelling*. Research Report 711. DfES.

Turbill, J. (2001). A researcher goes to school: using technology in the kindergarten literacy curriculum. *Journal of Early Childhood Literacy, 1*(3), 255–279.

United Nations (UN) (1989). United Nations Conventions of the Rights of the Child (UNCRC 1989). UN.

Vannebo, B.I., & Gotvassli, K. (2017). The concept of strategy in the early childhood education and care sector. *European Early Childhood Education Research Journal, 25*(18).

Wyse, D., & Bradbury, A. (2021). *The impact of the use of the Phonics Screening Check in Year 2*. Impact. Chartered College of Teaching.

Wyse, D., & Goswami, U. (2008). Synthetic phonics British and the teaching of reading. *Educational Research Journal, 34*(6), 691–710.

6

THE DEFICIT MODEL OF EARLY READING AND LITERACY

Chapter Objectives

This chapter is focused on the labels derived from policy-makers which often lead to a deficit model of reading for under-fives and a 'catch-up' culture. By the end of this chapter, you will:

- understand the deficit model of literacy and the impact this has for under-fives;
- review interventions as approaches to support literacy;
- recognise the importance of the environment to support early reading pedagogy;
- review literacy learning for children in reception classrooms;
- consider reading for pleasure for under-fives.

The Deficit Model of Early Reading and Literacy

We have so far explored early reading terminology and pedagogy and continue to establish this within the wider literacy context. Previous chapters have outlined some of the potential complications of literacy for educators working with under-fives, relating to the educational outcome's agenda and the government drive for raising standards in schools. This standards agenda is positioned within the curriculum frameworks from birth to five across the early learning goals (ELGs) for EYFS (DfE, 2021). In addition, a wide range of statutory requirements for training and development and the inspection and regulatory service in England, which is presently Ofsted, reinforces the assessment and monitoring of young children's reading. Chapter 5 focuses on the contentiousness of this policy agenda for early reading and systematic synthetic phonics (SSP), which then appears to become part of our provision within the early childhood education and care (ECEC) sector, long before it is relevant or appropriate for younger children. This is often referred to as the 'top-down' approach and is also part of the of the school readiness agenda described by Moss (2014, 2019), Roberts-Holmes (2019) and Wood (2019). Moss (2019, p. 95) defines school readiness as preparing children for the 'government norm' by assessing their literacy skills, thus positioning ECEC as only preparing children for school – 'readying' children for the measurement of their performance in primary tests and making this attainment available to the public and within inspection reports. The dilemma I have with school readiness is that the ECEC sector seems to accept these performance measures as a given and begins to prepare children to be ready for school, sometimes too early.

This chapter will review some of the 'labels' often used to describe children's attainment or perceived lack of attainment as a deficit model, which often then situates these within an intervention approach of 'catching up' as being the norm for children under-five. For example, you might have heard of the 'word gap', 'language gap', 'attainment gap' – mind all the gaps! This chapter explains how the deficit model of 'measurement', particularly for literacy and early reading, is not underpinned by early years pedagogy, seminal child development theories or international curriculum frameworks. In this chapter we will also explore 'reading for pleasure' and how this does or does not fit in with early reading pedagogy. This is a thorny concept for under-fives and involves some deeper reflection, given the literature associates reading for pleasure with school-age children who are already readers.

Activity 6.1: Deficit Model of Literacy

What is your understanding of a deficit model of literacy?

How does this position the child in their learning and development?

What impact does a negative view of attainment and outcomes have on the ECEC wider field?

Think about another way to measure attainment for under-fives – consider if we need to measure at all.

Find out more about 'school readiness' and consider how (if at all) this influences your own pedagogy.

Your reflections might have included the many versions of 'gaps' we often see in print, literature and research or the constant 'catching up' and intervention discourse. The notion that children are behind in something does not appear to align with the characteristics of effective learning (CoEL) within the original principles of the unique child in the EYFS (DfES, 2007), Te Whariki, Reggio Emilia, Froebel or Montessori principles for young children. This is because, nationally and internationally, we position young children as capable, individual learners from birth within our philosophy of early years pedagogy (Stewart & Moylett, 2022; McDowall Clark, 2016). However, we also need to accept that individuals, including practitioners/teachers and policy-makers, all bring a wide range of perspectives in shaping the ECEC curriculum and indeed have their own ideals about children's learning and development (Wood & Hedges, 2016). We need to think about how we position children: as competent learners, active investigators or empty vessels that need filling up with new knowledge (new knowledge being what adults perceive to be new here). It could be suggested that when we focus on word-gap ideology, which I would argue is an artificial practice, this ignores and devalues the many different communication, language and literacy skills that children already have. When we measure attainment in words (vocabulary) and count these, then superficially include assessing SSP at such an early age, the concepts of comprehension, cohesion, context, clarity and relevance do not appear to matter. Communication is not just focused on speech or vocabulary (outputs) – non-verbal communications coexist in all our interactions with very young children within the pedagogy of early reading. Shanahan and Lonigan (2010) summarised the findings of the report of the National Early Literacy Panel, published in the United States in 2008. The researchers carried out extensive analysis of 300 studies published in journals. In their summary, Shanahan and Lonigan (2010, p. 283) concluded that 'It is possible that what works in early literacy works for all children, no matter their status and background.' This suggests that the quality of the early reading provision, the literacy environment and those early interactions from birth to five are critical for how children learn and develop. If we do focus on early reading provision for all our under-fives, then we may not need to be so fixated on plugging the gaps.

Activity 6.2: Understanding Terminology in the Context of Early Reading

Think about the terminology of 'communication, comprehension, cohesion, context, clarity and relevance'.

Think of some examples from practice for 'cohesion' and 'clarity'.

Review the CoEL birthto5matters.org.uk/ Playing and Exploring, Active Learning, Creative and Critical Thinking and consider how they fit into your pedagogy.

What is your view of children and how they learn – how do you position children?

You may have defined clarity as being clear in our language, speech and communications and perhaps ensuring that the language we use is easy for everyone to understand. Cohesion is then about joining up the thoughts and ideas within these communications to have meaning and purpose. The interactions we have with young children are pivotal to their communication, speech and language development. These interactions are also important in supporting early reading and writing. We need to be mindful that if we are merely counting the first 50 words that children say, we are completely missing the point about the criticality of communication, responsive interactions, listening and understanding. Communication is more than words – it is how the words are used, understood, shared and have meaning. As such, communication and language can be both a barrier and an opportunity for many young children, especially if their language is different to the language spoken in the setting.

Research suggests that children's early language development is directly associated with very young children's later success with early reading and literacy in their school years (Fernald et al., 2013; Roulstone et al., 2011; OECD, 2012). We have already discussed in previous chapters that literacy and being literate have long-term social and economic dynamics, given that the focus on attainment gaps is more often linked to disadvantage. Yet this argument is sometimes flawed, as it is underpinned by academic success as a measure – early language, disadvantage, the need for children in disadvantaged backgrounds to 'catch up' – catch up to an ideal of expectations, without understanding the families, communities, or the individual child. If we believe that all children are indeed competent learners from birth, the discourse of gaps just does not fit in. We know that children learn and develop in many ways and that children's learning and development is not linear (Conkbayir, 2018; Hoff, 2014). Indeed, language development is not just about measured or perceived academic success. Researchers such as Ahrenkiel and Holm (2020), Gee (2014) and Hackett et al. (2021) suggest that language development is more equally related to meaningful communication and multisensory engagement with culturally appropriate experiences, which are diverse in nature and not just measured against norms that are not culturally relevant. In other words, the language measurements currently in place in England are inequitable: socially, morally and educationally.

Reflection Point

Think about how children's language is different within the indoor environment and the outdoors. What do you notice?

Don't forget about gesture, sign language or children who may be struggling with their communication and language at the moment. Think about how you could enhance your early reading provision outdoors to encourage further language and communication.

We already know that social and environmental factors have an impact on language development. However, social deprivation or disadvantage is not the only explanation for a deficit in communication and language experiences of children. Language deprivation can also impact on all families – for example, where professionals work long hours or work away from home or perhaps are just very busy working parents. Yet, there are a significant number of children already identified with speech, language and communication difficulties and studies (Communication Trust, 2020; OECD, 2012) highlight that this could be approximately 10 per cent of children in our settings. Therefore, making communication, language and literacy a key priority from birth is a sound investment for all children and their families, and this is where our early reading pedagogy connects everything together.

The word-gap concept is based on a perception that young children should be using a certain number of words at a certain point in time. For example, Roulstone et al. (2011)

propose that the language development at age two is a reasonable predictor of children's performance on entry to primary school. Yet, most of the research highlights that it is often the quality of input that children receive which is far more important than the quantity (Law et al., 2017; OECD, 2012). This debate takes us back to our early reading pedagogy again. Current educational measurements for literacy appear to prioritise the language of phonics, the mechanics of reading and ignore non-verbal communications, rhyme, song and rhythm which is an essential aspect of all young children's language development. In fact, we know that the recent EYFS reforms (DfE, 2021) have been adapted and enacted to specifically support communication, language and literacy (CLL) outcomes for under-fives – more gaps to plug. The Department for Education (DfE) in England is very clear about CLL being a concern relating to later literacy attainment, specifically reading. Equally speech and language specialist provision suggests that children's language in nursery settings is steadily declining overall and there is an urgent need to support all practitioners/teachers, families and their children. More recently the Royal College of Speech and Language Therapists highlighted that the impact of the global Covid-19 pandemic has led to more five- and six-year-olds needing specialist support (speechandlanguage.org.uk/). I would, however, argue that this is very different – and does require more careful consideration of support mechanisms after a global pandemic.

Activity 6.3: Word-Gap Expectations

Consider the children in your setting – what expectations do you have for children's vocabulary? Are you documenting the words the children use, say?

Think about a few of the children that you know well in these age ranges and complete the table below:

Age range	Words?	Expected achievement?
6 months		
12 months		
2 years		
3 years		
4 years		
5 years		

How many words are the children expected to know at six months old and two years old? Where is the evidence/research for this number of words?

I wonder if we compared this with the words that children use in their own environment whether it would be very different, particularly for children with English as an additional language (EAL)?

What about the children who are not yet ready to speak, yet communicate freely?

Find out about the first words checklist and the advice to support children's first words from speech and language therapists.

The problem with counting words in isolation is exactly that – it is an isolated activity and is often done without any context or culture. I think the most important message to come from the word-gap and language-gap discourse is that it has led to an increased recognition that strategic change needs to happen for all provision, which has also raised awareness of supporting every child's holistic language learning and development. For example, there are now many more accessible tools for assessing children's early language (if necessary), enhanced training for health visitors, speech and language therapists and all professionals who work with young children and their families. Language development is now strongly encouraged content for all training providers across the early childhood sector, alongside child development – the status of CLL has thus been raised. This also means that children's language is more carefully monitored, and perhaps individual children's struggles are observed and supported when it is most appropriate. I would like to propose that what is needed when we are supporting children's language and literacy development is less intervention and more quality early reading pedagogy. For example:

- always using gestures and facial expressions to help children make sense of new words and concepts, communicating clearly and not rushing any responses in two-way communications;
- make comments when playing and interacting with young children, rather than asking lots of questions. Questions can sometimes stop CLL;
- singing regularly with children – sing rhymes, poems and raps to playfully introduce vocabulary;
- encouraging more talk than is necessary with children and encourage children to talk to each other;
- encourage the use of sign language and gestures;
- include children with EAL or bilingual children in mixed small groups and encourage chatting;
- reading often to children; telling and retelling interesting stories;
- supporting parents, carers and families to understand how important it is to talk, sing, rhyme and read with their children;
- considering that for many children, not always in areas of high deprivation, there may be an absence of a culture of talk. The idea of talk might mean following instructions and perhaps not involving two-way interactions. Immerse children in quality talk, play and fun.

Activity 6.4: Influences on Provision

Think carefully about what has and does influence your provision in your setting – the pedagogical approaches, vision and culture you are creating or would like to create.

Make a list of the reasons why you do the things that you do to support literacy and reading specifically. What influences these approaches?

Concentrate on communication, language and literacy and the environment you have created for literacy – the colours, the materials, the layout, the sounds, noise levels.

It is useful to return to your pedagogical approaches often and to understand how your own rationale for what you do and why is embedded within the needs of the individual child, families and their communities as the key priority. As practitioners/teachers it is essential to stay true to these principles and to remind ourselves that the latest trend, newest educational programme, or top-down approach is sometimes not the best pedagogy for the children in your setting, based on your knowledge and the interpersonal relationships with the children and their families. It can be exhausting keeping up with the ECEC field at times, so my advice is stay true to your play-based, literacy-rich pedagogy and avoid getting involved in the school readiness culture.

The Gaps – 'Attainment Gap', 'Language Gap', 'Transition Gap'

The attainment-gap and language-gap discourse could be considered to be underpinned by the controversial practices of social class – middle-class status, power, single-language dominance and whiteness (Flores, 2016), coupled with a standardised English approach throughout primary education to rationalise language attainment. This discourse suggests unequal gaps in existence that hinder children from taking part in the enjoyment of learning through play, due to some perceived missed potential of government test-driven achievement. We need to go back to the earlier sections of this chapter to remind us about what these gaps are, where they originate from and how this language creates a deficit model of early reading. Cushing (2022, p. 20) suggests that: 'Word gap ideologies operate on the myth that the language practices of white, able-bodied, middle-upper class communities are objectively higher quality than those of racialized, disabled and low-income communities.'

In explaining the many gaps various simple solutions are offered as fixes – perhaps a ten-week language-intense programme in a small group or one-to-one, or another phonological-based fast-paced systematic approach, which undoubtedly involves more over-surveillance and some further reassessment (and more plugging of gaps) to reduce inequalities embedded within poverty and discrimination. Alternatively, if we are going to discuss a balanced approach, then we do need to also consider that some children may need to be supported in their learning and development at some point, particularly children who may have a special educational need or disability (SEND) and that this is inclusive practice, not necessarily an intervention.

Activity 6.5: A Critique of 'the Gaps'

Consider the philosophy behind the language gap, the word gap and attainment gaps. Develop a balanced argument and a critique for and against. Use your knowledge and understanding of child development and the principles of the EYFS or other frameworks to support your for and against arguments:

	Critique (against)	Argument for
Language gap		
Word gap		
Attainment gap		

What do you conclude from your critique?

Think about inclusive practice to support all children in their literacy development.

Interventions as Solutions?

Interventions are considered to be a desirable mechanism to provide tailored support for children identified as struggling in a specific area. However, many interventions consist of children being removed from play or utilising other time slots for support, such as lunchtimes or after school sessions. These interventions are designed to plug the gaps in the children's learning. Bradbury et al. (2021, p. 8) suggest a growth in what they term 'intervention culture' and refer to children 'being removed from normal lessons, assemblies or playtimes' in schools.

Interventions in ECEC settings usually focus on communication, language and literacy and can often begin at the age of two. Most interventions require training to deliver, and this is an important aspect. In addition to ensuring that the individual needs of the child are carefully considered for any interventions, it is also critical that parents, carers and families are involved in the intervention, given that we acknowledge the strength of the home-setting partnership.

Law et al. (2017, p. 49) conclude in their review of 45 literacy intervention studies that many interventions 'appear to have a positive effect', but this is dependent upon the training, implementation and measurement of these interventions. These researchers suggest that all these interventions feed into the development of early literacy and support children's language development in some way, which might add a degree of validity to the intervention approach overall – nothing to lose? Wood and Hedges (2016, p. 410) remind us that when there is an equal measure of 'dynamic working practices' based on the voices and choices of the children, 'play-based provision, through reciprocal relationships', 'responsive teaching' and inclusive pedagogy, the challenging and inconsistent policy curriculum documents of development goals and the curriculum content do not need to dominate. The researchers argue that practitioners/teachers need to continue to ask critical questions of inappropriate curriculum content and carefully consider pedagogy, play and learning alongside assessment.

Reflection Point

Consider a more creative approach to children's learning and development other than a quick-fix intervention.

Go back to your thoughts on inclusive practice and think about how this will support children in place of an intervention.

When thinking about how best to support communication, language and literacy development, we also need to be knowledgeable about all aspects of inclusive practice, rather than just focused on interventions.

Think about how to support children who are deaf, for example. The suggestions from the National Deaf Children's Society advocate for accessibility and fully inclusive practice for all children, rather than quick fix interventions. //www.ndcs.org.uk/

Case Study 6.1: Supporting Communication

Lily is a child aged three years and two months. She is happy and settled in her nursery setting.

Lily is able to communicate with her friends and her key worker with key words and some phrases. She understands many instructions given to her and carries them out. Lily has not yet spoken at carpet time, although when asked later on in the day on a one-to-one basis with her key worker, Lily will respond to the question or scenario in her own way. Because this has happened now for a full term in the setting, the staff have raised this during their assessment meetings linked to Lily potentially having a gap in working towards the ELGs for communication, language and literacy. The team decide to seek support from the special educational needs co-ordinator (SENCo) in the setting to initiate an intervention.

What do you think the SENCo's advice will be?
What do you need to consider in supporting Lily?
What are the critical questions you need to be thinking about here?

The following quotes have been taken from extracts of graduate early years practitioner reflective zines and interview transcripts, an essential part of the early reading research study. A reminder that a reflective zine is an empty-page booklet that the practitioners use to write their reflections related to the research question 'how do you support under-fives with early reading?'

> All we seem to focus on in pre-school room is that we need to get our children ready - ready for school, ready to read, ready to sit and write, ready to listen and follow instructions. I am still not sure what I am getting them [the children] ready for. Our assessments highlight that some of the children are not ready, but ready for what – they are on track developmentally, I think.
>
> Interview Transcript 2 (nursery teacher)

> I am not comfortable with all the 'interventions' I am being asked to do with our 3- and 4-year-olds – what is this about? I think we have tried them all now.
>
> Zine 3 (private day nursery)

> We have used all kinds of interventions and a wide range of strategies, and we still need to support some children with their rhyming and speech sounds.

We have considered that this might be because they are the youngest children in our pre-school class.

Zine 3 (private day nursery)

The ELG for CLL, literacy reading and writing steers me towards being more focused on getting children writing and teaching letters and sounds earlier.

Interview Transcript 1 (nursery manager)

These extracts from experienced graduate practitioners suggest that it is time to review school readiness and the heavy focus on attainment outcomes, leading to interventions for under-fives. There are 75 instances of 'getting children ready to read' within the five interview transcripts, four zines collated for the research project and 48 instances of 'interventions' within the data. It is worth considering who decides on what the catch-up activities need to catch up to or what the getting ready for reading activities should contain and whether an intervention is necessary in the first place.

Reflection Point

Is school readiness a product of the intervention and catch-up culture in schools?

Reception Children and Their Literacy Learning

Chapters 2–5 have explored the connections embedded in early reading which focus on the importance of rhyme to support literacy learning (reading and writing). The research tells us that rhyme detection, sensitivity and repetitive use, alongside alliteration play predicts progress in reading development (Bryant et al., 1990; Bryant, 2002; Goouch & Lambirth, 2017; Goswami, 2001, 2015). Sound discrimination, music-making and visual discrimination are also key factors in supporting early reading development. The breadth of research highlights that the following are some of the most important aspects in literacy learning:

- rhyme
- alliteration
- environmental sounds
- music-making
- rhythm
- steady beat
- repetition
- visual discrimination

- syllable discrimination
- phonological awareness.

Activity 6.6: Reception Children and Their Literacy Learning

Under each of the headings above, think about the activities/experiences you could provide to support children in their literacy learning.

Try to think carefully about culture, relevance and meaning for all children.

Your ideas may have included activities involving loud and quiet sounds, stamping, clapping activities, matching music instruments to their sounds, identifying animal sounds, sounds in the environment, shadow games, silhouettes, memory games (Kim's game – find the missing object, odd one out), jigsaw puzzles, sequencing activities, role play, treasure baskets and so on. You may have included alliteration activities using the children's own names (Lucy likes lollipops and lemons) and having lots of enjoyable experiences with language. Hopefully your ideas were also full of outdoor activities. The outdoors offers many more opportunities to support literacy and can be sometimes over-looked. These are all fun, relevant and meaningful activities to support children in their literacy learning long before the focus is placed on teaching SSP or any interventions.

As we have already reviewed, children in reception classrooms in England are expected to be formally and discretely taught SSP in large-group and/or small-group activities by following an approved scheme. These children are usually four- and five-year-olds. The advice is to ensure fidelity with the scheme within all approaches and throughout the school (staying true to the scheme and following it consistently). Children in Scotland, Wales and international settings will most likely continue with the wonderful early reading and literacy learning within their play. Australia will be joining England in their approach of teaching SSP in their classrooms with four- and five-year-olds.

Reception children need to continue to be immersed in literacy learning and early reading pedagogy specifically. Remember that rhyme, alliteration, music, steady beat and rhythm supports children with their understanding of how the letters (graphemes and phonemes), words and language patterns have meaning. If children are encouraged to enjoy learning about literacy – playing with rhyme, reading, writing and spelling as part of their play, both indoors and outdoors – SSP will have context and meaning. Without the playfulness of early reading, SSP is not relevant and may well put children off reading entirely. In order to do this, within the current context of policy and artificial measurement (DfE Phonics Screening Check), we need to be willing to take some risks, have a clear vision for early reading and be able to articulate this to all stakeholders, be courageous and support each other with our knowledge of playful learning.

Reflection Point

Think about teaching SSP with four- and five-year-olds in reception. Consider the best approach to support children with their reading.

Reflect on what you have already done in nursery before children get to reception to support children in their understanding of the principles of SSP. This is a controversial question – as you will already be aware, I do not think that nursery is preparation for school and early reading is not preparation for SSP. Think about early reading and how you feel about this in relation to SSP. It is getting very confusing now, isn't it?

Go back to your definitions of early reading.

Remember that you can teach SSP in Reception and follow the scheme with fidelity, but you can also teach incidental SSP to support all children at their point of learning.

Encouraging Reading Behaviours; Reading for Pleasure

Reading for pleasure (RfP) has been defined by the National Literacy Trust in the UK as reading that we do of our own free will, anticipating the satisfaction that we will get from the act of reading. RfP is considered to be relaxing and informative. RfP also refers to reading that 'having started out at someone else's request, continues because children are interested in it' (Clark & Rumbold, 2006, p. 6). Woods (2001, p. 74) proposes that:

> Reading can change your life, it can inform, motivate, inspire and elevate; but it must be reading you do for yourself, at your own pace, in your own way, and that has a bearing on your own background, interests, values, beliefs and aspirations.

Bruner (1996) suggests that when we read, we gain a greater insight into human nature, culture and decision-making, which has unique benefits when we choose to read what we want to read. Clark and DeZoya (2011) suggest that there is a significant positive relationship between enjoyment and later attainment in reading. It makes sense that children who read more may be better readers. However, research studies and the annual Programme for International Student Assessment (PISA) and Progress in International Reading Literacy Study (PIRLS) data suggest that reading for pleasure has been steadily declining – children feel forced to read as it does not have an important place in their busy lives and, as a result, fewer children are choosing to read. Yet, this is very much dependent on the definition of reading – reading as print-based and reading from books.

We know that many children now read online and also read online for pleasure and purpose. There are many multimodal texts freely available, often including sound, music (podcasts), blogs, print, imagery and videos. Children access a variety of different media on tablets, phones, computer screen, film, television, radio and books (audio and digital). Bearne (2003, p. 98) suggests that 'these multi-modal texts have changed the ways in which young people expect to read, the ways they think and the ways they construct meaning'.

Coiro (2003, p. 458) explains that accessing multimedia and the 'internet provides new ways to interact with information'. This suggests that there may be many new ways of considering more complex critical thinking skills developing in reading online. When you factor in social media, this is another avenue for new literacy skills.

Reading for pleasure is very much focused on children being motivated to read and this should include all reading. Cremin (2007) highlights that reading for pleasure adopts a personal meaning for some children in order to make sense of their world. RfP enables them to make connections, engage emotionally and think critically. Cremin (2007, p. 184) offers a framework for teachers in primary classrooms, planning to nurture positive attitudes towards reading for pleasure, and suggests that:

> Teachers will need to respond to children's interests, offer a diverse range of potent texts and engage them in the selection process. Seeking in addition to strengthen home-school-community partnerships and enable creative engagement through enriched pedagogical practice. In creating a reading culture which fuels delight and fosters desire, teachers will be supporting the development of life-long readers, readers who find both purpose and pleasure in reading.

Reading for pleasure tends to be focused on children aged five and above in primary schools; children who are already reading. Although I am a huge fan of encouraging children to read and reading anything they enjoy, RfP can sometimes feel a bit forced for some children who do not read for pleasure but read for information, which I would argue is equally as important, although this is also respected within the RfP discourse. RfP leaflets, booklets and supporting advice for settings and schools suggest that the important aspects of RfP, relating to Read Aloud for RfP (ourfp.org) include:

- bringing the stories to life, bringing all texts to life;
- utilising informal as well as formal interactions with texts;
- creating further opportunities for child choice-led reading;
- encouraging a reading community;
- inspiring imaginative engagement with challenging texts.

Case Study 6.2: He Used to Read and Now He Doesn't – He Just Doesn't Find the Books From School Interesting

My son used to love reading, reading stories together, picture books, thinking about the endings of the stories, the characters. He used to read and now he doesn't – he just doesn't find the books from school interesting. In nursery he read, he loved bringing home picture books, story sacks. He used to ask to go to the bookshop to buy books and we visited the library often. In reception he just seemed to stop enjoying reading. He didn't want to read the words or do the tasks the school sent home – blending and segmenting. He just lost the love of reading.

How would you support this parent with RfP?

Where does RfP fit into your provision?

Early reading in the early years involves engaging and supporting children under-five with their positive attitudes about and within reading. It is a significant time for young children to set the tone for joy, wonder and enthusiasm for reading for information, for pleasure, or both, in any format. We also need to carefully consider the reading materials offered to young children to enable positive attitudes towards reading within cultural representations and imagery. This will be explored further in Chapters 8, 10 and 11.

Review and Rethinking Pedagogy

- Why is education focused on outcomes and gaps? Why do you think that literacy is the prime focus for attainment, linked to disadvantage?
- If we do not have a deficit model of early reading – what does this mean? How might this position the child and the professional?
- Think about enhancing your early reading provision outdoors to encourage language, communication. You could suggest some further ideas in your reflective journal.
- Consider consulting your local families and communities to find out about how the children and families engage with early reading and literacy at home.
- Review some of the SSP schemes that are available and get to know the principles and the advice on how to teach these principles.
- Consider the interventions that you are aware of and the ones you have used with children. Make a list of the interventions you know about. Think about how have you measured the success of these interventions. Do some quick research into finding out about some more interventions for young children.
- Consider the differences between reading for pleasure and reading for purpose – reading for information. Is there a significant difference? Why? Why not?
- How is your provision designed to meet the needs of all children?
- Think more carefully about inclusive practice and review provision with your setting.
- Research further the deficit model of reading and literacy.

In Summary

This chapter has outlined some of the 'labels' often used to describe children's attainment or perceived lack of attainment as a deficit model of reading, communication, language and literacy. Hopefully this chapter has offered some alternative viewpoints for you to consider for your own critical literacy journey. Often, the intervention approach and the 'catching up' culture in settings and schools is based on policy directives and not necessarily the individual needs of the children or their families. The deficit model of 'measurement', particularly for early reading, is not underpinned by seminal or contemporary early years pedagogy and does need to be carefully considered within our discussions about children's learning and development. There is a distinct difference in supporting children who have individual needs, such as SEND. This chapter has also reminded us about reading for pleasure and the importance of how we define early reading and reading as a concept, not just based on print.

Further Reading to Continue Your Learning

Read more about interventions to support early literacy.

Early literacy approaches | EEF (educationendowmentfoundation.org.uk)

Education Endowment Foundation (2018). *Preparing for literacy: improving communication, language and literacy in the early years*. EEF.

This paper offers insights into some of the ways that education can marginalise language-minoritised students. It is a complex read, but worth it.

Flores, N. (2016). A tale of two visions: hegemonic whiteness and bilingual education. *Education Policy, 30*(1) 13–38.

Read more about Reading for Pleasure, creating inclusive communities of readers and developing your reading pedagogy.

Reading For Pleasure (ourfp.org)

Read more about inclusivity for all children – utilise the advice from The National Deaf Children's Society https://www.ndcs.org.uk/

This research report outlines how using ability groups takes place with children as young as three.

Bradbury, A., & Roberts-Holmes, G. (2017). *Grouping in early years and Key Stage 1: a 'necessary evil'?* National Education Union.

References

Ahrenkiel, A., & Holm, L. (2020). Documentation of children's language development: a critical analysis and discussion of the conceptualization of language in widespread language assessments. In M. Alasuutari, H. Kelle & H. Knauf (Eds.), *Documentation in institutional contexts of ECE: normalisation, power relations, and participation* (pp. 41–57). Springer.

Bearne, E. (2003). Rethinking literacy: communication, representation and text. *Reading, Literacy and Language, 37*(3), 98–103.

Bradbury, A., Braun, A., & Quick, L. (2021). Intervention culture, grouping and triage: high-stakes tests and practices of division in English primary schools. *British Journal of Sociology of Education, 42*(2), 147–163. doi: 10.1080/01425692.2021.1878873

Bruner, J. (1996). *The culture of education*. Harvard University Press.

Bryant, P.E. (2002). It doesn't matter whether onset and rime predicts reading better than phoneme awareness or vice versa. *Journal of Experimental Child Psychology, 82,* 41–46.

Bryant, P., & Bradley, L. (1990). *Children's reading problems*. Blackwell.

Clark, C., & DeZoya, S. (2011). *Mapping the interrelationships of reading enjoyment, attitudes, behaviour and attainment: an exploratory investigation*. National Literacy Trust.

Clark, C., & Rumbold, K. (2006). *Reading for pleasure: a research overview*. November. National Literacy Trust.

Communication Trust (2020). speechandlanguage.org.uk/talking-point/for-professionals/the-communication-trust/

Coiro, J. (2003). Reading comprehension on the internet: expanding our understanding of reading comprehension to encompass new literacies. *Reading Teacher, 56,* 458–464.

Conkbayir, M. (2018). *Early childhood and neuroscience: theory, research and implications for practice*. 2nd ed. Bloomsbury Academic.

Cremin, T. (2007). Revisiting reading for pleasure: delight, desire and diversity. In K. Goouch & A. Lambirth (Eds.), *Understanding phonics and the teaching of reading: a critical perspective* (pp. 166–190). McGraw Hill.

Cushing, I. (2022). Word rich or word poor? Deficit discourses, raciolinguistic ideologies and the resurgence of the 'word gap' in England's education policy. *Critical Inquiry in Language Studies*. doi: 10.1080/15427587.2022.2102014

DfES (2007) Early Years Foundation Stage. Learning and Development Requirements

Department for Education (2021). *Statutory framework for the Early Years Foundation Stage: setting the standards for learning, development and care for children from birth to five*. DfE.

Fernald, A., Marchman, V.A., & Weisleder, A. (2013). SES differences in language processing skill and vocabulary are evident at 18 months. *Developmental Science, 16*(2), 234–248.

Flores, N. (2016). A tale of two visions: hegemonic whiteness and bilingual education. *Education Policy, 30*(1) 13–38.

Gee, J.P. (2014). *Literacy and education*. Routledge.

Goouch, K., & Lambirth, A. (2017). *Teaching early reading and phonics: creative approaches to early literacy*. 2nd ed. Sage.

Goswami, U. (2001). Early phonological development and the acquisition of literacy. In S.B. Neuman & D. Dickinson (Eds.), *Handbook of early literacy research* (pp. 111–125). Guilford.

Goswami, U. (2015). *Children's cognitive development and learning*. Cambridge Review Trust.

Hackett, A., MacLure, M., & McMahon, S. (2021). Reconceptualising early language development: matter, sensation and the more-than-human. *Discourse: Studies in the Cultural Politics of Education, 42*(6), 913–929.

Hoff, E. (2014). *Language development.* 5th ed. International ed. Cengage Learning.

Law, J., Charlton, J., Dockrell, J. Gascoigne, M., McKean, C., & Theakston, A. (2017). *Early language development: needs, provision, and intervention for preschool children from socioeconomically disadvantaged backgrounds: a report for the Education Endowment Foundation.* EEF.

McDowall Clark, R. (2016). *Childhood in society for the early years.* Learning Matters.

Moss, P. (2014). *Transformative change and real utopias in early childhood education: a story of democracy, experimentation and potentiality.* Routledge.

Moss P. (2019). *Alternative narratives in early childhood.* Routledge.

OECD (2012). *Starting Strong III: a quality toolbox for early childhood education and care.* OECD.

Roberts-Holmes, G. (2019). School readiness, governance and early years ability grouping. *Contemporary Issues in Early Childhood, 22*(3), 1–10.

Roulstone, S., Law, J., Rush, R., Clegg, J., & Peters, T. (2011). Investigating the role of language in children's early educational outcomes. Research Report DFE-RR134. DfE.

Stewart, N., & Moylett, H. (2022). Interaction and talking for learning and thinking. In H. Moylett (Ed.), *Characteristics of effective early learning: helping young children become learners for life* (pp. 115–129). 2nd ed. Open University.

Shanahan, T., & Lonigan, C.J. (2010). The National Early Literacy Panel: a summary of the process and the report. *Educational Research, 39*(4), 279–285.

Wood, E. (2019). Unbalanced and unbalancing acts in the Early Years Foundation Stage: a critical discourse analysis of policy-led evidence on teaching and play from the Office for Standards in Education in England (Ofsted). *Education 3–13,4*(7), 784–795.

Wood, E., & Hedges, H. (2016). Curriculum in early childhood education: critical questions about content, coherence and control. *Curriculum Journal, 27*(3), 387–405.

Woods, P. (2001). Creative literacy. In A. Craft, B. Jeffrey & M. Liebling (Eds.), *Creativity in education* (pp. 62–79). Continuum.

7

BEING A 'READING' PROFESSIONAL AND A LITERACY ADVOCATE FOR UNDER-FIVES

Chapter Objectives

This chapter will support your understanding of how being a literacy advocate for under-fives is a vital role for all practitioners/teachers to undertake to support children, families and communities with literacy. By the end of this chapter, you will:

- understand the position of the ethics of care within routines and the agency of listening to children;
- consider access to early reading resources for all children;
- review where the voices and choices of children and other stakeholders feature in literacy policy and pedagogy;
- reflect on your own pedagogy as a 'reading' professional and literacy advocate for under-fives.

Being a 'Reading' Professional and a Literacy Advocate for Under-Fives

Previous chapters have summarised the position, policies and importance of early reading. This theory has been aligned with the wider literacy context for children under five and what this involves every day to support provision and pedagogy. Chapter 7 outlines some recommendations to support the reader in being a 'reading' professional and as such, a literacy advocate for under-fives. I do not presume that you are not already! This chapter invites the reader to consider how being immersed in routines, reading, writing and playful pedagogies encourages all children in 'being' readers, writers and literacy lovers. We will also review some significant suggestions for supporting and collaborating with parents, carers and families as an advocate for literacy.

It is necessary to begin this chapter with some key principles pertinent to the early childhood profession, linked directly with literacy and advocacy:

- the ethics and agency of listening to children – the child's voice within policy, provision and pedagogy;
- agency and access to knowledgeable adults and inclusive resources to support literacy advocacy;
- the ethics of care discourse and how we view daily care routines – rushed and necessary versus learning moments which are essential to the curriculum (Ailwood, 2020; Bussey & Hill, 2017; Dali & White, 2016).

Activity 7.1: Ethics, Agency, Access, Voice of the Child

Explore and review the concepts noted above. Think about how we often approach:

1 the child's voice within policy, provision and pedagogy;
2 agency, having ownership and access to high-quality, inclusive resources and experiences;
3 ethics of care routines.

Why is it important to consider all of these aspects for literacy in particular?
   Think about what the research tells us about agency and children's voice.
   What do you already know about the rights of every child, for example?
   What do we mean when we talk about the ethics of care for infants and toddlers?

Your suggestions may have been centred around how we gather very young children's opinions and how we actively listen to children when planning activities, room layouts or daily provision. You may have discussed the United Nations Convention on the Rights of the Child (UNCRC, 1992):

- Article 3 'The best interests of the child must be a top priority in all decisions and actions that affect children.'
- Article 12 'Respect for the views of the child'.
- Article 29 'Education must develop every child's personality, talents and abilities to the full. It must encourage the child's respect for human rights, as well as respect for their parents, their own and other cultures, and the environment.'
- Article 31 'The right to play'.

Obviously, we recognise that the UNCRC (www.unicef.org.uk/what-we-do/un-convention-child-rights/) has 54 articles in total, all relevant and meaningful for children, families, communities and government and not just the suggestions above.

You might also have considered how policies are written and enacted in settings for early reading or literacy and if key stakeholders are involved in the writing of policies at all, such as including the children, parents, carers and families as well as the practitioners/teachers. The research project which this book is based upon has initiated further discussion about practitioner/teacher's perceptions of reading and the extent to which both the children's voices and the practitioners' opinions are acknowledged, if at all, within reading or literacy policies in England. Boardman (2022) concludes that the children's voices and their choices about early reading are not considered in many ECEC settings' reading policies. Often the dominant, centrally determined government agendas and policies (SSP and the drive to get children reading earlier) is having a detrimental effect on the practices of ECEC settings and consequently influencing the opportunity and time to consider the child's voice.

When we talk about agency in relation to young children, we refer to the pedagogy and provision that enables children to make choices and decisions on everyday activities or future events (which should include their opinions). Agency involves respecting each child's right to make decisions, to initiate and direct their own learning – to have choices about what happens to them, when and how. It is often a puzzling concept for very young children and practitioners/teachers in practice, particularly when working with infants. However, it is integral to pedagogy and advocacy. We do need to ensure that we always provide real opportunities for young children to use their agency and have a voice. Many-ukhina and Wyse (2019) propose that 'agency is best defined not simply in terms of an individual's will and capacity to act, but as "the *socio-culturally mediated* capacity to act"' (p. 229, emphasis original). I always like to provide choices for infants about everything, when appropriate (which is a contradiction in itself). For example, choices about break-fast could be cereal, porridge or fruit, choices about mark-making or writing media could involve paper, cardboard, books, colouring books, which is often why writing areas have a variety of resources for children to choose from. Many schools now include a variety of ways to encourage children to make choices about the story at story time and use online forums with the pictures and titles of two or three books for the children to vote on. Alter-natively, in settings the books are on display and the children vote with mark-making or writing their names. It is certainly a good starting point. It would be useful to think about many more ways we can enable choices and the child's voice, particularly with under-fives.

As a literacy advocate or a 'reading professional' you might like to consider how you support access to knowledgeable adults and what resources you provide to support lit-eracy advocacy across your setting. Our role as professionals in ECEC is often based on how we ensure that the voice of the child, agency and the ethics of care are at the fore-front of everything we do – immersed within our ideal pedagogy, certainly for quality provision (Clark, 2011; Vygostky, 1986; Singer, 2013). Being an advocate for very young children, in general, is an essential part of our professional role. For example, you might hear statements like 'I don't understand her when she speaks – it's nonsense and I don't know what she is asking me for' or 'All I seem to do in the baby room is change nappies' and 'I am just constantly tidying up in the toddler room'. I have heard these statements recently from sixteen-year-olds and seventeen-year-olds spending time on work experience in private day nursery settings. Care routines are crucial and ought not to be viewed as detrimental machine-like practices to just get 'done'. Usually, this knowledge and understanding of the importance of care routines and transitions in ECEC develops and is enhanced with more experience and further study, but, until then, as advocates it is our duty to challenge these statements.

It is vital that all interactions are positive and that we encourage any talk – even when we may not understand the child. It is much better to engage in two-way conversations so that the child will continue and want to talk. A literacy advocate always offers plenty of opportunities for children to communicate – resist the urge to anticipate individual children's needs before they communicate their needs – talk, gesture and sign are effective ways to ensure that there are always two-way communications between infants and their caregivers. The ethics of care within daily routines, such as nappy changing, feeding, dressing, sleep and rest is integral to our work with very young children. Bussey and Richardson (2020) recently estimated that daily care routines can take up at least 80 per cent of the day for babies, infants, toddlers and their educators. Therefore, it is crucial that we carefully consider how these care routines are enacted as respectful communication, language, meaning-making 'connected' experiences.

Activity 7.2: CLL in Day Care Routines

Think carefully about the communication, language and literacy experiences the following care routines could/should offer and complete the table below:

Care routine	Communication	Language	Literacy
Nappy changing			
Toileting			
Mealtimes			
Bottle feeding			
Dressing			
Sleep			
Rest			
Self-regulating or soothing			
Wiping noses			
Choose one more			

Now check your responses against some of the information within this chapter or other chapters, discuss with your colleagues and enhance further. It would be useful if you continue this table and add as much information as possible to demonstrate the value of interactions.

Think about how you would explain the value of communication, language and literacy in mealtime routines and nappy changing to parents, carers and families.

Care routines can offer a wide variety of communication, language and literacy experiences if you consider these to be essential aspects of pedagogy, rather than routine tasks to be completed swiftly. For example, nappy changing can deliver key communications of eye contact, sensitive touch, affirmation with smiles, gestures, new language and repeated experiences of language in context. Nappy changing times are also great opportunities to sing songs and to enhance attachments, alongside playful literacy experiences. Indeed, Page's (2018) seminal work on 'professional love' highlights how developing and fostering positive interactions with infants promotes communication, emotional and social needs, prioritising the needs of the child.

Case Study 7.1: Nappy Changing

An experienced graduate practitioner notices that a fourteen-month-old has soiled her nappy:

P: (making eye contact) 'Shall we change your nappy?'

C: (avoiding eye contact) 'No, no no!'

P: 'Okay let's wait a few minutes then – it is a good idea to make sure you are comfortable so that you can carry on playing with your car. Shall we choose a book to take with us or would you like to sing a song?'

C: Continues to play for a few minutes than comes to the practitioner and holds her arms out to be lifted up.

P: 'Ahhh thank you (names child) – did you decide on a book or are we singing today?' Practitioner carries the child to the nappy changing room, puts her down on the floor so she can choose from a selection of board books from a basket. The child turns and put her arms up to be lifted again – clearly doesn't want a book on this occasion. The practitioner carefully places the child on the changing unit and narrates the procedure of changing her nappy – 'Let's take this nappy off, oops, up, down legs, just going to use your wipes to clean you up and then we will pop some cream on – shall we?'

C: The child is at ease, making eye contact and using gestures with the practitioner – pointing to the mobile on display up ahead, saying 'That … that' to the practitioner, eagerly awaiting her words.

P: 'Ball, dolly, car, rabbit – I like the rabbit. It has big ears and jumpy feet – boing, boing. The ball is bouncy too – boing, boing.'

'Can you see the blue car, you had a red car didn't you before in the playroom … You like cars (names child). Did Daddy bring you to nursery in his car this morning? Daddy has a black car doesn't he? Mummy's car is red – can you see this car has a number plate too?'

C: Nods and smiles during the nappy changing routine, pointing to the mobile objects above and listening to the practitioner.

P: 'What shall we sing (names child)? – Twinkle little star …'; waits for a gesture from the child.

C: Nods and hold her hand out as a star, smiling.

P: Sings the song, gently narrates the nappy changing procedure and finishes with 'All clean, all done – are we ready to go back to play now?'

C: Holds arms out, signalling to practitioner to pick her up, smiling happily.

The nappy changing procedure takes approximately ten minutes, with plenty of opportunities for communication, language and literacy and conversational interaction.

- What opportunities for 'literacy' can you highlight from this exchange?
- Think about the environment for nappy changing – what do we need to consider, enhance or change to support further literacy development?
- Consider the child's voice and agency here and discuss with your colleagues.

Case Study 7.2: Environment for Nappy Changing/ Potty Training

Reflection on staff development session led by a Deputy Nursery Manager with a team of practitioners working with infants and toddlers.

'I invited the team to review our nappy changing environment – bland, bleak and seemed to be based on the chore of changing nappies on a changing rota. It has also been a bit difficult getting the staff team to support with potty training sometimes. I attended a recent CPD session on quality environments and routines – seemed like a good place to begin. I posed some questions and asked the team to think about how we could make this experience better and improve the nappy changing space. At first it was really hard going. Nothing came from them except putting pictures/posters in there. Then with a bit more time and some steering to focus on this making the most of any language, communication and literacy experiences for our children, we discussed lots of suggestions – low-level posters, books, picture cards, favourite photos etc. while sitting on potty, mobiles on the ceiling, some transfers – clouds, stars etc., quite a lot of suggestions that could be easily sorted, and then we focused on how we do things differently – which was much harder! Eventually we produced some guidelines with some useful prompts on to support the team (our L2 and L3 staff mainly). I feel this is an area we can return to in the future, but for now, we are at least reflecting and acting on those communications.'

Case Study 7.3: Nappy Changing Routines

Reflection on new initiative led by Nursery lead, early years teacher status (EYTS), with a team of practitioners working with infants and toddlers.

'We decided that if we were going to get this right – attachment, tuning in to communications and supporting the language of care for all our babies and toddlers – we needed to review who was doing the nappy changing, sleep routines etc. So, we have lots of wonderful staff and although they love popping in and out of the baby and toddler rooms, they don't work in there as their expertise is utilised elsewhere, but they do love popping in and out. So, we thought they should also be part of the routines of the day – they are not strangers to our babies and toddlers, they cover breaks, they cover lunchtimes and also move around a lot. We began to think that, right, we need the right people to do the job – while they are covering and popping in – they need to change nappies and support the other staff with modelling good practice. It seems to work for us at the moment.'

Reflection Points

- Consider the last two case studies – what written guidelines or prompts would you find useful to support nappy changing, mealtimes, rest and sleep routines?
- When focusing on communication, language and literacy within all of your routines – what other ways can you support the staff team in your setting as a literacy advocate?
- What do you think about utilising the other staff across the whole setting (perhaps more experienced or more qualified) to support with routines? Would this work in your setting?
- Consider the experience and qualifications of the staff team that work with infants and toddlers. If you invest in staff teams that are highly experienced and highly qualified, what might change about these scenarios?
- Consider the value you place on the daily care routines, given they take up to approximately 80 per cent of the day when working with infants.

Consequently, the practicalities of each setting and their daily routines can also be a further barrier for careful consideration when linked to literacy for young children. Boardman and Levy (2019) suggest that reading and access to reading resources for under-threes is very much dependent on the sleeping and rest routines of the day for some settings. Graduate practitioners shared their insights into their daily routine and agency of children under-three as part of the research study:

> I hadn't realised that whilst the babies and toddlers are sleeping, the other children can't get access to the books! Unless they actually climb over the sleeping children, they can't get to the books.
>
> (Boardman & Levy, 2019, p. 450)

> We use the book area as our sleep and rest area, naturally as it is a calm area. We do have books in some of the other areas, but not in the baby room – bit of an oversight!
>
> (Two-year room lead, private day nursery)

> It's difficult when the children are sleeping for the others who are awake. We often take them outdoors, so they don't disturb the sleeping children. We realised while taking part in this research study that if they want to have any quiet time, it's not available to them. So, we moved our sleeping area away

from the carpet into a separate room, so we haven't prioritised sleeping children over those that are awake and not ready to sleep yet. That way, the children who are not sleeping can have quiet time with books or snuggle. We also reconsidered our routine to ensure that children can rest and sleep when they need to – not when we need them to.

(Deputy manager, private day nursery)

These extracts highlight the complexity of access and agency for infants and toddlers within routines. As such, Boardman and Levy (2019, p. 450) remind us that 'the physiological needs of under-threes – care, sleep, rest, healthy diet and exercise – are not discrete from education' and that the professionals in this particular small-scale study identified reading 'as a quiet and passive activity' for under-threes, given that 'they used the reading area for sleeping' (p. 451). This is a significant finding in that we may inadvertently be getting on with our busy routines in the setting and disadvantaging infants with a limited perception of early reading.

Being a reading professional and literacy advocate when working with young children can take many forms and ought to always consider the care and daily routine opportunities as key learning. I believe (although I am very biased) that every single part of a child's day is a key literacy learning opportunity not to be missed!

Case Study 7.4: Access

In a busy two-year-old provision setting, most of the children are asleep on the carpeted area. There are some two-year-olds awake and they have access to small-world play resources. The sand, water and messy play areas are all closed off over the lunch period, as part of the routine of the day. One child is trying to get across the carpet to reach his favourite book. Each time the staff member escorts the child back to the small-world play resources, unaware that the child is trying to access his favourite book. Another practitioner has been observing and realises what he may be trying to do and brings a few books over to the carpet area with the small-world resources, including his favourite picture book. The child sits and enjoys the selection of picture books provided.

Reflection Points

- What would you recommend in this scenario?
- Does this case study tell you anything about the value of early reading?
- Think again about child voice and agency.

You may have suggested that while the sand, water and other messy play areas are covered up, perhaps a basket of books, rhyming games or some musical activities could be accessible for the children that are awake, as essential resources to support early reading. Access and the value of early reading tend to go hand in hand.

Are you a Reading Teacher/Professional?

Whitehead (2009) refers to the crucial 'role of the adult in supporting early reading development as literacy informants, demonstrators, scribes, reading partners, models and facilitators' (p. 79). Therefore, it is vital that early years practitioners/teachers always encourage children's talking and listening skills and act as positive role models by engaging in rich literacy practices themselves (Roulstone et al., 2012; Tassoni, 2013).

Let us consider how you present your reading teacher/professional stance in action – if you are a reading teacher/professional – and how can you develop further as a literacy advocate. Reflect on the following case studies from practice.

Case Study 7.5: Modelling Visible Reading Behaviours

Practitioner has observed the children engaged in play in the home corner in a nursery class. The practitioner decides that it is time to do some more modelling 'visible' reading behaviours. They take a sample of reading materials in the home corner area and begin to use these, beginning with the recipe book. The practitioner sits at the table and looks at the pictures in the recipe book, turning the pages over. A few of the children come to join the practitioner.

Children (C): 'What are you reading?' 'What are you doing?'

P: I am looking for a delicious recipe in my recipe book. I am going to make some cakes I think or I might bake some bread when I get home.'

C: 'Can I see?' 'What is a recipe book?' 'What is a recipe?' 'I think you should make cakes.'

Practitioner responds to all the questions and then picks up the tablet and some recipe cards (collected from the local supermarket) and models these with the children.

P: 'Shall we search for some cake recipes together on here? – You can carry on looking through the recipe book, here are some recipe cards and perhaps we can choose the best?'

The children look together – some using the book, some the recipe cards and some the tablet. The practitioner then picks up a magazine and a leaflet and begins another conversation with some other children who have joined in about reading behaviours.

Scaffolding, influencing, leading or negotiating children's play is still very much a contested debate. Many seminal studies such as *Researching effective pedagogy in the early years* (Siraj-Blatchford et al., 2002), *The effective provision of pre-school education (EPPE) project* (Sylva et al., 2004), *Exploring effective pedagogy in primary schools* (Siraj & Taggart, 2014), *Effective leadership in the early years sector* (Siraj-Blatchford & Manni, 2007), *Effective pre-school, primary and secondary education project (EPPSE 3–16+)* (Taggart et al., 2015) and *Study of early education and development* (Callanan et al., 2017) all highlight a balance of child-initiated and adult-focused activity to meet the learning needs of young children. Although, the focus is on children aged three and above in many of these studies,

I would argue that, when it comes to literacy and being an advocate to support the whole early reading domain, that positive reinforcement and visible action is necessary.

Activity 7.3: Modelling Literacy

Consider the following questions about your own pedagogy:

How often do you model reading behaviours with under-fives? Or writing or other literacy activities?

Make a list of all the reading teacher/professional activities that you carry out in a day … a week. Consider if you perhaps need to rethink this and include more reading/writing/literacy modelling behaviours.

Think carefully about how you could specifically support children with English as an additional language (EAL) or dual language speakers?

One of the critical aspects of being a literacy advocate is to carefully consider the questions you ask young children; for example:

- are they open-ended (encourage more than one answer)?
- do you ask questions you already know the answer to (what colour is that?)?
- are you carefully observing and paying attention to the child's gestures, facial expressions and body language when engaging in all communications?
- consider how often, when and why you ask questions. Are you interrupting play, communication or writing activities or supporting communication, language and literacy?

Reflection Point

Many communication and language interventions encourage you to focus on quality talk and discourage the use of questioning when working with younger children.

Try the 'in five rule':

1 Make a comment
2 Comment
3 Comment
4 Comment
5 Now you could ask a meaningful question.

It is certainly not easy, but does encourage further language and two-way conversations, rather than the child just answering your questions. Try it out and share this practice with parents, carers, families and your colleagues.

Supporting Parents, Carers and Families

Now that we have explored a little about adopting a reading teacher/professional out-look on pedagogy, we should also consider how we can support parents, carers and families (PCF) with this aspect – which is our role as a 'reading teacher' literacy advocate. You might consider signposting to some resources or strategies to support interactions between babies and their carers or linking what you are doing in the setting to continue at home, in supportive and creative ways. You could:

- share how you are supporting children's communications through sounds, facial expressions and gestures on a display board or in your daily online communications;
- model how you know that early language, communication and literacy skills are learned through everyday activities – share photographs of you reading books, writing together, sharing conversations and playing together. Share these conversations with PCF;
- tell PCF about the new experiences the children have had. Invite and encourage PCF to develop a fun way of recording new language, new words or expressions;
- share the songs, books, stories and rhymes that you are singing with the children – you could make a favourite song book for individual children or share nursery rhymes weekly? It is important not to presume that PCF know the songs, nursery rhymes and finger play games that you do in settings. Remember to ensure that all images, resources and references contain positive representation to support children with inclusion, race, ethnicity and gender identity;
- talk often about how the children enjoy exploring books, images, magazines, tab-lets etc. Share pictures of this and display photographs where PCF can see these;
- send pictures home when children make marks and write, consider scribing for the children or make some notes on the back about the language that has accompa-nied the picture;
- talk about the children's favourite games and encourage PCF to share the things the children like to do at home with you;
- share how you use books as part of the children's daily routines. Make the routine visible to PCF – when story time or song time, rhyme time happens;
- invite PCF in to tell stories, read stories or do song or music time with all the children;
- create displays to support PCF with their learning about how reading behaviours develop, from birth, how stories and songs can be calming and settling;
- explain the principles of telling and retelling the same stories and singing the same songs over and over again and why this is important for young children, that deep learning happens with repetition;
- talk about the reasons why, when you are reading or telling a story, you give each of the characters its own interesting voice. This supports children with their early reading – tuning in to the different sounds, pitches, patterns and tones of lan-guage, as well as being fun.

It is also helpful for you to get to know what the children's home-learning environment already includes so that you can provide more meaningful exchanges and support. Conkbayir (2017, p. 84) suggests that an effective home-learning environment:

> should include some or all of the following elements on a regular basis: affectionate interactions, sharing books regularly, reciting nursery rhymes, playing games, providing a range of resources and activities that are appropriate to the child's age and stage of development, as well as trips to local parks, art galleries, museums, theatres, libraries and play groups.

This may not always be the case for all the children in your setting, so perhaps some children may require more support than others. Remember that families will be doing lots of other interesting activities that do fall under literacy, but they may not know this.

Given that we know that literacy is rooted in a love of, and interest in stories, books, rhymes, music, reading and writing, it is important to provide lots of positive experiences so that the children and their PCF want to keep on learning and sharing. Establishing a strong family-setting partnership is a window for advocacy. Some further suggestions to support PCF as a literacy advocate are:

- encourage families to make photo books using photographs of family members, nursery key workers etc. and other significant people or places in their lives. You could also do the same with nursery events, mealtimes, playtimes etc. to take home to encourage more communication;
- make fabric/wooden, sensory or tactile books to send home, with some communication prompts;
- make a sound, music bag, rhyming bag and encourage PCF to bring in things from home;
- share a selection of finger play songs, number songs, nursery rhymes and their actions to take home for the weekends. Again, do not presume that families know the rhymes or songs that you sing in nursery or school;
- create and model a literacy collage map/river/ocean made up of all the wonderful things that the children do, read, enjoy, sing and play – share with PCF over the holidays or weekends to continue raising the status and value of early reading.

Literacy Advocates for Babies and Toddlers

Let's go back to the earlier discussions in this chapter surrounding routines and those pivotal care moments for babies. Carefully consider how you could enhance these routines and daily activities and advocate further literacy interactions. You might also consider creating a home rhyming, reading or early reading journal to document literacy learning with babies and their families. Encourage families to bring in suggestions, photographs or favourite picture books, songs they have shared together. Although, as literacy advocates, we are concerned about language and communication, it is essential to remember and support colleagues with an understanding that babies do not have a daily word count to achieve. It is the quality of the interactions that matters much more – not how many words they say. Additionally, although I advocate for talking more than is necessary, babies do need to take part in conversations as turn-taking and be involved within these interactions – make these meaningful moments. Allow babies to take the lead and respond, give them your full attention, with warmth, enthusiasm and eye contact – remember professional love (Page, 2018). Find out what babies are interested in, notice, comment and talk about this together. Take notice and be responsive when babies point, as this is a key literacy milestone.

Activity 7.4: Leading Change

Consider leading a staff development session with your colleagues working with babies and toddlers – gather their 'big ideas' about prioritising early reading, which includes communication and language at the heart.

Encourage your colleagues to make one small change to each routine each week or add something new to the weekly planning.

Use the table in Activity 7.2 to enhance all routines and interactions.

Literacy Advocates for Two-Year-Olds

Exciting physical experiences are literacy 'moments'. Consider the two-year-old walking up and down steps and along the pathway – the patterns they are exploring with their bodies and the language of up, down, along etc., the whole-body movements supporting their understanding of position, place and their world. Think about children following a straight line, going round and round in circles, being upside down and moving in, out. These are all literacy moments to be celebrated. As in the previous sections of this chapter, interactions, conversation and physical responsiveness are key to supporting literacy – modelling, listening, scaffolding and creating space and time for those imaginative discussions. Remember the importance of rhymes and finger play songs with two-year-olds. We shouldn't underestimate the power of tracking in action rhymes to support early reading. Spratt (2012) refers to tracking as singing, looking at your hands and focusing on the actions as you sing, which is important to support early reading. Remember to introduce and/or enhance provision with lots of stamping, clapping and steady beat activities.

Reflection Point

Have you noticed how very young children who have experienced lots of talk at home continue to tell you their information, even when you may not understand – especially two-year-olds? They will keep going until you engage and attempt to understand what they are trying to say. How wonderful they are.

Can you think of an example when this has happened in your experience?

Literacy Advocates for Under-Fives

We have now reached a key point for some further reflection. Review and consider the following list of activities and think about when and how often you:

1 provide daily one-to-one activities to support eye contact and taking turns in conversations;
2 encourage children to identify and point out objects of interest;
3 encourage gestures and use sign language;
4 encourage eye contact, gesture and wait patiently for a response;
5 provide daily encounters with music, rhyme, rhythm, rap, stamping, clapping and steady beat;
6 tell stories, make up stories;
7 read stories and share picture books in small groups or one-to-one;
8 teach, create and share new rhymes and poems;
9 play games to encourage listening – guess the sound, environmental sound walks;
10 encourage more talk than is necessary, but also know when to tune in to thinking and silence;
11 introduce all genres of music and music-making for young children;
12 change the endings of rhyming words – Humpty Dumpty sat on a fence ... Twinkle, Twinkle little pot ...;
13 encourage play with letters and sounds;
14 write more than is necessary.

Activity 7. 5: Review of Pedagogy for Literacy

Consider the above list.
What is missing (if anything) from your current provision and why?
Consider why you might you need to talk more than necessary to children to support their language and also understand when not to talk – but to stop and listen, as a literacy advocate.
Create a poem with two-year-olds – it is fascinating and fun for the children and you.
Think carefully about other ways you ensure that you are a literacy advocate for under-fives.

Review and Rethinking Pedagogy

• Consider how would you challenge these statements:

'All I seem to do in the baby room is change nappies'

'There is no time to read with children on an individual basis.'

- Write your own case study about modelling writing with under-fives – consider how this looks and feels.
- Remember that some children may only experience orders/commands or instructions as communication exchanges and have not engaged in more talk than is necessary experiences. They may have busy working parents or have a unique family situation. How can you ensure that you support all children?
- Return to your Venn diagram from Chapter 3 (Figure 3.1) – review your pedagogical approach to supporting early reading and include some of the approaches we have considered as literacy advocates for under-fives.

In summary

This chapter has explored some recommendations to support the reader in being a 'reading' professional and, as such, a literacy advocate for under-fives. These suggestions have also been aligned with the many ways you might consider supporting parents, carers and families as literacy partners. We have also considered literacy and advocacy, the ethics and agency of listening to children – the child's voice within policy, provision and pedagogy briefly, alongside agency and access to knowledgeable adults and inclusive resources to support literacy advocacy. This also includes the ethics of care discourse and how we view daily care routines and physical development – rushed and necessary, versus literacy learning moments.

Further Reading to Continue Your Learning

Communication-friendly spaces is an established approach by Elizabeth Jarman, which may offer some further insights into an environment to support communication, language and literacy with children and families.

Jarman, E. (2013). The communication friendly spaces approach: re-thinking learning environments for children and families. Elizabeth Jarman.

These seminal research studies will enhance your knowledge and understanding of pedagogy and leadership in the ECEC sector:

Siraj-Blatchford, I., Sylva, K., Muttock, S., Gilden, R., & Bell, D. (2002). *Researching effective pedagogy in the early years*. DfES.

Siraj, I., & Taggart, B., with Melhuish, E., Sammons, P., & Sylva, K. (2014). *Exploring effective pedagogy in primary schools: evidence from research*. Pearson.

Callanan, M., Anderson, M., Haywood, S., Hudson, R., & Speight, S. (2017). *Study of early education and development: good practice in early education*. DfE.

This is also an interesting paper to explore some further thoughts about the relationships woven within care and teaching.

Noddings, N. (2012). The caring relation in teaching. *Oxford Review of Education, 38*(6), 771–781.

References

Ailwood, J. (2020). Care: cartographies of power and politics in ECEC. *Global Studies of Childhood, 10*(4), 339–346.

Boardman, K. (2022). Where are the children's voices and choices in educational settings' early reading policies? A reflection on early reading provision for under-threes. *European Early Childhood Education Research Journal, 30*(1), 131–146. doi: 10.1080/1350293X.2022.2026437

Boardman, K., & Levy, R. (2019). 'I hadn't realised that whilst the babies and toddlers are sleeping, the other children can't get to the books!' The complexities of 'access' to early reading resources for under-threes. *Early Years, 41*(5), 443–457.

Bussey, K., & Hill, D. (2017). Care as curriculum: investigating teachers' views on the learning in care. *Early Child Development and Care, 187*, 128–137.

Bussey, K., & Richardson, M. (2020). Attuned routine experiences. *Early Childhood Australia, 8*(3).

Callanan, M., Anderson, M., Haywood, S., Hudson, R., & Speight, S. (2017). *Study of early education and development: good practice in early education.* DfE.

Clark, A. (2011). Breaking methodological boundaries? Exploring visual, participatory methods with adults and young children. *European Early Childhood Education Research Journal, 19*(3), 321–330.

Conkbayir, M. (2017). *Early childhood and neuroscience: theory, research and implications for practice.* Bloomsbury Education.

Dali, C., & White, E.J. (2016). Group based early childhood education and care for under 2 year olds: quality debates, pedagogy and lived experience. In A. Farrell, S.L. Kagan & K.M. Tidall (Eds.), *The Sage handbook of early childhood research* (pp. 36–54). Sage.

Manyukhina, Y., & Wyse, D. (2019). Learner agency and the curriculum: a critical realist perspective. *Curriculum Journal, 30*(3), 223–243.

Page, J. (2018). Characterising the principles of professional love in early childhood education and care. *International Journal of Early Years Education, 26*(2), 125–141.

Roulstone, S., Wren, Y., Bakopoulo, I., & Lindsay, G. (2012). Interventions for children with speech, language and communication needs: an exploration of current practice. *Child Language Teaching and Therapy, 28*(3), 325–341.

Singer, E. (2013). Play and playfulness, basic features of early childhood education. *European Early Childhood Education Research Journal, 21*(2), 172–184.

Siraj-Blatchford, I., Sylva, K., Muttock, S., Gilden, R., & Bell, D. (2002). *Researching effective pedagogy in the early years.* DfES.

Siraj-Blatchford, I., & Manni, L. (2007). *Effective leadership in the early years sector: the ELEYS study.* Institute of Education Press.

Siraj, I., & Taggart, B., with Melhuish, E., Sammons, P., & Sylva, K. (2014). *Exploring effective pedagogy in primary schools: evidence from research.* Pearson.

Spratt, J. (2012). The importance of hand and finger rhymes. In T. Bruce (Ed.), *Early childhood practice: Froebel today.* Sage.

Sylva, K., Melhuish, E., Sammons, P., Siraj-Blatchford, I., & Taggart, B. (2004). *The effective provision of pre-school education (EPPE) project: findings from pre-school to end of Key Stage1*. DfES.

Taggart, B., Sylva, K., Melhuish, E., Sammons, P., & Siraj, I. (2015). Effective pre-school, primary and secondary education project (EPPSE 3–16+): how pre-school influences children and young people's attainment and developmental outcomes over time. *Research Brief*, June. DfE.

Tassoni, P. (2013). Tuning in. In S. Featherstone (Ed.), Getting ready for phonics: L is for sheep. Bloomsbury.

United Nations Convention on the Rights of the Child (UNCRC) (1992). UNICEF.

Vygostky, L.S. (1986). *Thought and language*. MIT Press.

Whitehead, M. (2009). *Supporting language and literacy development in the early years*. 2nd ed. Open University Press/McGraw-Hill.

8

LANGUAGE AND LITERACY – THE BIGGER PICTURE

Chapter Objectives

This chapter will consider language and literacy and explore the bigger picture in context for children under five. By the end of this chapter, you will:

- understand further the importance of language and literacy for very young children;
- consider the role of families in the wider aspects of language and literacy learning;
- review the lifelong learning discourse for literacy;
- understand the many aspects of language acquisition;
- recognise the importance of visual literacies for young children;
- be aware of literacy equality, race, diversity and inclusion to support your pedagogy;
- consider unconscious bias and anti-racist practice for literacy.

Language and Literacy – The Bigger Picture

This chapter reviews some bigger-picture thinking about language and literacy for life-long learning, and also for the here and now (the age and stage of children's learning and development). The context of the importance of language and literacy for very young children is reviewed in further depth within this chapter. Literacy equality, diversity and inclusion is also explored for some impactful pedagogy rethinking. This chapter also serves as a reminder that language and literacy for very young children is not just about those who are able to talk and use complex language, or those who are learning to read and write, or focused on those who struggle with these aspects – it is a much bigger picture, with huge implications for early years pedagogy.

We have already explored language development in previous chapters and situated this within the context of early reading, as part of the interconnected nature of holistic literacy. Communication is vital for literacy development in any form alongside the many theories of language acquisition – how children obtain and develop their language, which continues to be explored and reviewed by researchers such as Hamer (2011) and Hoff (2014). Remember that I include communication and language within an early reading discourse, given that no one area of development can be learned in isolation for very young children, if this is to have purpose, context or meaning. Children learn using all their senses as learning is not linear – it is holistic for very young children. Educational philosophy refers to this as embodied learning (Shultz, 2015). For example, research from Macedonia (2019) highlights that you cannot separate the cognitive processes from the body – 'the human mind does not work like a computer processing symbols' and as such abstract and real-life concepts are 'grounded in action and perception in the body' (p. 9). When you link this to what we have already outlined in previous chapters about infants and toddlers having social brains, this becomes more apparent. In addition, a research study from Hackett et al. (2021, p. 925) carried out with two-year-olds in a day care centre concludes that, for these children, language is 'more than words' and also involves 'something mobile, dynamic, relational and multisensory' and this is indeed more visible when children are immersed in the outdoor environment and given space to explore (and experience).

At this point, I would also like to suggest that we begin an important discussion about babies and their social brains and their pushchairs, which is a further argument I make for the value of embodied learning for very young children. We have explored how young children learn meaningful communication and language when we talk and sing to them, as an essential part of those playful interconnected back and forth experiences. We know that children communicate with facial expressions, gestures, words and also by listening (attuning to sounds). Language supports the connectedness of literacy in many important ways and has been the subject of many chapters focused on early reading in this book. Therefore, if we are going to communicate and support language development when out and about with children, it makes sense that pushchairs are parent facing – to enable this two-way interaction to take place and to develop further. The infant can see you, hear you and communicate with you face-to-face – use gestures and words, listens and responds to your interactions and the sounds within the environment. However, I would suggest that this is somewhat challenging when the pushchair and the child is faced forwards away from the parent/carer. Remember that language, early reading and literacy exchanges are all based on eye contact, gesture, or sensory communication. Evidence from my own research and a further contemporary research project exploring how best to support communication, language and literacy with under-fives (Boardman, 2023), highlights that most families position their pushchair to outward facing around the age of six months, or in between the ages of six and nine months. Prior to this, the study suggests that babies are all parent-facing in their pushchairs. Some families purchase pushchairs that only face forward and outwards and they are not sure why they made this decision. Yet, we know that children from birth need to be making eye contact and using facial gestures, pointing, signing (if relevant) and communicating with significant adults, as part of their learning and development. Many seminal theorists (Piaget, Bowlby, Bronfenbrenner, Vygotsky, Erikson, Froebel and Bandura to name a few) advocate the importance of establishing eye contact for language development and those infants learn best from these key interactions with significant adults to support babies' social brains and their communication (Parent Infant Foundation, 2021; Young et al., 2022). As such, this is always a real concern for me – forward-facing versus parent-facing pushchairs and the decisions made by families at the most optimum time to support communication, language and literacy development or indeed if this decision has already been made for them by manufacturers at the point of purchase. I am purposefully not trying to be judgemental of the decisions made by families, but I do think this is an important point for us all to consider when we think about language and literacy and the bigger picture.

Case Study 8.1: Pushchair as a Barrier?

While on holiday in Majorca, ten years ago, I met a lovely family who had three children, aged five months, two years and five years. We had initially met on the aeroplane, when I supported Mum with the baby who was crying as she needed to change the two-year-old's nappy (I was waiting to use the bathroom at this point). Therefore, I naturally offered to hold the baby for five minutes to enable her to support the two-year-old. I settled the baby (gifted in settling babies!) and handed her back fast asleep. One day while walking around the compound, the baby was crying and Mum was pushing the baby around in the pushchair trying to get her to sleep. We stopped to chat and she explained that she just would not settle in this pushchair at all, thinking it might be the heat (as it was about 28 degrees). The pushchair was facing forwards and I wondered if perhaps this may be the reason, so tactfully (I hope) suggested that she could turn the pushchair around so the baby could see her and might then settle better. We did this and it took us both quite a while to figure out a such a complex pushchair! Mum explained that she did not even know she could do this – she said she had three children and used the same pushchair for all of them and never turned it to face her, it was just how she bought it. The baby seemed to settle. We then met up again on the complex a few days later. Mum said the baby always settled now in the 'new, improved' pushchair and exclaimed that I was obviously a miracle worker. Up until this point, I hadn't given pushchairs and language development any considerable thought – except to think it was crackers to push babies outward facing from a personal parental viewpoint. I now have two grandchildren and I have only ever used their pushchairs in parent-facing mode, right up until they did not need to be in a pushchair any more (about two and a half to three years old). I struggle with why you would want to do this any other way – unless you purchased a forward-facing pushchair that could not move into parent-facing.

What are your thoughts on forward-facing pushchairs?

Clearly, I do have strong opinions on this aspect – you may have other considerations to bring into this discussion that I perhaps have not explored.

Discuss with a friend, colleague and perhaps a family member you know well. Perhaps you are a parent yourself and you have already thought carefully about this and reached your own conclusions. Might the decisions we make about pushchairs be a barrier to communication and language development? Remember your own critical literacy here – your right to question what you read in print.

Activity 8.1: Pushchairs and the Bigger Picture

Make a list of the benefits of parent-facing and forward-facing pushchairs for babies from birth to two years. Consider all aspects for the child, parents and families.

Present your arguments for or against in your reflective journal.

Should we consider highlighting these points with pushchair manufacturers? Why?

How can you support parent-facing pushchairs, without families feeling judged?

It is important to think about how to explain that development happens in response to relationships, environments – embodied learning.

Language and Literacy, Lifelong Learning

Language and literacy learning is most often associated with the lifelong learning discourse – the future, our contribution to society and global communities. Usually when policy-makers and educators talk about lifelong learning, what they mean is correct grammar, punctuation, understanding nouns and verbs, writing to communicate to an audience, spelling and of course reading, teaching phonics and reading fluency. The premise of lifelong learning is clearly evident within the seventeen United Nations sustainable development goals (SDGs) (UN, 2015). The SDGs are considered to be a global call to action to support an end to poverty, to protect the planet, and move towards success for everyone, regardless of their circumstances. SDG 4 focuses on ensuring 'inclusive and equitable quality education' and promoting 'lifelong learning opportunities for all' (WEF, 2016, p. 7). Hanemann (2019, p. 254) suggests that SDG 4 'seeks to ensure successful completion of basic education leading to effective and relevant learning outcomes for all children, youth and adults as a foundation of lifelong learning'. In addition, Hanemann outlines that:

> Literacy learning as a continuous and age-independent activity is relevant across all ages and generations. The acquisition and development of literacy is not limited to and completed with formal schooling: it occurs before, during

and after primary (and secondary) education, in and out of school, and through formal, non-formal and informal learning. Hence, with the lifelong learning principle in mind, we can argue that it is never too early and never too late to start with literacy learning.

(Hanemann, 2019, p. 259)

This literacy as a lifelong learning debate involves an understanding of literacy (language, communication, reading and writing) as a continuous learning process which begins from birth and continues throughout all age phases – not as stand-alone discrete activities to assess or measure at a particular age phase. We also need to be mindful that literacy, as a learning continuum, is incorporated within everything that we do on a daily basis, in the same way that I advocate that early reading pedagogy is for under-fives – you cannot separate the actions or the experiences from the learning. This is why I suggest that interventions such as short-term quick fixes are at odds with our early reading pedagogy. The values we hold, the environments we create and the experiences we provide for under-fives are critical to individuals, families, communities and society.

Reflection Point

Think about your own understanding of lifelong learning.

Reflect on what you think literacy is for under-fives and how this fits into the lifelong learning global debate.

I wonder if your ideas about language and literacy for lifelong learning involve how young children can 'carry' the skills they learn into their future or their communities and develop these skills and their knowledge further. Lifelong literacy learning can easily get caught up within the school readiness agenda, outlined in Chapter 6 as over-assessed and intervention driven towards an 'ideal' point of learning at specific ages. When we consider language and literacy learning, we need to be thinking more carefully about the here and now – how we support children at their stage of learning and development, not necessary for the future. This is another reason why I strongly advocate for early reading pedagogy discourse for under-fives – to keep it grounded in the now, the experiences we provide for children daily and not really for later (although we do know these experiences support later learning – it is not why we do it). In addition, the UNESCO *Institute for Lifelong Learning policy brief* (UNESCO, 2017) challenges the assumption that literacy (and numeracy) are stand-alone skills to be learned within a set timeframe and argues for a more holistic approach, encouraging a culture of learning within environments which include families, communities and societies to ensure that lifelong learning is meaningful for everyone.

Activity 8.2: Language Acquisition

Research some of the theories of language acquisition. You might like to find out more about:

- Behaviourism
- Nativism
- social interaction
- embodied learning
- neuroscience
- usage-based theories.

What do these theories tell us about how children learn communication and/or language?
Where do bilingualism and dual-language learning fit in?
Think about digital technology and language learning.
Consider communication outdoors – how might it be a different experience for some children?

Hopefully, you have concluded that most of the evidence on language acquisition and how children's language develops is based on the quality of communications, relationships and interactions with others – those interpersonal experiences with families, environments, spaces, places, communities and the wider world. As such, the emphasis for communication is often placed on those crucial moment-by-moment relational interactions (Walton, 2021).

Visual Literacies

Visual literacies involve active engagement or experiences with text, images, video and many other forms of multimedia – for example, television programmes, cartoons, maps, digital advertisements and environmental imagery. Visual imagery is everywhere in the worlds of under-fives. Think about sharing picture books, accessing online stories or retelling stories. For example, young children might enjoy joining in with the *Room on the broom* story by Julia Donaldson and Axel Scheffler and love to role play the 'whooshing' of the broom, falling off the broom, finding lost objects and thinking about position and place on the broom. Of course, this story is now accessible on television, video and online, so children can watch the story and see the three-dimensional characters – the setting, the relationships between the characters, the layout (of text, image and so on), feelings, colours and shapes (the shadow of the scary red dragon, for example). Kress and Van Leeuwen (2006) describe visual literacies as a set of abilities that enable us to find, use, interpret and create images using our sensory experiences and our cultural understandings of the wider world. Painter et al. (2014) propose that visual literacies are especially important when sharing picture books with young children. The visual imagery highlights the characters, how we feel about the characters, the places and the values of the story. Therefore, visual literacy plays an important part in our bigger-picture thinking and our pedagogy for language and literacy. Stafford (2011) further emphasises the active process within visual literacy, being much more than just something that happens in our daily lives, with the focus on understanding, interacting and interpreting, which is critical for very young children.

Visual literacy activities with under-fives may include active participation in:

- retelling familiar stories through role play and playful pedagogy;
- recreating images, stories, characters or picture books using mark-making, painting, writing, drawing or a range of digital platforms;
- imaginative use of images, photographs, shadow play based on characters in picture books or television characters – for example, taking photographs of characters (bears, dinosaurs etc.) from a different perspective, create shadow paintings of the bears, use tablets to play with changes in colours, links to feelings, mood;
- creating picture books, using mark-making, drawing or writing or digital sketchbooks about characters from stories from the children's perspective;
- encouraging pointing out interesting things in pictures or stories on screen – the features of the environment, animals, what the characters are saying and how they are feeling (remember accurate and positive representation in images and stories/ storytelling);
- using storyboards – digital and text – to put characters from a favourite story in a different context and retell the story – adding new characters and encouraging critical literacy.

Reflection Point

Think about how you use, introduce, plan and support children with their visual literacy.

Consider some of your favourite (or children's favourite) picture books or television characters to think carefully about the setting of the story, the relationships between the characters, who the characters are, the layout of text, the images, the feelings, colours, shapes, messages within the story. How important are these images?

Literacy and Equality – Race, Diversity and Inclusion

Literacy has always been embedded within the social justice debate and has in fact been used as a barrier to equality and freedom of speech for many parts of society worldwide. For example, during the 1800s in America, slave rules were enacted to make it unlawful for black people to learn to read and write. Furthermore, literacy tests were created from 1950s onwards to disqualify immigrants and African American voters, in particular – if they could not achieve a certain level of literacy, they did not 'deserve' to vote. This practice ended with the Voting Rights Act of 1970. Shocking, isn't it, that literacy was used as a barrier to human civil rights not that long ago in our history? As well as being a racial barrier, literacy was also gender dominant in that it was considered unnecessary for women across many cultures to read and write or communicate their own thoughts or opinions. We also need to consider religious inequalities and perceptions, given that Scheitle and Eckland (2020) report that Muslims and Jews face the highest discrimination behaviours within today's society. Inequality is still very much in action globally and is a feature for many of the lived experiences for under-fives.

Literacy, as the bigger picture within our social justice frameworks, must be accessible and inclusive for all, more so for under-fives. Yet, it appears there is still a long way to go with inequalities and social justice for all children and their families. The National Literacy Trust in the UK promotes the use of books (fiction and non-fiction) that reflect society and communities and also features characters that children can see themselves represented within. Thus far this practice is not established within our ECEC pedagogy, given the white cultural dominance within our education systems present in many of our settings and schools (CLPE, 2022; Cushing, 2022; Matthews & Jordan, 2019). Matthews and Jordan (2019, p. 49) discuss the practice of circle time as 'filled with cultural rules, such as children sit and listen quietly while the teacher reads the book', which the authors outline as not the cultural norm for many families, particularly for black boys. Matthews and Jordan's idea is an important one for us to consider – the quietness of listening during story time as a white cultural norm, which will be explored in more detail in Chapter 10. We already know from research that children as young as three months old notice ethnic differences and race (Kelly et al., 2005; Xiao et al., 2015) and that children are making associations about race from a very young age (Lingras, 2021). Therefore, we need to carefully consider this and talk about and act on race and representation within all our literacy learning to ensure that inequalities of power, privilege and racism are unpicked and addressed. This culturally responsive pedagogy (Escudero, 2019; Bains et al., 2018) requires teachers/practitioners to affirm, notice and design all children's learning experiences focused on children's individual strengths, paying close attention to the cultural inequalities that may arise in the local community. Some suggestions for you to be thinking about could include:

- ensure that you know the cultural heritage of the children and build meaningful home-setting/school relationships to find out more about this from the child and their family;
- focus on the lived realities of all children – the everyday cultural experiences (which can often not be represented at all in books, images, characters in stories);
- support children in valuing their own cultural heritage and experiences and the lived experiences of others;
- encourage empathy, empowerment, equity, justice and alternative viewpoints – respect for all is essential;
- recognise all children's strengths and know your own areas for development in talking about race, culture, religion and society.

Activity 8.3: Unpicking Some Terminology

Research literacy and equality and find out more about the impact of literacy worldwide – for example, in China, Switzerland, Asia, Iran, UK and Egypt. Make a note of your findings – what does this tell you about literacy in general?

What do we mean when we think about literacy and:

- equality
- race
- diversity
- inclusion?

Each of these terms means something completely different, yet is equally essential for literacy learning. We need to ensure that we support under-fives with equality, diversity, race and inclusion, but this is much easier said than done.

Note any new learning for your own pedagogy at this point. Go back to your Venn diagram from Chapter 3 (Figure 3.1) and reconsider your pedagogical approaches to early reading relating to these ideas of literacy equality.

What might you need to do more of and less of tomorrow in your practice?

Your thoughts may have included some recommendations for your own pedagogy. First, it is vital to ensure that you consider all children to be literacy learners, which includes children who are non-verbal and children with special educational needs and disabilities (SEND). To ensure that we are fully inclusive in our provision, we also need to carefully consider the following:

- responsive pedagogy: we have a responsibility for all our children in enabling and empowering every child to achieve and have an opinion – their voices must be heard and listened to as they are the experts of themselves;
- regularly audit and update the resources and materials you use – books, visual aids, digital resources to check the accuracy and diversity of characters in stories and the images that represent the children in your setting. You may also need to update your own knowledge on what resources are available to you to avoid being tokenistic in your representation of children and their families;
- think about how young children have access to an onsite or nearby library (or museum, art gallery etc.) to enhance your collections and the experiences offered to support literacy – some children enjoy visiting the library with their families and others may have never been to a library, perhaps due to access concerns;
- use storyboards, visual props and understand that story time for many children is active, exciting and fun – not a quiet listening activity;
- choose books, rhymes, songs and poems that have repetitive text so that it is fun for all children (verbal and non-verbal) to join in;

- support children who are non-verbal, using sign language, visual aids and by using energetic facial expressions to help communicate the feelings that the story, song or rhyme conveys;
- make some small adaptations to support children with accessing books and story time – for example, putting a small piece of foam on the pages of a book for children who may need support with turning pages, using foam grips on pens, modified writing surfaces such as slant boards and tabletop easels, braille letters and so on;
- ensure that there are opportunities for literacy access for all children within the whole classroom environment. Consider where your resources are placed, the height and accessibility for children that have physical mobility challenges;
- boost vocabulary learning for English language learners within mixed groups of children during activities, so they can begin to understand the context of the language and use some new words in conversations, with relevance;
- encourage talking pairs and talking triads for peer-to-peer support – young children need plenty of opportunity to talk to each other;
- have a range of tablets and e-readers available for children who prefer not to handle print;
- use stories with sound effects or record stories and create sound effects to encourage active listening.

In order to ensure that both our pedagogy and our literacy environment is more inclusive for all learners, we need to give due regard to the concepts of exclusion and highlight the principles behind inclusive pedagogy. Borkett (2021) refers to these concepts as the 'dilemma that is inclusion' in her guide to inclusive practice. Exclusion can mean many things in educational terms – children removed from settings/schools due to behavioural concerns or actions, children being removed from mainstream settings due to SEND or being removed from classrooms in mainstream settings and placed within specialist provision. We should also consider social exclusion, where families or individuals are unable to access or participate in key services or activities, which is also present within our education systems and is a vital aspect of the inclusion debate. Exclusion can also be a factor within the interventions we put into place for literacy, previously discussed in Chapter 6. When we remove children from the setting, classroom or activities that other children are taking part in this is exclusion and needs to be more carefully considered within the practice of interventions. As practitioners/teachers working with under-fives (and all children really), we need to be considering inclusive practice consistently for all the children in our settings. Often people exclude due to their own lack of experience or knowledge and do not always intend to do so. Borkett (2021, p. 23) also suggests that 'Children with SEND who have a Statement of Educational Needs or an Educational, Health and Care Plan are six times more likely to be excluded than other children.'

The principle aim of inclusion is to embrace all, regardless of race, gender, disability, medical or any other individual need. Inclusion is about making sure that we offer equal access and equitable opportunities to remove any barriers related to discrimination and/ or prejudice. For some families, inclusion ensures that parents and children have the right to access mainstream education if this is the choice they wish to make. UNICEF (n.d.) describes inclusive education as the right for every child to access and participate in quality education and learning, where parents request this, and children's needs can be met. UNICEF also acknowledges that disability is often one of the significant barriers to education globally.

Just to avoid any confusion, at this point we need to think about the terminology of 'inclusion' and 'diversity' – which is often used interchangeably, yet the words do have different meanings. Diversity is often focused more on representation, while inclusion is about how to ensure that everyone is included and feels as if they belong. The Centre for Studies on Inclusive Education (2004) encourages settings to adopt whole-school approaches for inclusion, which also includes aspects of diversity. An inclusive setting is working towards providing effective planning and adaptation of activities and/or experiences to meet all children's individual needs. I use the term 'working towards' as this is an honest reflection of what we can all do – we do not know every aspect of every child's individual needs until we ask them and include their families in decisions made about participation and experiences – every child is an individual. We can and should always be thinking critically about how we can foster a community of collaboration to support the design and development of the curriculum, learning spaces and experiences for all children and their families, which does include anti-bias and accurate representation.

As early years educators, we also need to be mindful of conscious and unconscious bias within our pedagogy and embed anti-racist practice within all our interactions. It is useful to carefully consider what we mean by unconscious bias, given this is often defined as actions (the things that we do) that are prompted by ideas and preferences that we are often not very aware of. These can be described as hidden influences, coming from our own life experiences. Unconscious bias influences our behaviours and the decisions we make. As a consequence, unconscious bias can lead to discrimination, inequality and illegal actions. The Equality Act 2010 ensures that there is scope to challenge inequality in all aspects of unfairness, which includes age, gender, religion, disability, race. Think carefully about how you can avoid bringing your unconscious bias into your actions, decisions and interactions with very young children. If you treat everyone as an individual, will this avoid unconscious bias in your interpersonal relationships? It is important to recognise that there is no one way to eliminate any bias – it needs to be first acknowledged and then acted upon responsibly. For example, you cannot just review your resources and book lists and complete several cultural environment tick charts! Although this is important and you must regularly review your resources, this task alone will not ensure that you meaningfully and purposefully represent the range of cultures, life experiences and the backgrounds of all the children in your settings. As teachers/practitioners working in early years settings, it is our responsibility to acknowledge racial, religious and cultural differences and to recognise the unconscious bias that we all have. We know this is a fact – and we also know that now we know this and are more aware of our unconscious bias – our pedagogy should be changed. Remember that this also includes our attitudes to inclusion. It is critical to respect diversity and encourage curiosity and uncertainty from children – it is inevitable that this is going to happen, and we need to be ready to be challenged and also be ready to challenge. Supporting children with their own critical literacy skills is an important part of this process and also ensuring that we embed anti-racist practice within all our pedagogy. Liz Pemberton (2022) outlines '4 Es' of the anti-racist framework:

- *Embrace* all children's racial, cultural and religious backgrounds.
- *Embed* a culture of belonging and value amongst practitioners/teachers and children.
- *Ensure* that practice is culturally sensitive, and that the child is positioned as the expert of their own identify.
- *Extend* learning opportunities for the child by showing interest, expanding conversations and using diverse resources.

Activity 8.4: Anti-Racist Practice

Consider Liz Pemberton's '4 Es' framework above – what does this look like and feel like in practice?

Think about 'white supremacy', 'oppression' and 'privilege' – what do these words mean and how does this terminology fit into your own thoughts or your own lived experiences?

Think about positive representation in leadership, in decision making.

Remember that just attending a workshop or taking part in some CPD will not embed anti-racist practice within your pedagogy – you will need to carefully consider this every day within all your interactions.

Consider finding an anti-racist mentor to support you and your setting for those ongoing, difficult and sometimes uncomfortable conversations.

Review and Rethinking Pedagogy – Impactful Pedagogy

- Find out more information about the sustainable development goals (SDGs) and consider these for your own pedagogy.
- We know that physical environments, space, indoors and outdoors have a major influence on children's learning, development, health and well-being (Evans, 2006). Think carefully about places and spaces for language and literacy – noise levels, artificial grass, natural features, access, inclusion and representation.
- Review Liz Pemberton's '4 Es' anti-racist framework and read more about Liz's work – how can you begin to bring these aspects into your setting? How are you involving and engaging your community, families and parents/carers into these discussions?

- How does your unconscious bias influence your interactions with children? What will you do about this?
- Consider early reading as embodied learning – explain this to another professional you are working with or have a conversation about this with your leader/manager.
- Think about how you can further support the children with their language and literacy learning. Think about how you will communicate this to the children's families.
- Supporting literacy is part of our collective societal responsibility for lifelong learning, but what does this mean in practice?
- Find out about children's relationships and affinities with books – how does this matter? How books feel and smell and have memories associated to them is important for all children, particularly children with SEND.
- Consider which actions bring about change focused on your relationships and interactions with children and their families.

In Summary

This chapter has considered the bigger picture for language and literacy – family contexts, literacy for lifelong learning, visual literacies, literacy and equality – race, diversity and inclusion. We have considered embodied learning and you have researched some theories of language acquisition to support your understanding of the contexts of language learning. This chapter has also explored an introduction to race, anti-racist practice, diversity and inclusion and offered some further perspectives for you to consider for your own pedagogy. Global inequalities still exist and impact on young children's life experiences and their learning, therefore it is vital that we carefully consider all aspects of language and literacy to support very young children, with inclusion at the heart of our provision.

Further Reading to Continue Your Learning

This blog post is an interesting conversation between five ECEC researchers who share some practical ways to support children to develop a positive sense of self, which includes how to talk about race and racism openly.

Gaywood, D. (2022). Developing a positive sense of self blog.

birthto5matters.org.uk/2022/01/04/developing-a-positive-sense-of-self/

Charlotte Hacking from the Centre for Literacy in Primary Education (CLPE) outlines the importance of picture books for literacy in this article.

https://www.teachearlyyears.com/learning-and-development/view/why-visual-literacy-shouldnt-be-overlooked

Read more about anti-racism from Professor Vini Lander and Professor Heather Smith in the Anti-racism framework for initial teacher education/training, which includes some useful resources to support pedagogy.

Anti-racism framework. Newcastle University. www.ncl.ac.uk/social-science/research/anti-racism-framework/

You can find out more about the United Nations SDGs and how these fit into the critical thinking for literacy globally.

United Nations sustainable development goals. sdgs.un.org/goals

This UNICEF website hosts many research reports and offers some advice for inclusive educational practices.

www.unicef.org/education/inclusive-education

References

Bains, J., Tisdale, C., & Long, S. (2018). *'We've been doing it your way long enough': choosing the culturally relevant classroom.* Teachers College Press.

Boardman, K. (2023). *Supporting communication, language and literacy with under-fives: Research Circle Project.* Edge Hill University.

Borkett, P. (2021). *Special educational needs in the early years: a guide to inclusive practice.* Sage.

Centre for Literacy in Primary Education (CLPE) (2022). *Reflecting Realities Survey of ethnic representation within UK children's literature 2017–2021.* Centre for Literacy in Primary Education. Arts Council.

Centre for Studies on Inclusive Education (2004). CSIE. csie.org.uk

Cushing, I. (2022). Raciolinguistic policy assemblages and white supremacy in teacher education. *Curriculum Journal,* 1–19. doi.org/10.1002/curj.173

Escudero, B. (2019). *How to practice culturally relevant pedagogy.* www.teachforamerica.org/stories/how-to-engage-culturally-relevant-pedagogy

Evans G.W. (2006). Child development and the physical environment. *Annual Review of Psychology, 57,* 423–451.

Hackett, A., MacLure, M., & McMahon, S. (2021). Reconceptualising early language development: matter, sensation and the more-than-human. *Discourse: Studies in the Cultural Politics of Education, 42,* 913–929.

Hamer, C. (2011). Face to face: why talking to babies, and giving them the chance to respond, will give them the best possible start. Early Education, *Spring,* 10–11.

Hanemann, U. (2019). Examining the application of the lifelong learning principle to the literacy target in the fourth sustainable development goal (SDG 4). *International Review of Education, 65,* 251–275.

Hoff, E. (2014). *Language development.* 5th ed. International ed. Cengage Learning.

Kelly, D.J., Quinn, P.C., Slater, A.M., Lee, K., Gibson, A., Smith, M., Ge, L., & Pascalis, O. (2005). Three-month-olds, but not newborns, prefer own-race faces. *Developmental Science, 8*(6), F31-6.

Kress, G., & Van Leeuwen, T. (2006). *Reading images: the grammar of visual design.* 2nd ed. Routledge.

Lingras, K.A. (2021). Talking with children about race and racism. *Journal of Health Service Psychology*, *47*, 9–16. doi.org/10.1007/s42843-021-00027-4

Liu, S., Xiao, W.S., Xiao, N.G., Quinn, P.C., Zhang, Y., Chen, H., Ge, L., Pascalis, O., & Lee, K. (2015). Development of visual preference for own- versus other-race faces in infancy. *Developmental Psychology*, *51*(4), 500–511.

Macedonia, M. (2019). Embodied learning: why at school the mind needs the body. *Frontiers in Psychology*, *10*, 1–8.

Matthews, K., & Jordan, I. (2019). Our children, our workforce: why we must talk about race and racism in early childhood education. *Focus on Race, September*. ExchangePress.

Painter, C., Martin, J.R., & Unsworth, L. (2014). *Reading visual narratives: image analysis of children's picture books*. Equinox.

Parent Infant Foundation (2021). *1001 days: Parent Infant Foundation*. parentinfantfoundation.org.uk

Pemberton, L. (2022). *The black nursery manager*. www.theblacknurserymanager.com/about

Scheitle, C.P. (2020). Individuals' experiences with religious hostility, discrimination, and violence: findings from a new national survey. *Socius*, *6*. doi: 10.1177/2378023120967815

Scheitle, C.P., & Ecklund, E.H. (2020). Individuals' experiences with religious hostility, discrimination, and violence: findings from a new national survey. *Socius: Sociological Research for a Dynamic World*. doi: 10.1177/2378023120967815

Shultz, S.A. (2015). Embodied learning. *Educational Philosophy and Theory: Incorporating ACCESS*, *47*(5), 474–487.

Stafford, T. (2011). Teaching *visual literacy in the primary classroom*. David Fulton.

UNESCO (2017). *Institute for Lifelong Learning policy brief: community-based learning for sustainable development*, *8*. UNESCO.

UNICEF (n.d.). www.unicef.org/education/inclusive-education

United Nations (UN) (2015). *2030 agenda for sustainable development goals*. UN. sdgs.un.org/2030agenda

Walton, J. (2021). The impact of Covid-19 on children in early years settings. BERA blog post. Part of series: Covid-19, education and educational research. 3 August. British Educational Research Association.

World Education Forum (WEF) (2016). *Incheon declaration and framework for action for the implementation of sustainable development goal 4: towards inclusive and equitable quality education and lifelong learning opportunities for all*. Education 2030. UNESCO.

Young, V., Goouch, K., & Powell, S. (2022). Babysong revisited: communication with babies through song. *British Journal of Music Education*, *39*. 2730285.s

Xiao W. S., Fu G., Quinn P. C., Qin J., Tanaka J. W., Pascalis O., Lee K. (2015). Individuation training with other-race faces reduces preschoolers' implicit racial bias: A link between perceptual and social representation of faces in children. *Developmental Science*, *18*, 655-663.

9

DIGITAL LITERACIES AND MULTIMODALITY

Chapter Objectives

This chapter will review the literature, research and provision for digital literacies and introduce multimodality. By the end of this chapter, you will:

- understand how digital literacies are embedded within early reading pedagogy for under-fives;
- consider the digital world for children and their families, including digital footprints;
- review multimodality;
- reflect on your pedagogy and provision for digital literacies to support under-fives and their families.

Digital Literacies and Multimodality

This chapter draws upon the literature surrounding digital literacies and reviews the research into multimodality, with a focus on the digital child and the notion of digital footprints. This chapter also explains how digital literacies are embedded into early reading for many under-fives, given the definition of early reading outlined in previous chapters. We will also explore some of the contemporary debates for access, benefit and the perception of the digital world for under-fives.

UNICEF's 2019 Scoping Paper, Digital literacy for children: exploring definitions and frameworks (Nascimbeni & Vosloo, 2019), highlights that digital literacy is becoming increasingly recognised as one of the key skills children require for school, work and life. Yet, this review also acknowledges that our understanding of what it means for children to be digitally literate is still developing – more so for children under five. For example, there are many different perspectives to consider:

- operational aspects (access, use, which digital technology is available to use and how);
- reading, writing, comprehension, information gathering;
- developing technical digital skills;
- holistic approaches, including social and cultural dimensions;
- risk, safety of access, access times and the dangers of independent access versus setting/school access;
- critical thinking development (understanding that not everything we read online is fact and having alternative viewpoints);
- sources of information, truth, values and ethics;
- intercultural digital literacies;
- access to and involvement with digital literacy in the home and in settings/schools.

Recent children's digital literacy debates also include the importance of child voice perspectives and the participatory rights of children, often linked to social media use and children's images. Most children today already have a digital footprint in action on social media platforms which begins with their families sharing their stories, often from conception or birth. Livingstone (2016) and Livingstone and Third (2017) have debated an emerging agenda of research demonstrating that the benefits associated with children's online participation may be overtaking the previous perceived risks connected to children being online, which is one aspect of the many debates concerning digital literacy. Later research from Livingstone et al. (2019) appears to confirm this; there are indeed more perceived benefits for children, families and communities. However, we also need to carefully consider these debates for children under five and their families, given that most contemporary research and many other literature studies are often focused on older school-age children.

Although there is overall agreement on the importance of young children being digitally literate (Marsh & Hallet, 2008; Marsh et al., 2021; UNICEF, 2020; UNESCO, 2017), there appears to be a lack of global data for children's digital literacy, particularly for very young children. Nevertheless, research studies are beginning to gather this data, with a more specific focus on children under eight. For example, research by Marsh et al. in 2015 suggests that pre-school children are usually accessing either a laptop or tablet by the age of two. This research paper, *Exploring play and creativity in pre-schoolers' use of apps: final project report* (Marsh et al., 2015), also outlines that approximately a third of under-fives own their own tablet at home, which is interesting data for 2015. Later research from Sefton-Green et al. (2016) states that:

> The vast majority of children with access to tablets use them to watch TV
> programmes and video clips or to play games and use Apps. Half of pre-schoolers

use Apps of some kind either on a smartphone or a tablet. More than one in three children under five are using mobile phones to access Apps and games.

(Sefton-Green et al., 2016, p. 8)

My own research about early reading provision also confirms that an increasing number of children under five access tablets and/or smartphones. All families surveyed in the Northwest of England (73 in total) as part of a communication, language and literacy study stated that their nursery children under the age of five accessed either a shared tablet, their own tablet or had access to a smart phone for approximately two to four hours or more per day to watch songs, rhymes, videos, digital book reading, access children's programmes and other TV associated apps. Given that under-fives and their families appear to be immersed in the digital world already, let's explore what digital literacy is and what this involves.

Sefton-Green et al. (2016) and Nascimbeni and Vosloo (2019) highlight three dimensions of digital literacy for children, which include, but are not limited to:

- operational skills of reading and writing within a wide range of diverse media;
- cultural elements, which include understanding literacy as a cultural practice;
- critical elements that emphasise the need for critical engagement.

These authors also suggest that it is vital to continue to ask questions about control of media, representation, culture and authenticity within the scope of digital literacies for young children, which are significant issues that do need to be addressed within our provision. The diversity and range of digital media is increasing rapidly and already includes smart toys and linked apps, augmented reality (AR), QR codes, personalised digital books, digital books and gaming resources, which sit alongside television, radio, podcasts and many accessible live streaming sites.

Activity 9.1: Digital Literacy Access

What is your experience of digital literacy and access to media (smart phones, tablets, computers, watches?) – how often do you access digital media and how do you use it?

- In your own home?
- In your setting/school?

Think about the advantages and disadvantages of accessing digital media for literacy? Or for any other reasons?

What are your thoughts on under-fives and access to digital media?

It would be useful at this point for you to go back to your reflective journal and review the definitions of early reading. Can you see where digital literacies fit in here?

Think carefully about music, television and popular culture.

The Digital Literacy World for Under-Fives

Definitions of digital literacy differ worldwide, yet they all agree that it is just as complex as literacy itself, with the additionality that an essential aspect of the digital literacy world includes our ability to effectively make use of technology and understand the holistic, social and cultural practices that sit alongside this. Does this sound familiar? Let's think about reading pictures, focus on language, print, text, finding out information, listening to rhythm, rhyme, steady beat and music – all key early reading concepts, also active within our digital literacy world.

As previously discussed, UNICEF's Digital literacy for children (Nascimbeni & Vosloo, 2019) suggests that digital literacy is not just about getting to grips with the technology, but it is the knowledge, skills and attitudes that allow children to be both safe and empowered in our increasingly digital world. Digital literacies offer enhanced access to the wider world and the opportunity to find out more about global perspectives on what is happening, why and how. For example, young children can observe and interact with cultural differences when accessing dedicated children's sites, music, songs and stories and begin to ask questions about other children's or families' experiences. With this in mind, we need to think about how we position children's play and how we incorporate digital literacy within our understanding of play for under-fives. We also need to consider active participation, social networking (benefits versus pitfalls), social connectedness, in addition to the critical literacy activity of searching and learning through digital technologies. I would also emphasise the strong links between culture, music, literacy and family lives, given the connectivity between children's cultural worlds and the easily accessible digital technology for music, for example. **Intercultural literacy** (Sorrells, 2016) often involves an embodied engagement with culture (usually different to our own), that may be unfamiliar, yet connected with widening access to multimedia. Intercultural literacy offers opportunities for children to develop open-minded attitudes and empathy towards other cultures, given increased digital access in the world today. Alternatively, there is also the perspective that young children may pick up negative intercultural viewpoints. I suppose this comes back to the quality of interactions, communications and interpersonal relationships with significant adults once again for young children. In 2009, UNESCO outlined that:

> Cultural literacy has become the lifeline for today's world, a fundamental resource for harnessing the multiple venues education can take from family and tradition to the media, both old and new; and to informal groups and activities and an indispensable tool for transcending the 'clash of ignorances.'
> (UNESCO, 2009, p. 118)

My understanding of cultural literacy here fits within Sorrell's (2016) outline of culture as a 'global dynamic resource' (p. 11) that is not inhibited by any traditional descriptions of people's characteristics or their cultural values as norms for young children – everyone is a unique individual with their own lived experiences. Therefore, we ought to respect intercultural literacy and embrace multiple worldviews in order to adapt our attitudes (as appropriate) and to view literacy from many diverse perspectives. It is useful to think about literacy and intercultural literacy as opportunities for change. For example, Sorrell's (2016) 'Intercultural praxis model' highlights challenging stereotypes, prejudices, systematic inequities and encourages curiosity about difference – with the focus on how we interact and act in our world to make that change. This is so important for under-fives, especially their engagement with and understanding of cultural awareness. Digital literacies offer young children these opportunities, with the challenge of deepening their understanding of themselves and others within their world.

Accordingly, UNICEF (2019) suggests that 'children need to be digitally literate, even when they are not online' (p. 1). Children need to understand the implications surrounding communication, information shared about them, travel, educational systems (electronically signing in, photo identity etc.), the impact socially and for their own digital footprints. It is equally important for young children to develop an understanding of the use of technology in their cultural and social worlds and to have an awareness of its advantages and limitations – for example, finding the right information from the right source initially (children choosing a site to watch a story or listen to a song), which then leads into and includes the ethics and practice of social media or online gaming (messaging, responding); concerns about online safety; cyberbullying (or digital harassment); and the ethical use of online resources. Hence the complexity continues for young children combined with their connectivity to a wider audience. Cyberbullying is where individuals or groups of people, often unidentified (masking their own identity), use negative behaviours (such as threatening or aggressive communications) online through social media, email, text messages, blog posts, or any other digital media; it is a real concern for many families and settings.

Although young children may be accessing age-appropriate websites, with the support of their settings or families, and may well be learning such a lot from these enjoyable and informative experiences, we might also need to consider the time spent engaging in these activities – as in how long is long enough for screen time and the potential risks associated with screen time. Perhaps this is this not something to be concerned with at all if we consider digital literacy to be a playful experience. This is an important debate to return to later on in this chapter.

Activity 9.2: Quick Digital Literacy Audit

Think of all the ways that young children could and do use digital literacies in their day. Remember to start from their home environment, including their local communities and then in your setting/school. Remember to include all their playful experiences with digital technologies here also.

Make a list using the table below:

	1-year olds	2-year-olds	3- and 4-year-olds	5-year-olds
At home morning				
In the community				
In the setting				
At home afternoon				
At home evening				
Before bed				
Other				

You may have pulled together a comprehensive list of engagement with digital literacies and a wide range of media. Perhaps there may be more activities in the home versus the setting or vice versa and this may not be linked to access at all. For example, Flewitt et al. (2014) argue that children who have access to iPads/tablets or other devices at home demonstrate much more intentional use of digital technology for literacy purposes than those who do not, which makes perfect sense.

Reflection Point

The table did not include babies (under the age of one), but it is also worth considering that these children and families may also have been introduced to digital media from birth and will already be engaging in their own ways. Consider their engagement and interactions for your provision.

The National Literacy Trust's *How digital technology can support early language and literacy outcomes in early years settings* (Billington, 2016) proposes that those early years settings that already use technology well ought to be considerate about how they support 'access to technology for those families who might wish to access it but cannot afford to, in a similar way that lending libraries are provided for book sharing' (Billington, 2016, p. 11), which is an important point to note. Given this is now a life experience for many young children, it is worth considering how we support children who do have access to flourish in this area and those who do not within our ECEC setting's provision.

Case Study 9.1: Favourite Songs

Chloe (aged three years and two months) enjoys exploring both the interactive whiteboard and the tablet in her pre-school nursery room on a daily basis. The practitioner notes how Chloe moves between digital activities and play experiences freely. Chloe uses the interactive whiteboard to choose some of her favourite songs, save them in her folder 'Chloe' and also makes a list of some of her favourite songs. Chloe types in her list the 'titles' of her favourite songs – 'Frzen', 'Ed Sheeram', 'Strs', 'Scrow'.

When Chloe accesses the tablet, she uses the tablet to search for songs and confidently moves between several apps – CBBC Music, Music Box 3 and YouTube.

Case Study 9.2: Letters and Sounds

Jack (aged four years and nine months) spends his free time in his reception classroom to play games on the tablet independently. He enjoys playing on a variety of apps, such as . SplashLearn Fun (number games), ABC Magic Phonics, Read with Phonics Games and Meet the Alphablocks – all these are educationally based letters and sounds games, with some aspects of mathematical learning. He spends a long time on the Letters and Sounds app (Richmond) and switches between this app and another similar app – Letter Sounds Songs & Game Lite (Critical Thinking Company). Although (his teacher reports that) Jack does not enjoy the formality of sitting still and being taught phonics, he frequently uses the tablet (and sits still) to explore letters and sounds and is very interested in playing games on these apps. He often spends up to half an hour independently using the tablet matching letters to sounds and sounds to words.

Case Study 9.3: CBeebies' Mr Tumble

Lola (aged two years and four months) regularly asks her key worker for 'Mr Tumble', while holding the tablet outstretched at key points during her busy nursery day. Lola positions herself on the key worker's knee, while her key worker searches for Lola's requests – 'Jack bean' (Jack and the Beanstalk), 'Dingle' (Dingle Dangle Scarecrow) and 'Cake' (5 Currant Buns). She will spend about fifteen to twenty minutes watching and joining in with these stories and rhymes and then slides off the key worker's knee to go off and choose something different to do.

When the key worker is busy, Lola will use the tablet independently and search the CBeebies site (which is already on the tablet), using images to find what she would like to watch. Lola is able to switch between songs, rhymes and stories, swiping across, tapping to make her choice and turning the sound up and down on the tablet, as required. Sometimes, Lola shares this activity with her friends, and they search together for stories, songs and programmes they would like to watch together.

Case Study 9.4: Children Playing Around the World

Tom (aged four years, eleven months) and Lily (aged four years, nine months) are exploring the interactive whiteboard in their reception classroom after being introduced to a topic about 'children around the world'. They have used the teacher's link from earlier in the day to look again at the images of children playing around the world (www.boredpanda.com/happy-children-playing/?utm_source=bing&utm_medium=organic&utm_campaign=organic).

Lily searches through the photographs until she lands on the image she wants to talk to Tom about. She stops at the image of a child fishing with a toy fishing rod, sitting on a box on the ice with a cat next to him. The image is from Russia. Lily talks to Tom about the cat waiting to eat the fish and they both talk at length about the fact that they have never been fishing 'and it looks too cold to go fishing'.

Tom then searches for the image of the boys from Myanmar playing football and he talks to Lily about them all playing football 'in the same colour'. Tom is fascinated by the image and makes lots of suggestions to identify themselves as different teams. They continue to scroll on, taking turns and tapping on the screen when they have found what they are looking for and discuss the images together and the experiences they see in the images, linking these to their own life experiences. Tom and Lily spend 35 minutes on this activity and when others join in, they narrate each image and activity for their friends.

Reflection Point

Think about the learning taking place, the activities the children are engaged in, and note the critical literacy skills that are involved in each of these four case studies.

There is a wealth of digital literacy learning for these under-fives – potentially, not easily replicated in any other format.

Think about intercultural literacy.

The digital world offers young children many multisensory learning experiences, alongside intercultural literacies. I would argue that these are all playful learning experiences that are essential for young children, as would many other researchers in the ECEC field. Let's not forget about the opportunities for digital experiences outdoors within nature (using digital microscopes, recording devices, taking photographs etc.), when visiting museums and art galleries (QR codes and imagery) or other places of interest – the digital world is in existence for many families and communities, therefore we need to embrace this to ensure it is a meaningful element of our pedagogy for young children.

Multimodality – An Introduction to the Digital Literacy Discussion

Multimodality is often explained as an interdisciplinary approach that recognises communication and representation to be much more than just about language – it is about play and interactions: physical, emotional, social, moral, cultural. Multimodality reflects the changes in our global society in relation to new technologies, media and digital literacies. For example, visual (seen), aural (heard), spatial relationships (physical), embodied interactions (gesture, communication by movement, space and place) and environments (physical layout, space) and the use of more than one 'mode' of communication.

We have already explored how young children are surrounded by and engage with many interpersonal experiences and communications in order to identify, interpret and express meanings as part of our early reading pedagogy and literacy learning. Most under-fives have a variety of significant interactions with others, enjoy exploring interesting objects and play with a wide variety of natural or man-made resources, indoors and outdoors, which probably already include digital technologies. As such children are constantly attaching meanings to everything they do and utilising more than one mode in order to enhance their learning. Just to be clear, multimodality is not concerned with learning styles; multimodality is relevant within all types of playful experiences for under-fives – toys, resources, devices, technology, social interactions, singing, musical play, picture books etc. This curiosity, awe and wonder within children's play fosters critical literacies – children become active interpreters and develop their own ideas about what they see, hear and experience. Vasquez (2017, p. 3) discusses critical literacies within multimodal learning and explains that critical literacy is a 'perspective that should be constructed organically, using the inquiry questions of learners, beginning on the first day of school with the youngest learners'. As previously discussed in earlier chapters of this book, language and literacy are holistic in nature (Kress & Jewitt, 2003; Mills, 2016; Wohlwend, 2011). Literacy incorporates many modes that go beyond the formal notion of reading, writing, communication and language, each experienced differently for individual children in their global communities. Therefore, early reading, reading (decoding and encoding) and writing are natural multimodal activities for young children and difficult to separate into one mode of learning.

Multimodality encourages lots of purposeful engagement and new learning opportunities associated with children's individual needs, their culture, language, environment, background and understanding – thus, enabling children to learn at their own pace, when supported by active, critical and knowledgeable adults (Vasquez, 2014); This is one of the many reasons that I advocate for early reading for under-fives in the literacy domain. For example, Wohlwend (2011) highlights that when very young children are engaged in back-and-forth conversations and encouraged to listen to music, environmental sounds, rhythm and rhyming patterns these experiences directly link to their interpretations of talking, singing and rhyming for a purpose within their wider literacy learning.

In many ways, under-fives are already 'digital natives' who learn and develop within their digital worlds, knowing from their experiences that literacy includes a wide range of modalities. They think, learn and understand the world around them differently. They already have a view of literacy which has been influenced by social, cultural and technological change. When we think about pedagogy that incorporates multimodalities, in order to support young children, it is worthwhile considering learning that encourages access to:

- online sources to find out about imagery, tasks, instructions, artefacts etc.;
- music, art, photography, dance, movement, nature;
- film-making, audio and television clips;

- interactive posters, storyboards, picture books or leaflets;
- podcasts, vlogs, mini-instruction manuals;
- media to create digital stories, comics/graphic novels;
- software to create newspaper articles, advertisements, e-posters, campaigns.

Remember to ensure that dance is included in your multimodal thinking; dance is a wonderful opportunity to create 'movement invitations' with very young children, commenting, connecting and reflecting, using whole bodies and spaces (Clark, 2022) and exploring rhythm and steady beat, linked to music. I would invite all practitioners/teachers to find out more about the value of dance, creativity and imagination in supporting communication, language and literacy. There are of course many more new and interesting ways to use media with young children – it is important to keep up to date with new technologies as a practitioner/teacher working with under-fives.

Activity 9.3: Thinking About Multimodalities

Find out more about multimodality learning. Make a list of some further examples that you can confidently build into your provision in your setting.

If you do not consider yourself to be a digital native or confident with using technology, what might you need to do about this? Is there access to current technology in your setting?

The Digital Child and Playful Pedagogies

Before considering further the playful pedagogies of children and their digital experiences, it is necessary to review practitioner/teachers' and parent, carers and families' perceptions of the role of digital technology for young children in settings and at home. For example, Mertala's (2017) study of Finnish trainee teachers' perceptions raised concerns about very young children accessing digital media linked to their physical health and well-being (being still and not moving). Yet for older children, this concern moved from physical to more particular concerns about their cognitive development (screen time). Kucirkova and Flewitt (2022) found that the teachers in their study of digital personalisation in young children's reading were highly concerned that accessing and creating such personalised technologies (smart toys, apps and digital books) would lead to teachers and parents' input being diminished and ultimately replaced. We do need to be mindful that practitioner/teachers' perceptions of and access to digital technologies has a particular influence on their pedagogy and provision for young children (Hannaway & Steyn, 2017; Marsh et al., 2021). The same could be suggested for families, given that Kucirkova and Littleton (2016) published a national survey of parents' beliefs about children's reading for pleasure with print and digital books, which revealed many concerns from parents. The survey data included the perceptions from 886 mothers and 625 fathers of UK children (825 boys and 685 girls) aged between birth and eight years old. While 8 per cent of parents reported that they had no worries about digital reading for their children, many parents were concerned that reading on screen would increase their children's access to screen time, perhaps lead to children losing interest in reading printed books and might expose their children to inappropriate online content and too much advertising. The study outlined that 92 per cent of parents surveyed described themselves as 'confident users of technology', yet 25 per cent reported using digital books to read with their children and 57 per cent reported never having used a digital book at home, despite having access to these resources. It appears that families favour the printed book and are still a little sceptical about digital learning for their children. Similar studies revealed that families preferred using printed story books and picture books with their two-year-olds (Nicholas & Paatsch, 2021). In 2017, Strouse and Ganea proposed that parents of one- to four-year-old children enjoyed reading much more with a printed book, suggesting that their children paid more attention to these picture books and story books rather than digital books on a screen. Strouse et al. (2019) also highlighted parents in their research study favoured printed books with their three- to five-year-old children at home. Many of these studies highlight that families consider printed books to be more educational, a lot of fun and included important opportunities to continue the parent–child bonding and interpersonal relationships. Perhaps some of these viewpoints are based on digital activities as passive experiences, rather than considering the holistic nature of digital technology. Children in today's digital world can and already are engaging in creative and playful ways which enhance their multisensory experiences. Consequently, we should really be including and embedding digital literacies in our pedagogy.

Recent international studies highlight the playfulness of the use of tablets (watching videos, songs and looking at photographs) in the home environment with under-threes and suggest that there is evidence that the use of digital tablets supports children in their play and also creativity of play (Geist, 2012; Harrison & McTavish, 2018; Gillen et al., 2018; Marsh et al., 2021). For example, Marsh (2020, p. 291) researched under-threes play with tablets and their findings include evidence of creativity supporting 'children's expressive language, music and art' and how under-threes engaged in holistic play 'across cognitive (including linguistic), bodily/affective, social and cultural aspects of their development'. This study also highlighted that practitioners/teachers and families need to be supported with their understanding of the value of the digital world for under-fives. We already know that many children are technologically savvy, are able to navigate with ease between apps and programmes, code robots (Beebots, for example) and use virtual reality to bring stories to life in three-dimensional ways when provided with time, access and support. We should be encouraging these children to continue to use their imagination to create their own stories, videos, moving photographs, using green screen and augmented reality and creating small-world play animations, for example. The children that have not yet experienced or have access to digital technology also need to be encouraged and enabled in their creativity and imagination. Yet, many practitioners/teachers and families think that it is better for children to be moving physically, rather than being still in front of a screen. The examples listed above do not involved children being still! Axelsson (2022) explains that the discussions about 'the usual "screen time is harmful" (because digital play is more than that) and that it is sedentary (which so is reading, and classroom teaching) need to be reflected on so that we are offering/encouraging a wide range of play'. Axelsson (2022) offers her updated definition of 'play-literacy' (Wilson, 2010) to support this stance as:

> Play-literacy is our ability to read, interpret, sense, and understand the essence of play; an ability to communicate in a common language about play. It is a set of skills and knowledge needed to recognise play, know when to interact and intervene, and how to avoid interference. It is the ability to evaluate and analyse play in order to provide credible and meaningful information about it to others and to be able to design and sustain an environment in which play is given time, space and validation. It is also recognising that the essence of play can and should be found in everyday experiences.
>
> (Axelsson, 2022)

Reflection Point

Reflect on Axelsson's definition of play-literacy – think about your own understanding of play. Think about play, play-literacy and digital literacy.

Activity 9.4: The Benefits and the Risks of Digital Worlds for Under-Fives

Complete the table below to make a list of eight benefits of the digital world for under-fives and also include any associated risks:

Benefits	Risks	Actions to mitigate the risks

Think about the risks you have identified and reflect further on some practical steps you can take to mitigate these risks.

Carefully consider the benefits and risks for under-threes.

Revisit the Venn diagram (Figure 3.1) from Chapter 3 and reconsider your culture and actions for early reading pedagogy. You may have already included aspects of digital literacy within your first reflection task.

Your list of benefits may have included some important transferrable skills, such as enhanced communication, problem solving, analysis and reflective narratives, alongside playful pedagogies. For many children that have specific individual needs, an increased focus on digital literacy may offer a more rights-based approach, increased autonomy and agency for individual learners (refer back to Chapter 7 here). Children that prefer creative expression, exploration and imaginative concepts can also benefit from accessing and engaging with digital literacies, as will all children.

The last section of this chapter will explore the concept of digital footprints a little further and offer some suggestions to support our own understanding of digital literacies. A digital footprint, which is sometimes referred to as an electronic footprint, is about the trail of information we leave behind when using technology, either as an active or passive participant. This includes accessing websites, emails, posting on social media, maps on your smartphones, fitness tracker activity on your fitness watches, subscribing to any online newsletters, online reviews, online shopping and basically any information submitted online. Companies can track a person's online activities and the devices used and sometimes this can be done without permission (through cookies or third parties). Therefore, digital footprints matter as they are usually permanent, given that the information shared is in the public domain. There are some instances of digital footprints as semi-public in the case of social media platforms that request permission. It is vital that we consider this when we are using digital technology with young children in our settings and also that we ensure that the children are aware of their own digital footprint, to be safe and secure. Some practical ways you can do this are:

- limit the amount of information you share on any digital platforms;
- always check the privacy settings on devices, apps and games and re-check often;
- when using search engines, make sure you always use https:// sites – the 's' includes a security certificate;
- always delete information not being used;
- only use current software checked and secured with children and always keep it up to date;
- talk to children about being kind, considerate and supportive in their actions in person as well as online;
- understand and know that once information is published online, it is forever;
- do not use any personal devices when working with children – use the settings' devices at all times;
- if using Twitter or other social platforms, take care with children's images linked to the setting/school as they can be tracked.

Clearly there are some concerns about digital literacies, but they can be managed and monitored so that everyone is aware. These concerns ought not to limit engagement with digital technology in our settings and classrooms – we just need to be more aware and continue to keep ourselves updated. It is also a good idea to support families with their use of digital literacies with a workshop, poster, leaflet and regular communications.

Review and Rethinking Pedagogy

- Consider your own digital footprint and what is shared with the rest of the world.
- Plan how you can support parents, carers, families and the children in your setting with digital awareness.
- Think about how you use digital literacy in your setting and make some suggestions to improve this.
- How do you position digital literacies? Playful learning?
- Enhance your knowledge further about multimodality and early reading.
- Remember dance, music and movement within your playful pedagogies.
- Think about how you can further support children who are digital natives already.
- Review your knowledge on intercultural literacies and keep this regularly updated.
- Think about how digital literacies are embedded within early reading pedagogy for under-fives.
- Remember positive representation in everything we do with under-fives.

In Summary

This chapter has presented some of the international literature and research linked to digital literacies and multimodality to support you with your provision for digital literacies. We have considered how digital literacies may already be embedded within early reading pedagogy for under-fives and explored the digital world for children and their families, including a brief discussion surrounding digital footprints. This chapter invites the reader to reflect further on early reading pedagogy and provision to include digital literacies to support under-fives and their families. The benefits, reflections and potential risks of children as digital natives within their playful pedagogies has also been explored.

Further Reading to Continue Your Learning

This website has some useful resources to signpost you to the Early Years Dance Network (EYDN) with a range of articles, blogs and videos to enable you to lead or support dance in your setting.

www.communitydance.org.uk/programmes-and-training/early-years-dance

These journal articles will enhance your knowledge of digital literacy and pedagogy.

Marsh, J., Lahmar, J., Plowman, L., Yamada-Rice, D., Bishop, J., & Scott, F. (2021). Under threes' play with tablets. *Journal of Early Childhood Research*, 19(3), 283–297. doi.org/10.1177/1476718X20966688

Kumpulainen, K., Sairanen, H., & Nordstrom, A. (2020). Young children's digital literacy practices in the sociocultural contexts of their homes. *Journal of Early Childhood Literacy*, 20(3), 472–499.

This National Literacy Trust online resource explores digital technology in early years.

literacytrust.org.uk/resources/digital-technology-and-early-years/

Further resources from the National Literacy Trust offer guidelines about multilingualism, talking and tips for supporting parents and families with literacy.

literacytrust.org.uk/early-years/

References

Axelsson, S. (2022). *The complexity of risky play*. www.interactionimagination.com/post/the-complexity-of-risky-play

Bearne, E. (2009). Multimodality, literacy and texts: developing a discourse. *Journal of Early Childhood Literacy, 9*(2), 156–187.

Billington, C. (2016). *How digital technology can support early language and literacy outcomes in early years settings: a review of the literature*. National Literacy Trust.

Boardman, K., & Hindley, C. (2023). *Supporting young children with their communication, language and literacy: a research circle study with settings, schools and families*. Edge Hill University.

Clark, L. (2022). *About Liz: our creative adventure*. www.ourcreativeadventure.com/aboutliz

Deklerk, K.C. (2020). Multimodality in early childhood education. *International Journal of Literacy, Culture, and Language Education, 1*, December, 73–87. doi: 10.14434/ijlcle.v1i0.29481

Dudeney, G., Hockly, N., & Pegrum, M. (2013). *Digital literacies*. Pearson.

Flewitt, R., Messer, D., & Kucirkova, N. (2014). New directions for early literacy in the digital age: the iPad. *Journal of Early Childhood Literacy, 15*(3), 289–310.

Geist, E.A. (2012). A qualitative examination of two year-olds interaction with tablet based interactive technology. *Journal of Instructional Psychology, 39*(1), 26–35.

Gillen, J., Arnott, L., Marsh, J., et al. (2018). *Digital literacy and young children: towards better understandings of the benefits and challenges of digital technologies in homes and early years settings*. University of Strathclyde.

Hannaway, D.M., & Steyn, M.G. (2017). Teachers' experiences of technology-based teaching and learning in the foundation phase. *Early Child Development and Care, 187*(11), 1745–1759.

Harrison, E., & McTavish, M. (2018). 'i'Babies: Infants' and toddlers' emergent language and literacy in a digital culture of iDevices. *Journal of Early Childhood Literacy, 18*(2), 163–188. https://www.unicef.org/globalinsight/media/1271/file/%20UNICEF-Global-Insight-digital-literacy-scoping-paper-2020.pdf

Kress, G., & Jewitt, C. (2003). Introduction. In C. Jewitt & G. Kress (Eds.), *Multimodal literacy* (pp. 1–18). Peter Lang.

Kucirkova, N., & Littleton, K. (2016). *A National survey of parents' perceptions of and practices in relation to children's reading for pleasure with print and digital books*. Books Trust.

Kucirkova, N., & Flewitt, R. (2020). The future-gazing potential of digital personalization in young children's reading: views from education professionals and app designers. *Early Child Development and Care*, *190*(2), 135–149. doi: 10.1080/03004430.2018. 1458718

Kucirkova, N., & Flewitt, R. (2022). Understanding parents' conflicting beliefs about children's digital book reading. *Journal of Early Childhood Literacy*, *22*(2), 157–181. doi.org/10.1177/1468798420930361

Livingstone, S. (2016). Reframing media effects in terms of children's rights in the digital age. *Journal of Children and Media*, *10*(1), 4–12.

Livingstone, S., Kardefelt Winther, D., Kanchev, P., Cabello, P., Claro, M., Burton, P., & Phyfer, J. (2019). *Is there a ladder of children's online participation? Findings from three Global Kids Online countries*. Innocenti Research Briefs no. 2019-02. UNICEF Office of Research, Innocenti.

Livingstone, S., & Third, A. (2017). Children and young people's rights in the digital age: an emerging agenda. *New Media and Society*, *19*(5), 657–670.

Marsh J. (2020). Researching the digital literacy and multimodal practices of young children: a European agenda for change. In O. Erstad, R. Flewitt, B. KümmerlingMeibauer & Í.S. Pereira (Eds.), *The Routledge handbook of digital literacies in early childhood* (pp. 19–30). Routledge.

Marsh, J., & Hallet, E. (2008). *Desirable literacies: approaches to language and literacy in the early years*. 2nd ed. Sage.

Marsh, J., Plowman, L., Yamada-Rice, D., Bishop, J.C., Lahmar, J., Scott, F., Davenport, A., Davis, S., French, K., Piras, M., Thornhill, S., Robinson, P., & Winter, P. (2015). *Exploring play and creativity in pre-schoolers' use of apps: final project report*. University of Edinburgh.

Marsh, J., Lahmar, J., Plowman, L., Yamada-Rice, D., Bishop, J., & Scott, F. (2021). Under threes' play with tablets. *Journal of Early Childhood Research*, *19*(3), 283–297. https://doi.org/10.1177/1476718X20966688

Mertala, P. (2017). Wag the dog–The nature and foundations of preschool educators' positive ICT pedagogical beliefs. *Computers in Human Behavior*, *69*, 197–206. doi:10.1016/j.chb.2016.12.037

Mertala, P. (2019). Digital technologies in early childhood education: a frame analysis of preservice teachers' perceptions. *Early Child Development and Care*, *189*(8), 1228–1241. doi: 10.1080/03004430.2017.1372756

Mills, K. (2016). Literacy theories for the digital age: social, critical, multimodal, spatial, material and sensory lenses. *Journal of Multilingual and Multicultural Development*, *38*(4), 372–373.

Nascimbeni, F., & Vosloo, S. (2019). *Digital literacy for children: exploring definitions and frameworks*. Scoping Paper No. 01. Office of Global Insight and Policy. UNICEF.

Nicholas, M., & Paatsch, L. (2021). Mothers' views on shared reading with their two-year olds using printed and electronic texts: purpose, confidence and practice. *Journal of Early Childhood Literacy*, *21*(1), 3–26.

Sefton-Green, J., Marsh, J., Erstad, O., & Flewitt, R. (2016). *Establishing a research agenda for the digital literacy practices of young children.* A white paper for COST Action IS1410.

Sorrells, K. (2016). *Intercultural communication: globalization and social justice.* 2nd ed. Sage.

Strouse, G. A., & Ganea, P. A. (2017). A print book preference: Caregivers report higher child enjoyment and more adult– child interactions when reading print than electronic books. *International Journal of Child-Computer Interaction, 12,* 8–15. doi:10.1016/j.ijcci.2017.02.001

Strouse, G.A., Newland, L.A., & Mourlam, D.J. (2019). Educational and fun? parent versus preschooler perceptions and co-use of digital and print media. *AERA Open, 5*(3), 1–14, doi: 10.1177/2332858419861085.

United Nations Educational Scientific and Cultural Organisation (UNESCO) (2009). *Investing in cultural diversity and intercultural dialogue.* UNESCO.

United Nations Educational Scientific and Cultural Organisation (UNESCO) (2017). Annual Report. Institute for Lifelong Learning, UIL.

UNICEF (2019). *Digital literacy for children: 10 things to know.* UNICEF.

Vasquez, V.M. (2014) *Negotiating Critical Literacies with Young Children: 10th Anniversary Edition.* London and New York: Routledge.

Vasquez, V. M. (2017). *Critical literacy.* Oxford Research Encyclopaedia of Education. http://doi.org/10.1093/acrefore/9780190264093.013.2

Wilson, P. (2010). *The Playwork primer.* Alliance for Childhood.

Wohlwend, K.E. (2011). *Playing their way into literacies: reading, writing, and belonging in the early childhood classroom.* Language and Literacy Series. Teachers College Press.

10

STORYTELLING, NOT 'HERDING SHEEP'

Chapter Objectives

This chapter explores the value of story times for young children. By the end of this chapter, you will:

- reflect on the value of storytelling and sharing picture books/digital books within the daily routine for under-fives;
- explore picture books/digital books and the essential links to desired reading behaviours for under-fives;
- review your provision for storytelling;
- understand the magic of rhymes to support the early reading journey for young children.

Storytelling, Not 'Herding Sheep'

This significant chapter refocuses you on the value of storytelling and sharing picture books and/or multimodal interactive stories regularly within the routine of early years settings, not just as a 'herding sheep', filling-in or settling-down activity, but as a key early reading component. This chapter is also a reminder of how rhyming, rhythm, poetry and steady beat should also feature within storytelling activities to support children in their early reading development.

I am referring to the overall concept of story times as 'herding sheep' because this is often what shared, whole-group story time is for many young children in educational settings. This is also the perception of many practitioner/teachers working in these settings and schools. The children know that the adults want them all in one place, settling down, ready for the next 'bit' of their daily routine. For example, just before lunch or at the end of the nursery/school day. The adults require the children to all be in one place sitting still, often as passive agents – to get children ready for lunch or ready to go home. In this scenario, which I know is the not the case for every setting or school, story time becomes more of a 'herding sheep' activity. As such, this is often considered to be more about the beneficial settling-down rationale for the children, rather than an intended educational literacy focus. I suggest that this construct of story times needs some rethinking to support early reading pedagogy in early childhood education and care (ECEC). Let's explore this a little further, linked to the early reading research project findings.

The research project I carried out in England from 2017–2021 included 147 surveys, six focus group workshops, nine reflective zines and eight interviews with graduate early years practitioners/teachers working in a range of settings with under-fives. Participants were encouraged to share their views about how they support early reading development in their settings. All the data sources included storytelling or sharing stories at some point to support early reading development. When asked specifically about how often, when and where practitioners/teachers tell stories, there was very little variation from just before lunchtime or at the end of the nursery/school day. One of the key findings from this research project overall is that the majority of settings planned one daily story time session for under-fives, yet planned two, three or more 'phonics' carpet time activities within their daily routines to support early reading. Consequently, it is necessary to reflect, recognise and deconstruct this pedagogy with a focus on the value placed on story times for young children in settings. Given that story times are considered by many researchers and educationalists as an essential feature of very young children's early reading experiences and their developing literacy attainment, the research data suggests that we may be devaluing the art of story times within our daily routines and just regarding story times as a routine activity – as a tradition. Seemingly, many practitioner/teachers are not really sure why this is the case and are often not entirely sure what children gain from their story times, except that it is preparation for educational transitions. Hopefully your reflections and your new (or enhanced) knowledge from completing the activities within each chapter of this book are supporting you with an understanding that sharing stories, picture books and/or digital stories often is one of the most important activities to support under-fives with their early reading development, especially when this involves rhythm and rhyme. The early reading journey needs to begin with the purpose of inspiring a love of language and an engagement with shared reading experiences, which as we already know from previous chapters is inextricably linked with communication, listening, speaking, rhythm, rhyme, music and steady beat. Story times are invaluable opportunities to enthuse all children and especially those children that may not have any prior experiences of sharing stories in their homes or communities.

Equally, it is vital to consider the voice of the child within your story times – not just focused on the routine of the setting (often organised to support the adults or as a 'settling the children down activity') and only purposefully shared once (or twice at the most) in the nursery/school day. The purposeful pedagogies of observing, interacting, reflecting and noting the children's interests, their engagement with early reading activities and resources and how young children incorporate stories, storylines, characters and imagery within their play are the crucial starting points in beginning any discussion about planning for and providing meaningful story times for under-fives. This can only be done if we provide ample opportunities for under-fives to engage with picture books and/or digital books alongside a wide range of meaningful early reading experiences.

Story times, for many young children, are associated with a quiet, settling down, inactive activity, sometimes linked to topics, but not as carefully planned as other more curriculum-focused activities to support literacy, such as reading, writing or spelling, for example. I argue that this traditional notion of story times needs a complete re-evaluation within many of our settings and a repositioning of the values we hold about the importance of story times for under-fives. Our role as practitioners/teachers is to make story times the key treasure, the most important activities in our daily routine, where children are active, busy, participant story-makers and collaborators, empowered and immersed in the literacy-rich activities of creating stories, characters, rhymes and stimulating storylines.

The following case studies are extracts from three focus group workshops with graduate early years practitioner/teachers responding to their own initiated discussions about 'story times'.

Case Study 10.1: Nursery School Setting

We have story time to settle the children down just before lunchtime and at the end of the day. The children love this gathering together and really enjoy a little bit of peace and some quality sharing a story time. It is our saviour some days. The children have such busy nursery days. They look forward to the story at the end of the day, right before the mayhem that is packing bags and going home time.

Case Study 10.2: Baby Room

We don't have a formal story time as such, we look at books throughout the day when the babies bring them to us or before sleep time when we can. We often share a picture book with the babies just before lunchtime, when we just about get them all at the table or in their highchairs. Some of them love this – others are just hungry and waiting for their lunch. We also sing songs to settle everyone down. When they move up to toddler room, they will have a small group story time there, so it is good to get them ready for this transition.

Case Study 10.3: Pre-School Room (Three- To Four-Year-Olds)

We love our story times – we have three built into our routine, one at carpet time in the morning just before snack time, one just before lunch and again at the end of the day. The children choose their own books for the day, and we read as many as we can. Sometimes they bring them from home too. Sometimes we will read a few at a time and put them out in continuous provision so the children can act them out, use the puppets etc. The end of the day story is chosen by the staff though as part of our planning. We know how important story time is for pre-school children and it also helps them with their transitions to school – sitting and listening and concentrating.

Case Study 10.4: Forest School Story Time

We have a Forest School story time every day as part of our Forest School provision. We are out for about two to three hours building dens and doing lots of natural activities, the children are free to choose what they do out there, but before we go back inside, we always have a story around the fire pit. It just finishes the session off nicely, we love it, the children love it and then we are settled and ready for the mayhem that is getting dry, wellies off etc.

In addition, the following reflections are extracts from the interview data focused on when participants talked about sharing stories or story time:

Reflection 10.1: 'We are Using Story Time to Herd the Children in One Place, a Bit Like Sheep' (Nursery School Headteacher)

We have given this such a lot of thought while being involved in this research project – when, how and why we support children with their early reading development. When it comes to story time, we need to revisit this as a whole team. It is a little bit like we are using story time to herd the children in one place, a bit like sheep, especially for our three- and four-year-olds. It is like, oh wow, I haven't given this the depth of thought that it needed before. I have been so concerned with the formality of reading, writing and communication that the timing and the point of sharing stories is getting lost.

Reflection 10.2: 'I'm Not Sure Why They All Need to Be in One Place!' (Room Leader, Two-Year-Olds)

We share stories and picture books with two-year-olds at key points in our nursery day. I really enjoyed listening and taking part in the focus group workshop the other day and some things shared really made me think about what we do. Like, I am not sure why they all need to be in once place, why we see story time as a fill-in activity and a settling-down activity. Don't get me wrong, I know the benefits of settling children down and getting them ready for the next part of their day, but we could do some more thinking about this. We have some two-year-olds who would sit a long time if the story is interesting, for example, and others that need support with this – I am thinking about doing this a bit differently now and the children do not all need to be in one place at the same time, I think …

Reflection Points

Consider the case studies and the two reflections about provision for story time in their settings.

Think about how and when you plan your storytelling whole-group activity/small-group activity and why you have made the choices you have made. Think about the children.

Evaluate how (and if) you are 'herding sheep', using story time as 'settling down' or 'filling-in' activity for the children or getting them ready for their next transition point. Does this matter?

Are the children active participants in their story times and will they feel empowered, included, valued? What do you conclude?

Story times should not have the focus on getting children ready for school – school readiness is not the purpose of story times!

Telling Stories

Storytelling often has its roots within our very early childhood experiences. Stories have been told from the beginning of time, as we already know from historians, handed down from generation to generation. What I mean by storytelling here is making up your own stories, without a storybook (or you could use a storybook and enhance/extend), using your knowledge of the children and perhaps using interesting props, bringing new characters to life in different ways to enable children to be inspired, curious and interested to learn more. Storytelling for me is not a quiet, inactive activity where children sit still and listen. This inactivity of story times is a real issue for many children and is certainly an important cultural issue to discuss and evaluate within your teams. Stories are an essential aspect of our daily activities where we learn to connect with each other to support us with making sense of our world. Storytelling often presents itself in a wide variety of ways in our daily routines – in our settings/schools, workplaces, television, films, advertisements, songs, literature, advocacy, fundraising, theatre, gossip – the list is endless. Think about how animated our adult stories are when we are together in social situations. Stories can establish a sense of belonging, develop familiarity, trust and empathy, inviting the listener to join in and visit another story world for a short while. Storytelling, in my opinion, is a tried and tested method to spark children's curiosity for literacy learning, alongside the magic of rhymes. Over a 40-year+ career in working with children aged from birth to eight years and over, my experience of storytelling is that telling stories can provide the fun, awe, wonder and curiosity that can be both motivating and aspirational for many young children – the key to getting children immersed in the literacy world. Obviously, this is only when the adult enjoys this activity, understands the value storytelling has for young children in their literacy learning and is well rehearsed with communication and interactions with children.

Likewise, it is important to note that under-threes (babies, toddlers, two-year-olds) also love being immersed in our storytelling worlds. Alongside sharing printed or digital picture books with under-threes, the art of storytelling is very much undervalued and certainly more so within ECEC settings. Yet, storytelling is often taking place in family homes and within communities. Reggio Emilia annually invites Italy, Europe and the rest of the world to engage in their 'Night of Tales' storytelling themes. This is an invitation for communities to gather around sharing stories, tales, adventures – reading, narrating and listening together to celebrate the value and the magic of tales. This annual celebration involves lots of colour, shadows, light, animation and creativity (#NottedeiRacconti). In my most recent Research Circle project with nursery and school settings in England (Boardman, 2023), families and communities talk about telling stories to their children more often than they share picture books, particularly families with dual languages or in families where English is not their first language. Families explain that they tell stories to their children to support their culture, their heritage and their world view. I strongly advocate that it is time to bring in more storytelling opportunities with under-threes.

Here are some of my musings about telling stories with under-fives, the benefits and some practicalities.

- Stories excite imagination, build vocabulary, develop relational social and emotional skills and can also support with values.
- It is essential to ignite the children's curiosity about the things they are interested in, or even things that children might not have heard of. For example, my stories involved lots of mystical characters such as dragons, fairies, elves, trolls, giants. I also included animals such as bears, squirrels, moles or hedgehogs, based on interactions and observations with children. The children loved stories about the squirrel that they could see in the school grounds daily.
- Story times need to be planned, yet they can also be unplanned, spontaneous activities, child-led and child-focused. Outdoors there are wonderful spaces for telling stories.

- Story time is not a sitting still activity – my stories have lots of actions, large movements, joining in moments, using the space around us, loud bits, quiet bits, props, puppets etc. Children are participants, story-makers and collaborators – they are expert story-makers if you allow them to be.

- Try to use stories as teachable moments with some challenges to think deeply about and overcome. You could make suggestions, leave children wanting to find out more which often leads to the vital impact of connectedness. There doesn't need to be a right answer – it could be a moral dilemma.

- Have lots of fun with language, include varied communications (sign language) and use a wide range of fun vocabulary, such as made-up words, rhyming words, alliteration and nonsense words. Through the magic of storytelling, you are also supporting children's phonological awareness and introducing new vocabulary, but that is a bonus and not the sole purpose.

- You might like to think about a social justice theme to support children with understanding society, such as sharing, homelessness, crime, culture, equity. Take great care with positive representation of characters here.

- Stories need to fuel children's imagination, they need to be fun and contain some laughter, some light and shade and be magical! Be careful not to frighten the children! *I have a dragon puppet and tell lots of stories about this cheeky dragon and his funny antics. One day one of our nursery children didn't want to come in because they were concerned about what the dragon might do next. I quickly reflected and he became a kind and considerate dragon in our next story adventures, with a focus on what this particular child would be interested in finding out.*

- Invite the children to get involved in storytelling, creating the storylines and the characters. Beware, this may take a long time, but you will get there. You will also build the children's concentration, imagination and creativity.

- Don't tell the ending of the story every time you share a story, particularly if you are telling stories to older children. Hold their imagination for as long as you can. I used to stop the story at a pivotal point near the end and then invite the children to meet me at a given time and place the next day to share the ending. For example, outside, on a step, in the library etc. As you can imagine, the children gave a great deal of thought about what the ending might be. Some children wrote the ending of the story for me the next day, drew pictures of the ending or just burst into school the next day with a whole series of endings. I also do this with storybooks and picture books to keep the stories meaningful for the children – they can think about alternative endings for the characters and use thought bubbles for the characters to focus on feelings. Remember story time is about the awe, wonder and curiosity of the world and needs to be meaningful for the children.

- Try to ensure that story time is not a 'grab and gather' approach (McCormick & McIntosh, 2020), that it has meaning to the children to continue their learning. Think about the concept of story times as herding sheep, the purposefulness of telling stories to children – what do you want the children to know and to learn, why and how?

- Consider creating stories about nursery rhyme characters for under-threes. Think about making up stories about some nursery rhyme characters – spiders, bears, stars, a bus, Humpty Dumpty etc. You can begin your story with the rhyme and build in lots of opportunities for more rhyming words, rhythm, steady beat – stamping, clapping, tapping, music, rap.
- Build storytelling baskets with props, puppets, imaginative play toys and everyday objects and link storytelling to nursery rhymes, poems or favourite picture book characters.
- Invite parents, carers and families to come and tell their own cultural stories to the children, or to record them digitally for the children to listen to.
- Encourage children to create and retell their own stories.

Activity 10.1: Telling Stories

Find out more about the difference between telling stories and reading/sharing picture books. Why are both activities equally important for young children?

Consider planning your story term with a range of themes linked to the children's interests, social justice and/or interesting events. Plan how you will ensure that the stories, the picture books or storybooks always include meaningful experiences that are representative of the children's lived experiences.

Think about the images, the characters, the value and the hidden (take away) messages within.

Sharing Picture Books

Serafini (2010, p. 10) explains that sharing picture books is a 'unique literacy experience', an experience that offers 'a range of visual interpretations' to engage and promote 'analytical thinking in young children's learning'. These are powerful words, supported by many other researchers. Arizpe and Styles (2016) describe 'the delight a child takes from a picture book is what is most important and should always be encouraged' (p. 187). Equally, Torr (2023) advocates that it is the interactions and the communications which sit alongside picture book sharing as an activity where the learning really takes place for very young children. Many researchers also believe that the literacy experiences offered in sharing picture books (print or digital) with under-fives cannot be replaced by any other experiences, as these are such rich and distinctive learning opportunities. Yet, we also know that this is very much dependent upon children's prior experiences with picture books and their own interests, given that many children may not have had the opportunity to engage in shared picture book experiences in their home environments or in early years settings. When I talk about sharing picture books with very young children, I refer to shared reading as an activity where:

- the picture book is the provocation that engages, motivates, interests and enthuses the child/children, as well as the act of holding the book (or tablet), turning the pages, interacting with the images, the sounds, the scenes and the story;

- the adult, practitioner/teacher, parent or family member reads aloud the printed words and engages in talking about the pictures, the characters or storylines and the words, connecting the experiences to the child's;
- the child/children are active participants – listening to the story and the pattern of the words, looking at the detail in the pictures, pointing, talking, interacting and imagining, connecting to their own experiences, and making meaning.

This is different, of course, to the one-to-one experience of the child choosing to access a picture book and interacting with the picture book themselves. It is also significantly different to reading as decoding, which is often the focus of reading definitions and reading activities. I cannot stress enough the critical value of picture books for under-fives in supporting the wide range of language and literacy-rich experiences necessary to create awe and wonder and to foster a love of language and literacy. Clemens and Kegel's (2021) contemporary research suggests that the 43 parents in their automatic language processing technology study produced more talk during shared picture book reading with their children, aged between nine and eighteen months old, than any other daily activities engaged with such as singing, playing, mealtimes or within other caregiving routines.

Reflection Point

Think about why picture books produce more talk than any other activities or routines for under-threes. Review how you can build more opportunities for sharing picture books with the children in your setting. Consider print and digital resources.

Reflect on the practical ways you can support parents, carers and families with the value of picture books with their own children at home.

Given that picture books introduce children to the wider world, often beyond their own lived experiences, it is imperative that we carefully consider accurate representation and images within all picture books. We already know from many global research studies (Birthrights, 2018; UNICEF, 2021; Zero to Three, 2022, 2023) that black and brown babies, their families and young children worldwide achieve far less positive outcomes across the many metrics used to access early childhood well-being than their white peers (birth rate, maternity care, poverty, achievement, income, employment) (Zero to Three, 2023). Therefore, we need to ensure that we are fully inclusive in our provision – particularly within the picture books and early reading resources we introduce to the children.

Case Study 10.5: Choosing Picture Books – Getting It Right

Many of our private day nursery settings are situated within socio-economically deprived areas and some are in an advantageous position within our nursery chain. Our children and their families are predominantly white. This is becoming a concern for us when we are trying to focus on being inclusive and anti-racist in our provision. The staff teams have all attended training, we engage in regular CPD, but we still feel like we are opening a can of worms – this is not any of our lived experiences. We don't want to be tokenistic in our approaches and really want to tackle disadvantage and white privilege in the early years, as we know this is where inclusivity needs to be embedded. We really want to teach all our children about their wider world, but every time we try it just ends up being tokenistic. We have bought new books, lots of positive black and brown images and inclusive characters and we review the messages in the stories about disability, race, culture, religion. It just all feels so political and it's so difficult. I just don't know that we are getting this right at the moment. I don't know how to get this right – is there a right? We are using the National Literacy Trust guidelines for picture books and Book Trust websites to support us. We get involved in all the literacy and book initiatives (Book Trust, World Book Day etc.). What more can we do? We know we do need to do more.

Activity 10.2: Choosing Picture Books

Imagine this is a conversation you are having with a colleague. What advice can you offer? Can you make some suggestions based on your reading and tasks from previous chapters?

We do need to get this right, but what is the right thing to do?

Do some research about how to choose picture books for under-fives.

Consider producing a quick checklist to support practitioner/teachers in your setting with selecting picture books. Consider the story line, strength of the characters, images, hidden messages, accurate representation and the learning intentions.

We will also discuss the concept of supporting colleagues further in Chapter 11.

Anti-racist and inclusive pedagogy is not without its challenges in our ECEC settings. It is a challenge we need to continue to confront, to debate and to support each other with. I certainly do not have all the answers to support the sector, but I do think that if we continue to discuss and explore this and consistently evaluate our resources, pedagogy and provision, we have a good chance of better supporting the children, families and communities alongside enhancing our own understanding.

Furthermore, the importance of sharing picture books with babies from birth (and even before birth) can also be heavily misunderstood by many practitioner/teachers, educators and families alike. There is often an underestimated perception of the cognitive abilities of babies (Copple et al., 2013) and sometimes when we discuss babies as competent from birth this can be a difficult concept to grasp. For example, it is easier for practitioner/teachers to see and measure the knowledge that is visible (language, names, physical movements, objects, numbers and labels), given that Mandler (2004) advocates that how babies learn is not always transparent within our early observations and interactions. The following reflective zine entries from the early reading research study illustrate the concept of observable behaviours from babies accessing picture books leading to further engagement from practitioner/teachers taking part in this study, rather than ensuring that sharing picture books is established pedagogy.

Zine 5

I am trying to put books in all areas of the room now with our babies – it's just difficult really as they are not looking at them, reading them – they take them to their mouths, empty and fill the book basket and then they start to play slip and slide, so we move them out of the way, because it's dangerous as the books are slippy. It's easier with toddlers and older children as you can see they are looking at them and pointing to the pictures, making sounds and so on.

(Boardman, 2017, p. 285)

Zine 2

The babies don't really enjoy looking at books unless we sit with them. We observed the babies eating the books, putting them in their mouths, tearing the pages of the books and pushing the books away. When we do look at the picture books with our babies, they easily get bored and crawl away – they will sit for a short while.

One of the babies brought a book over to the staff member and they looked at the picture book together. The baby pointed and patted the book.

The zine entries highlight that these graduate practitioners/teachers react to and respond to observable behaviours from the babies' interactions with picture books, which often leads to further engagement and interactions with book-sharing activities, as this is what interested the babies. Although there is convincing evidence that sharing picture books and sharing stories is an essential element in shaping attitudes to reading (Clark, 1976; Evans, 2012; Goouch & Lambirth, 2011) the practitioner/teachers did not appear to value this as a strong rationale for sharing and reading stories with under-threes, particularly babies. The practitioner/teacher's responsiveness to observable behaviours does not appear to be the result of purposeful pedagogy in these (and many other) scenarios. This is such an important finding to reflect on within our provision for babies, given that most researchers advocate that sharing interactive picture books with babies is a crucial activity to support children's language and cognitive thinking. Picture books provide and meet many of the principles of valued pedagogy for under-fives. Remember, when we are talking about pedagogy, we are referring to the ideas and values that underpin our teaching, learning and provision. This includes our understanding of learning (how children learn) as a result of our purposeful communications, interactions from birth, hands-on sensory and practical experiences, real-life and meaningful exchanges and that we are planning, adapting and reflecting on the experiences we provide to support this learning. The value of sharing picture books is vastly underestimated, and we need to address this within our pedagogy and provision for all babies.

Picture Books and the Link to Reading Behaviours

So far in this chapter, we have explored the fundamental value of stories – sharing stories and telling stories with young children and how these activities promote and encourage children's early reading and wider literacy development. There are also, of course, some very obvious links to wider desired reading behaviours that arise from sharing picture books. Yet, these are often not so easily explained or understood. I am repeatedly asked the question about readerly behaviours of under-fives and the visible observed benefits of these. This is very much dependent upon how you define reading, previously discussed in Chapters 2, 3 and 4. If you consider reading to be about young children enjoying stories, rhymes and singing, reading pictures, handling paper and screen texts, understanding concepts (comprehension) and having fun with language in a play-based environment and not just focused on decoding print, then there is a vast array of benefits. Alternatively, if you do focus on decoding and print-based reading, there are certainly benefits for under-fives engaging with picture books. Here is a brief overview of how sharing picture books connects to reading behaviours. Picture books help to:

- spark, build and maintain children's interests, noticing and commenting on the awe and wonder in the pictures, the story, the event. Reading pictures is how children will intentionally notice and point out the detail in the pictures;
- build language skills and introduce new vocabulary in context (pictures, words);
- connect pictures with words, connect stories with real-life events when the adults talk about the story, the characters and the pictures. Words on their own have no meaning without pictures, purpose and meaning;
- build phonological skills – alliteration, letter, sound correspondence, language patterns;
- develop children's comprehension skills;
- sequence stories, understand the characters and actions;
- make predictions and inferences, interpret and understand empathy, feelings, actions and consequences;
- support children with summarising and using contextual cues;
- social and emotional learning and self-regulation, comfort, calmness;
- support children with understanding how words and language work in practice – words are read from left to right, top to bottom, words swirling around the page – single words in capital letters, demonstrating emphasis etc.;
- value the act of holding, turning pages, carrying a book, having control over which pages to revisit and concentrate on, the feel of books, the smell and texture of books.

The Magic of Rhymes

In the same way that I cannot stress how important story times and sharing picture books with under-fives is, rhyming is also central in supporting children with their early reading development. There are many more picture books that currently include a variety of rhyming texts to share with young children, which is an exciting development. The job is already done for us here, if we choose our picture books wisely. Here is a brief outline of the potential of rhymes for young children.

1 Poems and rhymes support under-fives with language patterns and how language works – they begin to notice and then identify the endings of words, letters, sounds, matching words, common sounds and patterns in words to make the sounds.

2 Children love reciting nursery rhymes, action rhymes and poems and when they are practising rhymes, they are learning to anticipate words, memorise rhymes and learning new concepts.

3 Children experience the rhythm of the language in rhymes, so they can make predictions, notice rhymes, continue a rhyming string (cat, fat, sat, bat), identify rhyming words and also identify words that do not rhyme.

4 Rhymes teach children about expression, rhythm, steady beat – children can join in, listen for and keep a steady beat, use rhythm, music and take/wait turns within rhyming games.

5 Rhymes are all about communication, speaking, listening and developing strong oral skills.

6 Rhymes support children's imagination, awe and wonder – fun!

7 Learning rhymes and patterns in language supports sound discrimination, rhyme discrimination – identification of what makes the sounds, the words, the pattern.

8 Rhymes support children with new vocabulary and can teach children new words, phrases and their meanings in a context that can be understood.

9 Making up or reciting poems and rhymes can be done anywhere – on journeys, in the bath, at the dentist, getting dressed, in the playground. I use rhyming word games everywhere when I am teaching – in all the routine down-times, especially lining-up for activities, as we appear to line up children a lot in our settings.

10 Phonological awareness is developed through rhyme, rhythm, steady beat and musical activities.

11 Children also learn about shape, colour, size and other key mathematical skills when singing number songs and rhymes.

12 Children learn to decode print (read) and encode (spelling) through rhyming games and rhyming play.

13 Rhyming can teach children about onomatopoeia (when a word suggests the sound it makes – bang, crash, pop etc.) and alliteration in language.

14 Rhymes are short stories – so children are learning to sequence a beginning, middle and ending.

15 Rhyming makes things easier to remember for many children, so they are developing their memory and processing skills.

16 Children can also learn about abstract concepts within rhymes, particularly when carrying out action rhymes.

I am sure that you can also add a few more to this list. Rhymes are just magical as an essential component in how children understand communication, language, literacy, reading and writing.

Review and Rethinking Pedagogy

• Consider how you can change the narrative about 'herding sheep' for storytelling.
• Think about how you can enhance your own storytelling skills.
• List and share the essential early reading skills that under-fives gain from story times, picture books, rhyming games and poems.
• Reflect on how you are planning to ensure that you provide a wide range of experiences that include language, rhythm, rhyme, music and steady beat for under-fives.
• How will you be including parents, carers and communities in your provision for story times?
• Outline the benefits of sharing picture books with babies. Create an infographic to share with your colleagues.
• Plan a 'hands-on' PCF event where you share the magic of rhymes for young children's early reading development.

In Summary

This chapter has explored the value of story times within the daily routine of ECEC settings, enabling us to critique this pedagogy and provision. The fundamental importance of sharing stories, storytelling and sharing picture books with young children has been developed further within our early reading knowledge and understanding, impacting on how we position these as vital early reading experiences, which cannot be replicated elsewhere. This chapter has outlined some strategies for enhancing storytelling provision, re-evaluated and grounded within the voice of the child and the purpose of story times – why and how these are critical experiences for under-fives. We have also highlighted the essential links to some desired reading behaviours when children are engaged in sharing picture books and quality story time experiences. We have explored some voices from professionals and their opinions about provision for story times in their settings in order to support our own pedagogy. This chapter has outlined some of the benefits of rhymes in supporting under-fives with their early reading, with an understanding that there are many more potential learning outcomes to be gained from rhyming and rhythm.

Further Reading to Continue Your Learning

This PACEY blog outlines the benefits and offers some suggestions for 'the importance of nursery rhymes in early childhood'.

www.pacey.org.uk/news-and-views/pacey-blog/2019/october-2019/the-importance-of-nursery-rhymes-in-early-childhoo/

The Centre for Primary Literacy (CLPE) booklists are useful resources to support you with planning story themes, rhyming, early reading, wordless picture books, poetry etc.

clpe.org.uk/books/booklists

To enhance your understanding of music, rhythm and steady beat, you may find these resources useful.

dynamicmusicroom.com/rhythm-activities-for-kindergarten/

Lawrence Educational (2018). *The beat baby handbook.*

Lawrence Educational (2019). *Ros Bayley's beat baby raps.*

Dyke, J. (2019). *Songs, rhymes and finger plays.* A Froebelian Approach. Froebel Trust. www.froebel.org.uk/uploads/documents/FT-Songs-Rhymes-and-Finger-Plays-Pamphlet.pdf

Read about some ideas to enhance your storytelling provision from Imagine Forest.

www.imagineforest.com/blog/storytelling-activities-kids/

References

Arizpe, E., & Styles, M. (2016). *Children reading picture books: interpreting visual texts.* 2nd ed. Routledge.

Birthrights (2018). *Systemic racism, not broken bodies: an inquiry into racial injustice and human rights in UK maternity care. Executive summary.* www.birthrights.org.uk/wp-content/uploads/2022/05/Birthrights-inquiry-systemic-racism_exec-summary_May-22-web.pdf

Boardman, K. (2017). 'I know I don't read enough or even pick up a book in the baby room sometimes': early years teacher trainees' perceptions and beliefs about reading with under-threes. Doctoral thesis. University of Sheffield.

Boardman, K. (2023). *Supporting communication, language and literacy with under-fives: Research Circle Project.* Edge Hill University.

Clark, M.M. (1976). *Young fluent readers.* Heinemann.

Clemens, L.F., & Kegel, C.A.T. (2021). Unique contribution of shared book reading on adult-child language interaction. *Journal of Child Language, 48*(2), 373–386.

Copple, C., Bredekamp, S., Koralek, D.G., & Charner, K. (2013). *Developmentally appropriate practice: focus on pre-schoolers.* National Association for the Education of Young Children.

Evans, J. (2012). 'This is me': developing literacy and a sense of self through play, talk and stories. *Education 3–13: International Journal of Primary, Elementary and Early Years Education, 40*(3), 315–331.

Goouch, K., & Lambirth, A. (2011). *Teaching early reading and phonics: creative approaches to early literacy.* Sage.

Mandler, J.M. (2004). *The foundations of mind: origins of conceptual thought.* Oxford University Press.

McCormick, C., & McIntosh, S. (2020). Tailoring traditional tales as tools for our trade. In T. Bruce, L. McNair & J. Whinnett (Eds.), *Putting storytelling at the heart of early childhood practice: a reflective guide for early years practitioners* (pp. 31–63). 1st ed. Routledge.

Serafini, F. (2010). Understanding visual images in picture books. In J. Evans (Ed.), *Talking beyond the page.* Routledge.

Torr, J. (2023). *Reading picture books with infants and toddlers: learning through language.* Routledge.

UNICEF (2021). www.unicef.org/social-policy/child-poverty

Zero to Three (2022). stateofbabies.org/

Zero to Three (2023). www.zerotothree.org

11

TAKING THE LEAD ON 'LITERACY' FOR UNDER-FIVES

Chapter Objectives

This chapter will provide lots of case studies as the voices of early years professionals leading on literacy learning in their settings. By the end of this chapter, you will be able to:

- review some additional ideas to engage and support children, families and colleagues with literacy for under-fives, shared by graduate professionals;
- explore how equity and inclusion is a consistent thread throughout all literacy provision;
- support all practitioner/teachers as leaders of literacy;
- create/enhance your leadership vision for literacy;
- develop an action plan to support your setting/school with literacy learning.

Taking the Lead on 'Literacy' for Under-Fives

Chapter 11 provides some new stories from early years professionals in a wide range of settings to support with your understanding of enhancing and leading literacy provision for under-fives. Leading literacy has a different focus to being a literacy advocate in that you can be an advocate for early reading and literacy, have an interest and a passion for supporting literacy learning, yet all practitioners/teachers need to be leaders of literacy learning – this is where leadership comes into effect. We have already explored how literacy is the key in linking knowledge across all subjects to enable children to gain access and connect with the learning within each subject. Literacy is a whole-setting/school issue, and improving literacy has a curriculum-wide impact. As such, literacy is recognised as the most valued of skills worldwide for all stakeholders across many metrics – speaking, listening, reading, writing, spelling and digital literacies (refer to Chapters 4, 5, 8 and 9). Taking the lead on literacy in your setting requires you to support all stakeholders (children, colleagues, families, communities, governors) with their understanding of their role and the impact that literacy has for all children's learning and development. The role of the leader here is not necessarily having to come up with all the ideas and strategies, but to create an environment where ideas, accountability, advocacy and creativity thrives. We have discussed the advocacy of ethics, agency, access and the voice of the child in Chapter 7. This chapter is focused on how we can now take action and be accountable for creating and implementing a whole-setting/school literacy-rich environment, providing literacy-rich experiences for all children and especially those children, families and communities that are often marginalised. What I mean by this is that leaders of literacy learning are always thinking about how we can ensure that every setting/ classroom enables every child to participate and actively contribute, so that all children are able to connect to the learning taking place, regardless of gender, ability, language, culture, race, religion, and be fully included. This chapter is not about the theories of leadership, it is about how everyone can take the lead on literacy in their own classrooms/settings/schools to make a difference for all children, families and communities.

Taking the lead on literacy for under-fives involves:

- building your expertise to effectively develop others and lead a successful whole-setting/school literacy strategy, which carefully considers and implements the views of all stakeholders;
- developing the skills to support your colleagues to enhance literacy provision across the curriculum (without creating unnecessary workload or tension);
- valuing and knowing that literacy learning happens everywhere – outdoors, within setting/classroom routines, relationships, homes and communities;
- becoming a specialist in your role – developing your own knowledge and understanding of early reading and literacy (language, communication, speaking, listening, reading, spelling and writing);
- collaborating with others (in similar roles) or wider external literacy networks to develop a range of practical tools and guidance to support your setting/school's approach to literacy;
- encouraging everyone's ideas and utilising research-informed evidence to support literacy learning from birth;
- ensuring equity and inclusion for all children, families and communities;
- having a strong knowledge and understanding of the Equality Act 2010 and those protected characteristics within (age, disability, sex, gender reassignment, race, religion or belief, sexual orientation, marriage/civil partnership, pregnancy and maternity);
- making effective plans, using data and your knowledge of the children, their learning experiences (child development) to support literacy-rich teaching – starting with the child;
- adopting challenging texts and providing a wide range of opportunities to develop the knowledge of all children, including those from diverse linguistic and cultural backgrounds;

- regularly analysing and evaluating the resources used to teach literacy and literacy experiences provided;
- embedding quality talk in all teaching approaches and learning experiences;
- utilising useful questioning approaches, such as critical thinking to focus on what the children think, rather than there being one right answer. This approach enables all children to participate and share their ideas;
- nurturing social justice to make a valuable difference in education;
- expanding digital literacies to support all children;
- making more connections between in-school and out-of-school learning;
- creating and maintaining a culture of valuing literacy learning from the perspective of the child;
- planning focused professional development for the whole setting, which includes support materials from external sources, such as research studies, blogs, networks, evidenced-based outcomes and also includes co-construction with families and communities;
- a passion for literacy learning and advocacy;
- developing a distinct early reading policy in settings/schools, either alongside or within the wider literacy policy, which considers the voices and choices of the children, their families and the professionals working in the setting (Boardman, 2022);
- potentially informing future educational policy.

Although I appreciate this is a big ask, professionals working in the ECEC sector are putting most of these leadership strategies into practice every day.

Axelsson's (2022) *Original learning* approach may provide a reflective tool to support you with some aspects of taking the lead on literacy within your own context. Axelsson (2022) suggests that there are ten essential threads that enable children to learn and play naturally and at their own pace. These threads can be applied to any pedagogical philosophy or context. I advocate that these threads ought to be woven throughout your literacy pedagogy for under-fives and revisited often:

Wonder   Curiosity   Joy   Knowledge   Imagination

Interaction   Risk   Time   Reflection   Listening

Activity 11.1: Leading Literacy Learning

Using the ten essential threads above from Axelsson (2022), explore how these aspects are/can be woven into your pedagogy for literacy. Think carefully about how research-informed evidence can support you with each of these threads.

Consider your own professional development – what support might you need to begin to take the lead on literacy in your setting?

Plan a continued professional development (CPD) schedule for yourself and for your colleagues. Think about the protected characteristics within the Equality Act 2010 and our roles as practitioners/teachers. You may find the table below useful:

Focus	CPD plan Include suggested research to support
Developing communication, speaking, listening and language	
Early reading – rhythm, rhyme, poetry, rap, steady beat, picture books/digital	
Music development	
Developing reading – decoding, encoding, reading fluency	
Developing writing	
Enhancing digital literacies	
Quality, well-qualified staff	
Reading as an enriching process of communication, imagination, creativity and future planning	
Include your own focus here	
Enhancing social justice – protected characteristics	

The next section of this chapter provides some examples to illustrate the wonderful work that practitioners/teachers are doing to support under-fives with their early reading and literacy learning. These examples highlight how practitioners/teachers are leading literacy in their settings in a wide variety of ways.

Voices From the Field as Leaders of Literacy Practitioner/Teacher Case Studies

The following case studies have been shared by graduate practitioners/teachers as examples of leading on literacy in a range of settings. All the practitioner/teachers have been involved in the early reading research project, so you could suggest that they already have a sound knowledge and understanding of the importance of supporting children with their early reading development and literacy learning.

Case Study 11.1: Building Effective Home–Setting Relationships, Private Day Nursery

It is so important to communicate with parents, carers and families about what we are doing in our setting and to build effective home–setting relationships. We try hard to find out about every child in our nursery setting – what children are reading at home, the stories they share, favourite TV programmes etc. We make home visits, which are very time consuming and sometimes a real barrier, yet are such powerful opportunities to share values, ideas and really get to know our families. Some of the ideas we have recently put into practice have come directly from conversations we have been having with families – we recently created a display board with pegs on so that we can share books, comics, interesting readings, leaflets for our parents, we have also developed a rhyming booklet. We presumed that our families know the rhymes we share in our nursery and often they don't, so we give out our rhyming booklet during our home visits and model sharing a rhyme with the child. We follow this up with online communications and the staff team share quick videos of us singing the rhymes so that if the families don't want to do this, they can share the videos with the children.

We have also developed our self-registration activity based on conversations with families – we use a large whiteboard and encourage all our children and their PCF members to sign in, make their mark, draw a picture, write their name etc. together. Our families raised concerns about teaching the children to write their names. Ok, so we know that there are many stages in writing before this happens, but we put this in place to support and we have lots of really interesting discussions at self-registration. We have also put up a chalkboard outdoors so that this can be 'practised' outside with families. It is so lovely to see the messages, the drawings, the mark-making on a daily basis.

Case Study 11.2: Mosaic of Mark-Making, Two-Year-Old Provision

We set up a display board of the children's mark-making and called it 'a mosaic of mark-making'. The display board is in the corridor ready for drop-off and pick-up time. There seemed to be some pressure from our families for the children to be writing. We really wanted to demonstrate that we are always 'writing', making marks etc. and to display the journey of mark-making. We just don't want to lose the joy of mark-making. This simple addition has meant that we can value mark-making as writing, we can talk more about this with our parents and visitors. We listened to everyone's ideas and actually our staff team have learned a little bit more also. We are all talking more about writing as communication – all marks and all communications have meaning. We are thinking about producing a photo book of this to share with new parents also. Some of the things we are capturing on our mosaic of marks to support with the journey to writing are mark-making with water, paintbrushes, sticks, mud, water bottles, plungers, rolling and moving things (tyres), crates, large outdoor building, woodwork, tools, mud kitchen stirring, mixing – the list is endless.

Case Study 11.3: Self-Portraits Outdoors, Reception

When our children start with us in reception, we invite parents, carers and families in to make self-portraits outdoors together to set the scene for their children's learning. It is a big ask, but it is now something that the parents look forward to. We have grandparents joining us also. We then set some 'getting ready' homework self-portraits for those PCF who have not been able to attend. We go outdoors and use natural materials to create self-portraits of themselves, portraits of their children or anyone they want to talk to us about. It is more about the value of learning outdoors, quality talk and storytelling than any other end result, although we do have fun. We have many willing volunteers to tell stories using their characters. We have story prompts on rocks if anyone needs them. We encourage asking questions and making comments and we position these as critical literacy skills that we are encouraging in their children. Ok, there is some reluctance initially, but we scaffold and it works. The PCF leave the session with some understanding of the benefit of outdoors for their children, the space and the freedom to be creative, to talk in a more relaxed environment and the values we have shared about our literacy aims. Usually, over coffee afterwards, we get lots of opportunities to talk more about literacy. We think it has been such a valuable start for our children and a good inroad to building those relationships with families.

Case Study 11.4: Leading On Quality Talk, Pre-School Room (Three-Year-Olds)

All our data year on year suggests that we need to focus on quality talk and language. We have tried a variety of interventions and often although they might work for some children, they are just quick fixes. When I took over the lead for the pre-school room, I felt really strongly that the focus needed to be on literacy and quality talk. We unpacked what we meant as a team by quality talk and held a focus group with our parents (a bit like we did for the research project). Wow, it was really complex. We decided that if we chose all our picture books and literacy resources wisely, we could be halfway there.

We revisited sustained shared thinking (SST) as a team and focused on how we could and should be introducing more quality talk, thinking about our own skills first. We thought about trying hard to ensure that we didn't continuously ask children questions that we already know the answer to and focused more on critical thinking, open-ended questions. We also found that when we introduced more nursery rhyme props and story prop baskets talk did become more focused. We sent picture book packs home with the children once a month, with some prompts and some suggestions for thought bubbles – how the characters might be feeling, what they might be saying, thinking. The packs contained a picture book, some prompts as critical questions, a white board 'thought bubble' for recording talk and a talking tin (to digitally record some of the talk, interactions). We used these to plan sessions with families and also with the children. I cannot tell you how much we have all learned from this.

Case Study 11.5: Story Ribbons, Children's Centre

We have introduced some targeted planning for our story times. We wanted to have more of a focus for our children and a move away from topics. We plan each term, based on an aspect of the *characteristics of effective learning* (CoEL) as a starting point. We also ask our families what they like to read about, talk about or hear more about. We do a lot of stay and play with families and we also share stories. We introduced story ribbons so that our children could choose a theme also. We came across these on Etsy.com. We started with a few and now we make our own, our parents, grandparents and most of our families help us. Some are beautifully embroidered, have pegs on them, knitted, crocheted, have badges, pictures etc. – we have quite a collection now. The children can interact with these, retell the story, make up a new story and talk about the feel, the texture of the ribbons. We have really gone to town on these and they are so effective in supporting our staff team. We've just made a set with character pegs so the story can be retold in any way. It's so lovely listening to the children tell each other stories – this resource has just helped us to focus on talking and story-making.

Critical Reflection Points

What do each of these case studies tell you about the value of literacy?

Which aspect of leading on literacy learning could you introduce into your setting? You may already be doing this, but may not see this as leading literacy.

Think about equity and inclusion in each of these case studies. There are obvious benefits for children with English as an additional language, children with SEND – it would be useful for you to highlight these.

Some of these ideas involve deeper engagement with parents and families – which ideas might you like to introduce in your setting?

Here are some more literacy leaders sharing their ideas for you to consider.

Case Study 11.6: Visual Tracking Support, Private Day Nursery, Toddlers

One of the important things we have introduced for early reading, because we hadn't given it much thought before, is lots of visual tracking activities indoors and outdoors to support the children. So, we have things like water play funnels, ramps, shadow-matching activities, torch games. We do lots of ball play, throwing, catching, bouncing, marble runs, target practice, balloons, bubbles – we know how important these physical things are for our children to read and write.

Case Study 11.7: An Early Reading Model, Nursery Manager, Private Day Nursery

I introduced our early reading (ER) model diagram – each year we start with this model, and we revisit this to see if it is working or not. We share with everyone – parents, families, staff. It is just a reminder about what is important. We find it really useful to support us and we get great feedback from our parents (and also Ofsted). I must confess it is not mine – I borrowed it from a training session and have adapted this to suit our setting.

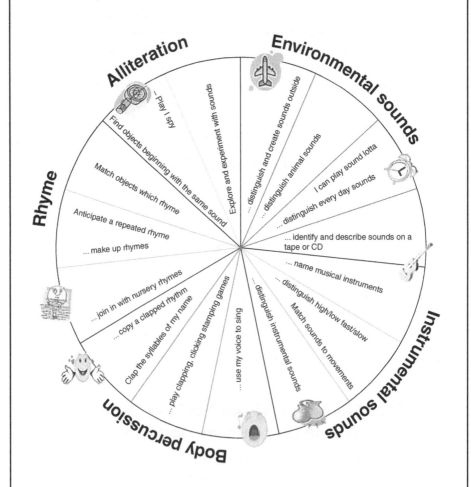

Figure 11.1 A model for early reading

Case Study 11.8: Tuff Spots are Not Worksheets! Reception Classroom

We seem to have gone full on with tuff spot trays, indoors and outdoors. We decided to utilise tuff spots to focus on our literacy targets – writing, letter formation, phonics, storybooks etc. Then we realised that we were just using them like worksheets with one task, or a few tasks that the children needed to complete. We have now gone back to basics with imaginative play as the focus for tuff spots. We do use them for storybooks and rhymes, but more open-ended resources. It is just so easy to be drawn into something and then lose sight of what it is for. Now we find that giving a more open-ended approach means that the children think for themselves – they write their own captions, add their own resources and use the activities in a more useful way. We made a decision not to use them at all outdoors, which has meant that the children need to be much more creative and imaginative in their play.

Leading Literacy for Under-Threes

You could suggest that leading literacy might take a different approach when working with under-threes. I would argue that if you are already focused on child development and play pedagogy as the foundations of everything that you do, then the principles of literacy leadership remain consistent for all children and their families. The only difference might be the focus for under-threes to be on early reading and should always consider the voices and choices of the children and their families in striving to be meaningful. Let's explore how and why there are some other things to consider when we think about leading literacy with under-threes:

- the voices of under-threes are under-represented in many policy decisions (Boardman, 2022; Murray, 2019; Shier, 2001) – they are silent and certainly not visible;
- we need to ensure that we develop a 'pedagogy of listening' Rinaldi (2006, p. 12), which values and actively seeks the views of young children. For example, what are the children's interests, how do we gather children's views about the picture books/digital resources we share, when and how often we have story times, how the children feel about reading, talking, listening, the music we choose? Who decides on how often children ought to access screen time and on what basis have these decisions been made?
- 'The notions of listening to under-threes with their developing language skills demands a different approach and one that is also culturally relevant, particularly within early reading policy development' (Boardman, 2022, p. 133). How we gather the views of babies, toddlers and two-year-olds in order to prepare our early reading policy needs to be visible and ethically sound;
- the mosaic approach is often used to capture the child's voice in any participatory research (Clark & Moss, 2011) and can actively involve children in research projects

and any other activities seeking the views of the child as part of the design, data collection and interpretation. This approach has also recently been used to include parents, families and educators about their views (Rogers & Boyd, 2020);

- how do we ensure that we seek and respect the viewpoints of ECEC practitioners/ teachers and all colleagues working with under-threes? Often the focus for literacy is on attainment, educational outcomes led by policy-makers. Where are the voices and choices of children and professionals in local and global policy development for literacy?

- it is crucial to carefully consider when and where the voices of under-threes are considered in early reading policy development in your setting – this needs to be explained within the policy for transparency and developed with all stakeholders. Perhaps we also need to build in review points;

- Vandenbroeck (2020, p. 418) suggests that when it comes to the ECEC sector, 'the daily practices of professionals and parents is decided without discussion with the direct stakeholders: parents, early years practitioners and local communities'. You can change this perspective. Include a section in all your setting policies about stakeholder involvement which outlines how you sought and have implemented the views of children, families, communities.

Hopefully some of these thoughts will support you in developing your own pedagogy and policy approaches to early reading and literacy in your setting/school. Policies are not just focused on strategic data; they should also include the voices of all stakeholders to have a purpose, to achieve the collective vision and to be able to make a difference for all the children, their families and the settings. Remember that decades of international research consistently highlights that the main influences on children's well-being is the quality of the interactions, relationships and experiences we have with our families and caregivers from birth. Therefore, this must be a factor for all our work with children, families and communities – the quality of our interactions, how we build reciprocal relationships and how we can strengthen these within pedagogy, provision and policy.

Voices From the Field as Leaders of Literacy Practitioner/Teacher Case Studies

The following case studies may support you with some further ideas about leading on literacy for under-threes.

Case Study 11.9: Communication, First-Hand Experiences, Private Day Nursery

I'm leading on literacy in my role as baby room leader. The main concern we all have for our babies and toddlers currently is their communication and language. We have one focus now – communication and first-hand experiences. We have introduced sign using Makaton and lots and lots of sensory experiences. We share a sign a week with our parents and use a lot more physical communication strategies. We go outside every day, and we plan for natural resources. I have told the team all I want to see is interaction, communications and first-hand experiences – never mind the observations, learning stories or assessment. These mean nothing without interactions, and they are what we are there for. Our job is to communicate, have loads of one-to-one conversations, introduce new vocabulary, use language and play.

Case Study 11.10: Steady Beat Experiences, Two-Year-Old Provision

Our literacy focus this term is steady beat – stamping, clapping, rhythm, tapping. We do this with our parachute games, ribbons, indoors, outdoors, within routines, when we are rhyming, as much as we can. This is helping to engage all our two-year-olds and we have such fun.

Case Study 11.11: Puddle Jumping, Private Day Nursery

Our toddlers love puddle jumping – we have just focused on the joy of talking, noticing the shape of puddles, talking about the colours, how many jumps we get until the puddle goes away, the noises the splashes make – squish, splat, tap. We get so much talk about puddle jumping.

Creating a Vision for Literacy

I anticipate that you may now have lots of knowledge and understanding about literacy and potentially could be thinking about leading literacy in our setting for under-fives. In Chapter 3, we started to think about our pedagogical approach to early reading. It is now the perfect time to review your thinking from this activity (Figure 3.1) and adapt this model to begin to create a starting point for a vision for literacy. Remember that this is just a starting point, as you now need to involve all your stakeholders in crafting, developing and implementing this vision. Before you begin to have these critical conversations about what your vision for literacy might be, here are some more ideas you might like to consider before developing your vision:

- the need for improvements can be overwhelming – start with what you know, what the data tells you, what your stakeholders tell you, observations, child-led initiatives, relationships and interactions;
- consider setting up a literacy working group to support you with establishing your literacy objectives, agreeing and arranging relevant CPD and suitable resources, monitoring and evaluating your suggestions and communicating with all stakeholders;

- less is more – vision statements are aspirational in nature and do need to be challenging, yet achievable as a collaborative, shared vision. Pick out some key themes across a year, perhaps some short-term, medium-term and long-term goals. Think about communication, reading, writing, fluency, oracy, quality talk etc. Think about how you are supporting children with additional needs and how to ensure you are fully inclusive;
- all stakeholders need to understand the direction for literacy and how their individual and collective contributions impact on the end goals;
- consider impact and accountability – how this will be measured and monitored, by whom and how often. It might be useful to think about an openness to new ways of working here;
- utilise evidence-informed practice and critique how this will support your vision and your practice in the setting/school – what works and why for your children and their families and the staff team you have;
- remember to highlight and give due regard to equity, inclusion, ethics and social justice;
- consider the curriculum or statutory guidance set in your local and regional area for literacy outcomes. However, remember that educational policy is often driven by an agenda of what works for outcomes/attainment for policy-makers, rather than children and families, so think carefully about who has decided on those end goals and where child development comes into play. Lots of policy decisions are made without key stakeholder involvement;
- build the CoEL into your literacy pedagogy;
- consider the environment you provide for literacy – spaces, play spaces, connectivity, quality interactions and the ways of communicating in order to enact your vision for literacy.

Your vision (or position statement) for literacy should be relevant, personal, clear, challenging, realistic and concise, yet aspirational and motivational. Your vision should also be clearly aligned to the setting's vision, and this is particularly important for everyone to see this alignment, how it all fits together within their individual/collective contributions. Although your vision may need to change slightly on occasion to meet the needs of a group of children or a community, your vision for literacy can usually remain, if it is working. Your vision will set out your purpose and outline how you will meet the needs of all stakeholders, For example:

'We aspire for our children to be …'
'We strive to develop our literacy community with …'
'Our literacy learning environments inspire learning, sharing, creativity and inclusion, and are the foundation for …'

You may already have a vision in place and perhaps you are enhancing this vision by embedding it into everything you do, given that it is up to the team, as individuals to put this vision into action on a daily basis, every day for every child. Here are two examples of how experienced practitioner/teachers developed their vision statements.

Case Study 11.12: Developing Our Vision (Focus Group Workshop)

We started to think about our vision for literacy while taking part in this research project – we haven't had any input into this before as a nursery staff team. We wanted to make sure that the whole-school vision had a separate bit for our young children – babies, toddlers and pre-school children – and that what we do with our children feeds into the whole-school vision for literacy. I just asked the head teacher, and he said 'great idea – let's do this'. We had a whole-team morning discussing what it is we do to support literacy and what our vision is for literacy in each phase. We found this helpful. We shared some ideas with our governors at the next governors' meeting and asked our parents' governors to gather the parents' perspective. We focused our vision on a welcoming and supportive environment and a commitment to ensuring that every child experiences quality talk and engages in quality interactions.

Case Study 11.13: Developing Our Vision (Focus Group Workshop)

We already have a vision in place in our setting for literacy – this came about in discussions about planning for our Ofsted inspection. Our vision for literacy is to ensure that every child achieves their potential by creating a nurturing learning environment, fostering a love of reading and writing and promoting enriching communications and interactions. We made some changes to our vision when we talked to the pre-school teams and some of our parents – we added: for our pre-school children, we intend to focus on early reading experiences such as rhythm, rhyme, poetry, music, steady beat, alongside sharing picture books and storytelling activities to support their literacy development. We now know that we need to think about how we bring in the children's perspectives into this vision.

Activity 11.2: Creating a Vision for Literacy

Think about creating or developing your vision for literacy and how you might go about this if you haven't already got something in place. Consider your starting point – will you have some critical questions for the team? How will you include all stakeholders?

If you already have a vision for literacy – take some time to review this.

As part of your vision, you might like to decide how you will evaluate your current resources for literacy, how will you choose resources, purchase future resources to support literacy? Think about those essential aspects of equity, inclusion, social justice, race, positive representation, quality vocabulary, rhyming text to guide your choices.

Have a go at writing your vision statement with the knowledge and understanding you already have about the children in your setting. In my experience, it is much easier to have a starting point of a few ideas, words and phrases ready to include in your vision discussions with everyone else. Sometimes a blank screen or blank paper is a tricky concept.

Action Planning with an Outcome

Now you have started to consider or created/developed/enhanced your vision statement for literacy and have more clarity about what your overarching goals are for your setting/school, you could begin action planning to set out what it is you all need to do together to achieve this. An effective action plan is simple, concise and should not create any additional workload for your setting/school – it is best if this is already embedded into your provision. For example, you might utilise staff meetings to action plan, review and discuss impact, rather than set up separate meetings for this.

Action plans usually include SMART (specific, measured, achievable, realistic, time) targets, actions, timeframes, resources, impact/outcomes and a review point to support you in meeting the overarching vision statement. However, you can action plan in any way you like. Once you know what it is you need to achieve (your vision), then setting SMART targets can be challenging and take a lot of practice. Let's review what we mean by SMART:

- *Specific*: Your goal should be clearly defined and specific. So, if you are focusing on data, it would be useful to set the threshold you ideally would like to reach. For example, an improvement of 10 per cent or ... our children say they enjoy .... Assessment data.
- *Measurable*: Make sure your goal can be measured. If your goal is to improve an aspect, you might need to consider how this will be tracked. You need to clearly articulate what evidence base you are using to measure success here – survey data, children's voice, achievement, practitioner/teacher assessments, baseline assessment, observations.
- *Attainable*: Challenge is good, but achievable is realistic within the timeframe that works for the setting.
- *Relevant*: Your goals should align with your vision and values and be relevant for the children, their families and the setting.
- *Time-specific*: Most settings/schools work to a specific timeframe for data capture, the end of year/phase, termly or ready for assessments.

There is a vast array of action planning templates for you to choose from, and it is likely that all stakeholders may want to have some input into this. Here are some headings you could use for your action plan template:

Vision:
Goal/target:
Action plan:

- actions (steps you plan to take to achieve your goals)
- responsibility (staff members who will be handling each step)
- timeline (deadline for each step)
- resources
- outcomes (desired result for each step)

Evidence of success:
Tracking and evaluation process:

A reminder that the important outcome here begins with the children and ends with the children. Even if the goal is to support the staff team, the outcome should always be child focused. I am not usually in favour action planning, but I am always an advocate of an action plan for literacy. This is a good way to remind everyone that we are all leaders of literacy and this needs to be our focus for the well-being of the children.

Review and Rethinking Pedagogy

* Plan how you will review your literacy resources, using the basis of the protected characteristics from the Equality Act 2010 to support.
* Explain why it is important to have a vision for literacy. What is the purpose, relevance and significance for children?
* Everyone is a literacy lead – consider how you will take the team with you on this journey (or review how you are already doing this and if this can be enhanced).
* Consider and evaluate the research you can utilise to support practitioner/teachers with literacy.
* How can you make sure that your staff team develops the necessary expertise to lead on literacy?

In Summary

This chapter has focused on leadership for literacy with under-fives. We have reviewed a wide range of case studies from early years practitioners/teachers leading on specific aspects of literacy learning in their settings, which included suggestions for further collaboration with families. Some of their ideas are simple, yet effective. We have also explored how and why equity and inclusion is essential as a consistent thread throughout all literacy provision to enable all children to connect to the learning taking place, regardless of gender, ability, language, culture, race, religion and be fully inclusive. This chapter reminds us that we are all leaders of literacy, given that the curriculum cannot be accessed without the key components of literacy. We have reviewed the importance of setting a vision for literacy, strengthened with an action plan to support your setting/school with inclusive literacy learning.

Further Reading to Continue Your Learning

Find out more about the mosaic approach, listening to the voices of children and seeking the views of all stakeholders – children, parents, educators and communities.

Clark, A., & Moss, P. (2011). *Listening to children: the mosaic approach.* National Children's Bureau.

Rogers, M., & Boyd, W. (2020). Meddling with mosaic: reflections and adaptations. *European Early Childhood Education Research Journal, 28*(5), 642–658. doi: 10.1080/1350293X.2020.1817236

Read more about the research to support quality talk.

Cartmill, E.A., Armstrong, B.F. 3rd, Gleitman, L.R., Goldin-Meadow, S., Medina, T.N., & Trueswell, J.C. (2013). Quality of early parent input predicts child vocabulary 3 years later. *Proceedings of the National Academy of Sciences of the United States of America, 110*(28), 11278–11283. doi: 10.1073/pnas.1309518110.

McGillion, M.L., Herbert, J.S., Pine, J.M., Keren-Portnoy, T., Vihman, M.M., & Matthews, D.E. (2013). Supporting early vocabulary development: what sort of responsiveness matters? *IEEE Transactions on Autonomous Mental Development, 5*(3), 240–248. doi: 10.1109/TAMD.2013.2275949

Reflect further on leadership in ECEC settings, focused on under-threes.

National College (2013). *Being and becoming: under-threes in focus*. National College for Teaching and Leadership.

Read more about Suzanne Axelsson's approaches to original learning in action.

www.interactionimagination.com/original-learning

Remind yourself about sustained shared thinking to support literacy.

Brodie, K. (2014). Sustained shared thinking in the early years: linking theory to practice. David Fulton.

References

Axelsson, S. (2022). *Original learning*. www.interactionimagination.com/original-learning

Boardman, K. (2022). Where are the children's voices and choices in educational settings' early reading policies? A reflection on early reading provision for under-threes. *European Early Childhood Education Research Journal, 30*(1), 131–146. doi: 10.1080/1350293X.2022.2026437

Clark, A., & Moss, P. (2011). *Listening to children: the mosaic approach*. National Children's Bureau.

Murray, J. (2019). Hearing young children's voices. *International Journal of Early Years Education, 27*(1), 1–5.

Rinaldi, C. (2006). *In dialogue with Reggio Emilia: listening, researching and learning*. Routledge.

Rogers, M., & Boyd, W. (2020). Meddling with mosaic: reflections and adaptations. *European Early Childhood Education Research Journal, 28*(5), 642–658. doi: 10.1080/1350293X.2020.1817236

Shier, H. (2001). Pathways to participation: openings, opportunities and obligations. *Children and Society*, *15*, 107–117.

Vandenbroeck, M. (2020). 'Measuring the Young Child: On Facts, Figures and Ideologies in Early Childhood'. *Ethics and Education*, *15*(4) 413 – 425.

12
FINAL THOUGHTS

Chapter Objectives

Final thoughts are outlined in this chapter, with a section dedicated to planning your next steps for provision, with some signposts to further activity to support and promote literacy as a continuum of learning. These final thoughts seek to remind the reader about the significant learning within this book and include some further discussions related to the chapters. By the end of this chapter, you will:

- understand how all the chapters link together to support the overarching themes of early reading and literacy development for under-fives;
- examine your own attitudes and pedagogy about early reading and literacy to support children in your setting/school;
- consider your own key learning and evaluate the next steps for your own professional development.

It is important that you understand that there is a lot of 'me' in this book – my thoughts, my ideas and my own pedagogy. Alexander (2001, p. 540) defines pedagogy as 'the performance of teaching together with the theories, beliefs, policies and controversies that inform and shape it'. This book is exactly that – it contains all my developed theories, beliefs, policies and controversies from my 40 plus-year career. I have my own viewpoints, shaped by my own opinions and practical experiences, and I have shared these with you. However, it is important that you use your own critical literacy skills to delve deeper into your own learning – ask yourself about the validity, robustness of the evidence, the ideas presented, think about the limitations that might arise and make your learning relevant to you. Adams (2022, p. 108) suggests that pedagogy is a 'thorny issue at the heart of education' and this requires some serious unpicking, further discussion and evaluating from your own perspective. As I stated in the beginning of this book – I am not an expert. I have tried to balance my own ideology with the voices from many other professionals currently working with under-fives. I decided to set the baseline of graduate practitioner/

teachers for all my research participants, and I do think this works. Graduates will have undertaken a period of study for at least three years, which usually involves reflection on practice, curriculum and pedagogical input and will have achieved some key graduate attributes (subject specific, innovative, creative, proactive, digitally literate and reflective). This graduate-'ness' is what makes them different from those without a degree and is an added value, given they have already started their journey of personal development in making a commitment to being responsible for their own future learning, often financially and professionally. This is not to say that I do not value all practitioner/teachers at whatever level, because I do – the sector is full of amazing talented professionals. It is important to have an ethical baseline for my research project and this felt right. It has been such a privilege to listen to, acknowledge and really hear the voices of these passionate practitioner/teachers. As such, I have learned such a lot from their reflections and their openness to delve deeper into their own pedagogical journeys.

This book is about co-collaboration in order to convey all the critical elements of early reading to ensure that this sits well within the context of literacy. When we think about terminology such as 'language-rich', we need to think carefully about what this means – who decides on what is 'rich' language, from which perspective and why. Hopefully this book will support you in unravelling some of this terminology and considering all viewpoints, including all those children, families and communities marginalised by our educational systems and policies.

Talking About Play

When I talk about play in this book, I am not referring to any particular type of play (role play, risky play, imaginative play, loose parts play etc.), I am referring to play that happens everywhere and not necessarily linked to an organisational context (Hedges, 2001): play that is happening outside, on the bus, in the bath, in nursery, at school on the playground, play with resources and play without resources. Canning (2020, p. 102) states that 'children having choice in what they want to do, having access to resources they want to play with and having time to follow their own interests is significant'. Play is hugely significant for literacy learning and I may not have stressed this enough within each chapter of this book, so I would like to state this clearly now – play is how children learn on their literacy journeys. Children learn to read and write when it matters to them and has meaning for them. The emphasis for literacy learning needs to be placed on the child, what they enjoy, what they already know and what they are interested to find out more about.

Thinking About What Early Reading is for Under-Fives

In Chapters 1 and 2, we explored some definitions of early reading to support our developing understanding of what early reading is. Chapter 2 encouraged a review of what this might mean for pedagogy and provision for young children under five. The main points outlined within this chapter are:

- there is no agreed definition of what early reading is for under-fives across the early childhood education and care (ECEC) sector;
- early reading experiences begin from birth and often take place in homes with families and in cultural communities;
- it is not useful to consider early reading as pre-stage, pre-reading or emerging skills. This devalues early reading learning. We highlighted that early reading pedagogy is not focused on print-based learning;
- the early reading environment is much more than the resources we provide, but resources do need to be carefully considered. It is about the language, communication, critical thinking and social interactions as crucial components to support our understanding of early reading;
- literacy-rich environments encourage and enable communications, listening, reading and writing and need to be co-created and co-designed with the children;
- early reading does not happen by accident and is very much dependent upon interactions and lived experiences;
- early reading involves planned and unplanned experiences and activities to support under-fives with learning to listen, interact, lots of time for talking, music, movement, storytelling and sharing stories, rhythm, rhyme and singing are some examples;
- access to high-quality resources is essential to support positive representation for all children and communities.

Final Discussion 12.1: Early Reading is …

Make sure you are clear about what you think early reading is.

Use the activities, case studies and ideas from the voices of professionals to continue to develop your own ideas about early reading. I obviously have my own thoughts about what I think early reading is.

Write your definition of early reading now.

A Reminder About What Early Reading is Not for Under-Fives

In Chapter 3, we developed an understanding that when we talk about early reading, it is not about teaching phonics. We explored how early reading needs to be separated from the phonics discourse for under-fives. The main points outlined within this chapter are:

- formally teaching phonics is not early reading. Early reading pedagogy, which can involve teaching systematic synthetic phonics (SSP) is relevant only when children are interested, and it is meaningful for them to understand the alphabetic code, read print, write and spell;

- introducing the formality of teaching phonics too early is never a good idea. Children need to develop an interest in language and stories (which many would suggest is the point of teaching phonics in the first place);
- the values and culture you create for early reading is crucial and sets the tone for how children under five engage with reading and writing;
- reflecting on the values, culture and the environment for early reading pedagogy for children from birth ensures that the resources provided are representational and inclusive to support equality, race, diversity, inclusion, religion and culture.

Final Discussion 12.2: Early Reading is Not

Take the time to re-read the experiences from the voices of professionals from Chapter 3.

Why is it important to separate early reading pedagogy from the pedagogy of formally teaching SSP?

A Valid and Useful Definition of Early Reading for Under-Fives

Think carefully about your learning from Chapter 4 and why reading, writing and literacy is important for very young children. Chapter 4 emphasises how important it is for young children to engage with reading and writing in whatever format and how quality early reading experiences support all children's cultural worlds. Some further highlights from this chapter include:

- traditional literacies are usually still rooted within the printed word within our pedagogies in ECEC settings and this needs some rethinking;
- children's literature has not yet caught up with families' and communities' lived experiences, therefore it is vital that we review the early reading resources we provide, using a critical lens;
- places of interest, such as art galleries, museums, zoos and farms offer a dearth of literary experiences for under-fives, which is often overlooked;
- outdoor literacy experiences offer a wide range of additional early reading experiences, which provide young children with interesting sensory and natural resources;
- writing is physical for under-fives, involving experiences of large manipulative resources, malleable and sensory materials, painting, mud play, rolling tyres, building crates and threading, and requires an acknowledgement that writing needs no end product;
- mark-making is meaningful for all children in whatever format – all materials are writing materials. Communication, language and interactions are embedded within mark-making experiences for many under-fives.

A valid and useful definition of early reading for under-fives encompasses communication, language and positive interpersonal interactions to nurture engagement with – and impactful love of – reading and writing.

Exploring the Educational Focus of SSP, Word-Gap Ideologies, Interventions

In Chapters 5 and 6, we explored some national and international educational debates. **Some of the main points outlined within these chapters are:**

- how teaching SSP formally fits into the early reading debate, if at all, given that one size does not fit all. Children are individuals with lots of prior experiences and we usually operate the principles of the unique child (EYFS) across the ECEC sector. However, when teaching SSP, the alphabetic code is the same for all children, so we do need to teach this well and be consistent with the SSP scheme authors' guidelines;
- the perpetual school readiness culture is leading to a more formal top-down approach from policy-makers who are primarily focused on attainment, outcomes and closing gaps;
- teaching SSP is still very much a contested pedagogy for many professionals. SSP is valued when it is meaningful to the children – the key question is when is that and do we get to have a choice, with the current SSP policy directive in England?
- there is still some confusion for many professionals about how early reading and SSP fit together within the broader literacy debate;
- international perspectives for teaching literacy (reading and writing) are varied and do not compare to the prescriptive method mandated by England;
- attainment gaps, language and word-gap discourse tends to be focused on a standardised educational approach based on policy-makers' expected outcomes for children. This often results in far too many interventions to support this catch-up culture, which impacts on children's well-being – in particular when children are removed from valuable teaching sessions and play experiences, which is usually the case;
- interventions can be a valuable pedagogy to support children with individual needs and/or SEND;
- reading for pleasure, although a valuable initiative, is more often than not focused on children who are already able to read, which misses some key opportunities to encourage readerly behaviours for under-fives. Positive attitudes to reading begin from birth in the experiences provided (or not) within families, communities and settings.

Final Discussion 12.3: Interventions

Use the activities, case studies and ideas from the voices of professionals to continue to develop your own ideas about interventions.

How do you feel about interventions for under-fives?

What interventions do you consider to be useful, valid and supportive for under-fives? How do you know?

Thinking More About Literacy Advocates and Why We Need More Literacy Advocates in Our Settings

Literacy advocates avoid 'theme of the week', 'story of the week', 'sounds of the week' approaches. There are many reasons for this – for example:

- this practice may devaluate the lived experiences of children and their interests;
- learning for most children takes longer than a week, needs revisiting, repetition, context and meaning;
- children's learning can take many forms and only when learning becomes meaningful to the child will it make sense and be relevant – learning needs to connect children to their interests and experiences;
- learning in themes may not be developmentally appropriate for some children – particularly children who do not learn in this way – as it is not inclusive pedagogy.

Literacy advocates:

- are passionate about play and understand 'the centrality of play in early childhood' (Stewart, Corr and Henderson 2023, p. 4)
- are reading professionals and literacy partners for all stakeholders;
- encourage and model communication, reading and writing, reviewing and focusing on the quality of interactions, experiences, spaces and resources;
- support parents, carers and families with their understanding of literacy for under-fives, ensuring that the children's and families' cultural worlds are carefully considered, valued and represented;
- place ethical values within care routines as crucial literacy learning moments that are often overlooked. As such, listening to children, gathering their viewpoints and hearing their voices is pivotal to ensure effective literacy pedagogy and policy development.

> ## Final Discussion 12.4: I am a Literacy Advocate Because ...
>
> Explore the many ways you are already a literacy advocate.
> Make a list of five clear actions you will take to develop this further.

Further Thinking About Literacy And Equality – Race, Diversity and Inclusion

Inclusive and authentic representation in literature (books, images, labels) offers a wider range of perspectives linked to children's backgrounds, cultures, race, religion, gender and disability and, as such, contributes to the children's and families' sense of identity and belonging. Literacy is a social justice concept that needs to be continuously reflected upon and adapted, especially for under-fives. We need to be constantly thinking about how our conscious and unconscious bias impacts on our pedagogy and provision. In doing so, the focus of regularly analysing and reviewing early reading and literacy resources needs to be embedded within pedagogy and provision for under-fives. This ensures that we are creating and maintaining a culture of valuing literacy learning from the perspective of the children, their families and the local community.

Final Discussion 12.5: Literacy Equality, Race, Diversity and Inclusion

Use the activities, case studies and ideas from Chapters 7 and 11 to continue to develop your own ideas about how we can be much better at supporting children, families and communities with their positive identity.

Outline six measures/actions you will take to improve your knowledge and understanding in this area.

Personal Note 12.1: Positive representation: I am always thinking about positive representation because I am aware of my 'whiteness' and the power dimension that sits with this. I try hard to consider the **critical race theory (CRT)** lens and always be open and honest in my conversations and actions. I am aware this is a weakness in my thinking, pedagogy and provision and unless this is challenged at all levels – policy, settings, experiences, resources – it doesn't really matter how much I reflect on this, I know that I need to do more – be more accountable. I think it is essential for all early year practitioner/teachers to get to a comfortable space to discuss their own attitudes and feelings and to understand the effects of racism on young children. Houston (2019, p. 123) suggests that there are particular 'aspects of the hidden curriculum that influence racialisation', such as:

- 'The ethos of the setting, displays and notices'
- 'Curriculum delivery, content, organisation and resources'
- 'Interactions, relationships'
- 'Communications with parents – enrolment, settling in procedures'
- 'Recruitment, retention, roles' and support of staff teams
- 'How play and learning resources are selected and provided'
- 'How daily routines provide for diverse cultural norms'.

This is such a lot for early years practitioner/teachers to be thinking about, but especially when it comes to literacy and the teaching of literacy and phonics.

Digital Literacies

In Chapter 9, we explored how digital literacies are embedded within early reading pedagogy.

The main points outlined within this chapter are:

- digital literacy is a key skill that society requires for all children, which is still very much in development for very young children;
- many under-fives and their families are already accessing and benefitting from digital resources on a daily basis in their own homes;
- cultural literacy is a powerful resource. Intercultural literacy supports children and their families with accessing and acknowledging a variety of world views and encourages us to think about intercultural literacy as an opportunity for change (in attitudes, thinking and behaviours);
- the ECEC sector could consider making better use of digital literacies to support under-fives in their settings/schools;
- there are considerable benefits and learning opportunities within the digital literacy world, given that many under-fives are already digital natives.

Final Discussion 12.6: Digital Literacies

Review Chapter 9 and highlight five key learning points to support your pedagogy with under-fives.

Thinking About the Value We Place on Story Time, Rhyme Time, Songs and Music-Making

In Chapters 4, 8 and 10, we explored story times, storytelling, the magic of rhymes and songs, music-making, dance, rhythm and steady beat. Some impactful learning is embedded across these chapters to support your understanding of early reading and literacy.

The concept of story times has been outlined further in Chapter 10, to reflect on how story times are valued by the children and professionals, when this forms part of the daily setting routine as a settling down or filling in activity. This chapter provided an opportunity to critique this pedagogy, with the voices from professionals shone a light on the value of story times from their perspectives. Picture books and the benefits of these experiences from birth, linked to reading behaviours, highlight that sharing picture books is a fundamental aspect of early reading for under-fives. The huge potential of rhymes, rhythm and steady beat to enhance early reading pedagogy suggests that there is literacy learning everywhere for under-fives within our interpersonal communications. Rhymes and rhyming games are also a wonderful source of fun!

Thinking About Leading Literacy

In Chapter 11, we explored taking the lead for literacy learning and supporting our colleagues as leaders of literacy for all children. This chapter showcases lots of voices from professionals who are leading on literacy in their own settings in many ways. The main points outlined within this chapter are:

- as literacy leaders, we value that literacy learning happens everywhere: outdoors, places of interest, within routines, interpersonal relationships and communications, homes, communities and across digital literacies;
- leaders of literacy build in aspects of knowledge, curiosity, wonder, joy, imagination, interaction, time, risk, listening and reflection within their pedagogy for literacy learning;
- leaders of literacy create and develop policies and practices which involve all stakeholders;
- crafting a vision for literacy begins with the stakeholders, the setting and the aims you wish to achieve, which are child centric;
- ensure that equity, inclusion, ethics and social justice is valued, respected, reviewed and embedded with your vision and pedagogy for literacy;
- although leading literacy can be complex, the aim is to build and sustain a literacy culture that values all stakeholders' viewpoints, is co-constructed and regularly reviewed by the stakeholders;
- leaders of literacy welcome the importance of setting an inclusive vision for literacy, strengthened with a responsive action plan to support the children and their families in their literacy learning.

This book intends to highlight the significance of early reading as responsive, intentional pedagogy for under-fives. Thank you so much for reading all the way to the end. I really do hope this has been a useful critical literacy experience for you to engage with. The world of early literacy is in your hands – change the world, reflect on your provision and make those necessary adaptations for the under-fives in your setting. Remember that young children can be locked out of wonderful opportunities embedded within literacy learning if they do not learn to communicate, read or write. It is that critical.

A few more critical prompts to conclude.

- If children are starting school at a younger age (before the term after they are five years old) how can we ensure that the pedagogy and provision meets the children's needs? What adaptations are we making for children with SEND and second-language learners, particularly for literacy?
- How can you safely explore children's ideas about their own identities?
- Explore further your ideas of inclusive environments. Consider how you enable all children to have a voice.

- Evaluate your provision for quality talk.
- Evaluate literacy-rich environments as a concept to support your early reading pedagogy.

Planning Your Next Steps for Your Provision and Your Pedagogy

Planning your next steps can take many forms. You might like to consider:

1   gathering the voices and opinions of all your stakeholders on a regular basis to support your knowledge, development and provision for early literacy. Sometimes fresh eyes uncover something wonderful. Think about how you plan to do this;

2   focus on writing – research and develop your mark-making pedagogy. Support parents, families and communities with all the possibilities of mark-making indoors and outdoors;

3   plan more outdoor experiences: Forest School, Beach School, visits and outings. Encourage the children to find and collect lots of natural resources to make mythical and imaginative characters for storytelling and create story worlds with them;

4   encourage more parental and family involvement in all your early reading provision – storytelling, reading with children, mark-making, art, design, singing, music, rhythm and steady beat;

5   nurture more literacy learning opportunities within all the care routines in your setting. Support your colleagues in highlighting where the possibilities are.

References

Adams, P. (2022). Scotland and pedagogy: moving from the anglophone towards the continental? *Nordic Studies in Education, 42*(1), 105–121.

Alexander, R. (2001). *Culture and pedagogy: international comparisons in primary education.* Blackwell.

Boardman, K. (2020). 'Too young to read': early years practitioners' perceptions of early reading with under-threes. *International Journal of Early Years Education, 28*(1), 81–96.

Canning, N. (2020). *Children's empowerment in play: participation voice and ownership.* Routledge. TACTYC Book Series.

Hedges, T. (2001). *Teaching and learning in the language classroom.* Oxford University Press.

Houston, G. (2019). Racialisation in Earlly Years Education. Black Childrens Stories from the Classroom. London: Routledge TACTYC.

Stewart, N. Corr, K. and Henderson, J. (2023). "The centrality of play in early childhood' in Nutbrown, C. (Ed) Early Childhood Education. Current realities and future priorities. London: Early Education. 3–13.

GLOSSARY OF KEY TERMS

Accountability is about being responsible for what you do and the things that happen that are intentionally planned/unintentional, with a satisfactory reason for your actions.

Alliteration is a string of words that begin with the same sound. Alphabetic code is how the letters in printed words represent sounds in spoken language. It is the relationship between individual letters of the alphabet (or groups of letters) and the smallest units of sounds in spoken language – letter-sound correspondences.

CPD refers to **continued professional development**, which is training or continued training to improve your knowledge while working.

Critical race theory is based on research that suggests that race and racism is not biologically natural but is a socially constructed (culturally influenced) theory.

Cultural literacies refers to having an understanding of the traditions and history of a group of people from a given culture other than your own. It also means engaging with these traditions and activities across a range of cultural spaces such as museums, galleries and presentations. Cultural literacy is an awareness that everyone is a unique individual with their own lived experiences and that engaging in reading, writing and other communications away from any cultural knowledge shapes our thinking.

Decoding is about translating printed graphemes (letter shapes) into phonemes (sounds) to sound out the words in order to read.

Digital literacies are the opposite of traditional literacies of reading, writing and understanding printed text. New literacy concepts such as computer literacy, media literacy and information literacy overlap. Digital literacies include all elements of the digital world to support communication.

Discourse refers to our thinking, understanding and communications or conversations in any form.

ECEC is an abbreviation for **early childhood education and care**. This term is used to outline pre-school years from the birth of the child usually up to the eight years in some countries or six years in others. In this book, ECEC is more than just preparation for primary education. UNESCO refers to ECEC as the holistic development of children's' social, emotional, cognitive and physical needs to support nurture caring, capable and responsible future citizens.

Emergent literacy refers to the knowledge, understanding and skills that young children have before formal literacy teaching and learning.

Encoding is about translating printed units of sound (phonemes) into words (graphemes) in order to spell.

Grapheme is the letter, or combination of letters, in print that represents a sound (phoneme).

Holistic refers to the whole picture of something and not just one aspect – everything all together.

Ideology is a set of beliefs or principles, thoughts and ideas about a subject or concept.

Intercultural literacies refers to the understandings, attitudes, language abilities, participation and identities that enable successful engagement with a second culture, other than your own.

Marginalisation is when we treat (a person, group, or concept) as not important.

Modalities refer to a particular ways of doing or experiencing something and can be used in all forms of communications.

Multimodality is an approach that understands communication and representation to be much more than about language. New media and technologies include visual, aural, embodied and spatial aspects of interaction, relationships and environments for learning.

Multisensory refers to an approach that encourages a range of senses, such as sight, hearing, touch, movement to share new information.

Pedagogy refers to the practice, method and art of teaching, alongside the theories that underpin this.

Phoneme is the smallest unit of sound in the alphabetic code. *Sh* represents one sound, for example.

Segmenting is splitting up an unknown word into individual sounds (phonemes) in order to spell.

Socio-cultural refers to the different groups of people across society – their activities, beliefs and traditions.

Systematic synthetic phonics (SSP) is one way to teach phonics. Systematic means to teach directly and regularly in sequence and synthetic is the blending, synthesis – bringing together of the sounds (phonemes) to read and write printed words.

INDEX

Note: Page numbers followed by *f* and *t* refer to figures and tables, respectively.